REAL ESTATE PRESENTATIONS THAT MAKE MILLIONS

Jim Remley, ABR, ALHS

AMACOM

American Management Association

New York • Atlanta • Brussels • Chicago • Mexico City • San Francisco
Shanghai • Tokyo • Toronto • Washington, D.C.

Special discounts on bulk quantities of AMACOM books are available to corporations, professional associations, and other organizations. For details, contact Special Sales Department, AMACOM, a division of American Management Association, 1601 Broadway, New York, NY 10019.
Tel: 212-903-8316. Fax: 212-903-8083.
E-mail: specialsls@amanet.org
Website: www.amacombooks.org/go/specialsales
To view all AMACOM titles go to: www.amacombooks.org

This publication is designed to provide accurate and authoritative information in regard to the subject matter covered. It is sold with the understanding that the publisher is not engaged in rendering legal, accounting, or other professional service. If legal advice or other expert assistance is required, the services of a competent professional person should be sought.

REALTOR® is a registered collective membership mark that identifies a real estate professional who is a member of the NATIONAL ASSOCIATION OF REALTORS® and subscribes to its strict code of ethics.

Library of Congress Cataloging-in-Publication Data

Remley, Jim, 1969-
 Real estate presentations that make millions / Jim Remley.
  p. cm.
 Includes index.
 ISBN-13: 978-0-8144-7401-3
 ISBN-10: 0-8144-7401-2
 1. Real estate business. 2. Sales presentations. I. Title.
HD1375.R456 2007
333.33068'4—dc22

2006032610

Printing number

10 9 8 7 6 5 4 3 2

Contents

Introduction

I was drowning. Blackness would come at any moment. My stomach rolled as I realized suddenly with a pang of fear and dread that nothing and no one would save me. I had no life preserver, and there were no rescue swimmers. I floundered, thrashed, and fought for control. But nothing helped. I was sinking, and now the seller unmercifully tied an anvil to my ankle by asking me the worst possible question at the worst possible moment:

"Are you okay?"

A dark abyss opened beneath my chair. As I looked down at the papers scattered all over the dining room table, my lap, and now the floor, my mind screamed, "No! No, I'm not okay!" but instead I mumbled weakly and continued searching frantically for the missing property disclosure forms.

It was my first listing appointment, and I was sure it was going to be my last. The family had invited me to their home after I had randomly stumbled upon them while doing something that my coworkers had referred to as cold calling. But now, as the sellers quietly watched my frustration turn to desperation, I could feel them looking at each other as if signaling in silent couple code, "How do we get this idiot out of here?"

The rustic farm home was a fixer, or, as I would later learn, something that we call in the business a "handyman special." The home had a broken-down collage of cracked windows, unpainted walls, missing doors, and worn-out carpets. But for me, fresh out of real estate school, all I could see was a dream opportunity. Preparing for the appointment back at the office, I could see the flyers, the advertising, and the brand new "For Sale" sign with my name on it. But as I walked across the threshold of the home, something strange happened.

My excitement melted into a mush of anxiety bordering on absolute panic. Inside my mind, everything that I had so carefully prepared to say slid away into a well of mental darkness. I felt disoriented, nauseous, and short of breath. For a moment I flashed back to an eighth-grade speech where I had choked so badly that I was unable to speak and had taken a failing grade rather than face the humiliation of making a second botched presentation.

Sitting near the home's sole source of heat, an ancient potbellied wood-stove that seemed to glow red with blast-furnace intensity, the sellers waited patiently until I finally found the disclosure statement, which had been hiding conveniently on the top of my briefcase. Taking a deep breath, I began to explain the fascinating history of the Latin term *caveat emptor*, otherwise known as "buyer beware," when the bearded husband with schoolteacher glasses and a short ponytail raised his hand. It was the universal sign for stop. I stopped in midsentence.

"You know, Jim, I think we need some more time to think about this." He paused, glanced at his wife, and continued. "So why don't we give you a call in a few days."

My new colleagues at the real estate office had told me that this listing appointment should be a slam dunk, a lay down, as the sellers had explained on the phone that they needed to sell fast because of the family's new pregnancy. Taking a listing is easy, the veteran agents had all said. Just tell them a little about the company, tell them the price, and then get out the paper-work—"You should be done in less than an hour!"

But I had been in the home nearly two hours, and now, as the couple stood in unison and looked down on me and my paperwork, I knew that the end had come. Without a word, the expectant mother stepped behind me and disappeared into the kitchen. Within seconds I began to hear the clanging of pots and pans. As I stood awkwardly in the middle of the small home, the husband opened the door for me to go. I looked past him to the outside. It was raining.

"Thanks for coming by." He shook my hand, and our eyes met. Without saying more, we both knew that I wasn't coming back; there would be no phone calls or office visits. This wasn't just good-bye. It was good riddance.

It was a hard lesson, and, like most spankings, it made a deep impression. Sure, in the real estate business we all lose listings, but for me this first one was an experience that I never, ever forgot. Why? Because it burned into my psyche a realization: *Presentation is the key to performance.*

Consider your own real estate career for a moment. When you think about your greatest successes and worst failures, the common thread that probably links these two experiences together is your presentation. In any client meeting, your display of the information, services, and benefits you can provide is absolutely fundamental in determining the outcome. For instance, a great presentation can separate you from your competition, differentiate your services, and get the client excited about working with you. On the other hand, a poor presentation can lead to your standing in the rain outside a house wondering what just went wrong and how close the nearest fast-food restaurant is (or maybe that was just me).

Some agents and brokers would argue that what makes a superstar real estate agent is a successful prospecting plan, or a terrific marketing idea, or the ability to build a deep database of past, present, and future clients. And to them I would say yes, yes, and yes, but those are only parts of the story. Let's think about this for a moment. Assume that you have a terrific prospecting plan, and you can find a steady stream of qualified leads. Getting to this point is no easy task in itself, but once you have done so, you have to ask yourself the next question: What is the goal of prospecting, or, for that matter, what is the ultimate goal of marketing, or of building a successful sphere of influence? Isn't the goal to set appointments with buyers and sellers to present your services? Of course it is.

Your presentation, then, is the focal point of all your efforts. It is where your business balances between terrible failure and incredible success, where you can literally *make millions selling real estate* (oddly enough, the title of my first book) or go bankrupt watching others outshine you in the marketplace. These crucial moments are the dividing line between greatness and mediocrity. As Christian Bovee once said, "The method of enterprising is to plan with audacity, and execute with vigor." A planned, well-thought-out presentation is a top-producing real estate agent's touchstone, the centerpiece of his or her career.

For me, this first disastrous listing appointment was a turning point, a jolt to my arrogant ignorance of what it would take to become a successful real estate professional. When I replayed the whole scene in my mind, it reminded me of my driver education classes in high school: the vivid scenes of horrible crashes, deaths, and dismemberments combined with the low voice of an off-camera narrator pointing out the drivers' fatal mistakes—their failure to heed warnings, to pay attention, to use a seat belt. If only they had turned left instead of right, stopped at the red light, or waited a second longer before crossing the railroad tracks. My presentation errors continued to flash across my mind with the same intensity as the deep voice of the narrator pointing out my own errors: "Notice how the agent fails to maintain eye contact. . . . He is unfocused. . . . The driver is now losing control of the conversation. . . . He is panicking. . . . Now he's overcompensating. . . . He can't steer the client back around. . . . He's all over the road. . . . He has crashed and burned."

Of course, in high school we all tried to pretend that we didn't care about the people on the screen, but if you looked around the room carefully, through the darkness, you could see some students turning green. We cared, just like real estate agents care when they lose a listing. Yet, ignoring the fundamentals, some real estate agents, not unlike teenagers, drive their businesses with reckless abandon, careening into client meetings as if they were on their way to grab a burger with friends, blaming lost listings on the client's failure to stay focused, or accusing buyers of disloyalty when they purchase a home from another agent.

Not me. From that day on, with the intensity of a drowning man, I committed myself to learning from the best and brightest minds in the industry, to becoming a sponge in the pond of presentation ideas, and to discovering how to master the client meeting. Surprisingly enough, it worked, and although I certainly had days when I coughed up water and thought for sure that someone had put cement shoes on my feet, I did go on to master the skills that enabled me, a 19-year-old college dropout, to reach the top 1 percent of real estate agents nationwide and to take over 150 listings in one 12-month period of time.

But this book isn't about me; it's about you and what you are capable of doing. Are you capable of earning a million dollars selling real estate? Are you one of the few who can become a real estate superstar, a person who can successfully master presentation skills and rise above the mediocrity that surrounds you? I think you are. I think that's why you bought this book. You can smell opportunity; it's all around you every day, waiting to be ravenously devoured by the select few agents who have the skills to sit down at the meal.

For people like you and me, success isn't something that we can sit passively on the sidelines watching happen to others. We want to be a part of it; we want the sense of achievement, fulfillment, and euphoria that comes with crossing the finish line first.

So how can I help? By using this book, you will be able to tap into the strategies, techniques, and ideas that I have learned during 17 years in the industry as a multimillion-dollar-producing agent and as the broker owner of the largest independent real estate network in southern Oregon—ideas that the best and the brightest in the real estate industry, the veterans and the young lions, are using at this minute to win the battle for motivated sellers and qualified buyers in markets across the country. With an easy-to-follow, step-by-step process, you will discover exactly what it will take to move your business to the next level and gain complete confidence at every client meeting that you have from this day forward.

Are you ready to begin? Let's get started.

Flash Point

How many presentations have you botched in your career?

Wait! When I say botched, I don't just mean that you lost the listing or didn't begin working with the buyer. I want you to also include in your total the presentations where you might have taken the listing or started working with the buyer, but you still failed to properly set the stage for success. For instance, perhaps you failed to discuss the importance of negotiations, concessions, financing, compliance work, escrow, or some other key facet of the transaction, which, of course, led inevitably to a failed sale. Be honest; unless you're a brand new agent, it's a huge, scary number, right? Now rewind a moment and consider how much more income you might have earned during your career if you had been able to successfully convert those failed presentations into successful closings.

> **$49,300**
> Median earnings among all Realtors in 2004.
> ___
> In 2004 the top 5 percent of Realtors earned
> **$250,000 +**
> According to the 2005 National Association of Realtors member profile.

Ouch. It hurts a little, doesn't it?

The brutal truth is that buyers and sellers today don't care about our glamour photos (but I look so sexy), our S-class Mercedes (but I just waxed it), or, shockingly, how much money we made last year (but I was the top agent at my company). Buyers and sellers care about only one thing: what we can do to help them. One example of this is the 2004 National Association of Realtors Profile of Home Buyers and Sellers study, which revealed that the quality that buyers preferred most in their next agent was knowledge of the purchase process (95 percent), followed by responsiveness (93 percent) and knowledge of the real estate market (92 percent). Amazingly, not on the list was the agent's hairstyle, his vehicle make and model, or even his latest ranking in the company.

With nearly $2 trillion changing hands each year in the sale of both new and existing homes, and over 80 percent of those transactions involving a real estate professional, the importance of creating and using a powerful presentation can't be overstated. For the profit-driven superstar, building a successful presentation is not an option, it is a necessary investment of time, money, and energy that will provide proven benefits, including more closings, better client relationships, better time management, and, best of all, more referrals.

Of course, it's easier to just blow off building a presentation. Most agents won't find the time or have the patience to conceptualize a powerful client meeting strategy, much less create a systematic plan for making it happen consistently. Instead, most of us are experts at coming up with every excuse known to man to avoid building (or, harder yet, using) a presentation in the field. In fact, if you listen real close, you can almost hear the voice in the back of your head right now. Shhh . . . shhh . . . listen. . . . "Presentations are for rookies, newbies, or the weak. You don't need a presentation. You're way, way too cool to use a presentation."

Yes, you do, and no, you're not.

Mastering the real estate business means gaining mastery over your presentation skills. Just as professional athletes spend their time preparing to do battle on the playing field, successful real estate agents spend their time preparing to perform at their highest and best level during each of their client meetings. And whereas athletes may spend 90 percent of their time training and only 10 percent of their time competing, we, the real estate athletes, are likely to train 10 percent of the

> **$1,150**
> Median amount spent by Realtors in 2005 on promotion and marketing.
>
> ---
>
> 9 percent of Realtors spent over
> **$10,000**

time (if we're lucky) and spend 90 percent of our time competing in the fields and homes of our marketplace. Because of this, in superstars' eyes, everything they do in business is leading either up to or away from a successful client meeting. They understand the fundamental truth that presentation is the key to performance. During these relatively few minutes in front of buyers and sellers, you define your entire career. This is the critical flash point on which a superstar's business profitability hinges, a natural and necessary extension of any great marketing plan. Most important, a high-quality presentation ensures that every lead generated by your prospecting and marketing efforts will be given the best chance at developing fully into a closed sale. (This is important, since the median amount spent by Realtors in 2005 on promotion and marketing expenses was $1,150, and most of us spent several times that!)

I know, it all sounds so rosy, doesn't it? Build a presentation and buyers and sellers will lie down end to end across your office parking lot and wait patiently for their turn in line to work with the almighty, the chosen one, the greatest living real estate agent to walk the earth—in other words, you. Sorry, no; your presentation will not create a tsunami of new clients beating a path to your door. But what a great presentation will do is give you the tools to effectively and persuasively talk to any prospect with whom you do come into contact. Fortunately for me, it was early in my career when, with the dull thud of a hammer hitting something soft and squishy, I came upon the undeniable yet simple truth that I could prospect until I was blue in the face, spend a zillion dollars on personal marketing, invest in the best technology, and still end up "living in a cardboard box down by the river" unless I built and began using a presentation.

So there I sat in mid-1989 behind my brown desk, looking at my brown phone and the brown walls, enjoying a full head of hair, a flatter stomach, and clearer vision while considering my next step. With each idea came thoughts of Michael Jordan making a three-point shot, Joe Montana throwing a touchdown pass, or Martina Navratilova knocking down another ace (it was 1989), which made me wonder: Do these sports stars get performance anxiety? Do they sweat each shot, question each play, or wet the bed after a really bad game? Or, instead, are they machines, gods of the game, made of inner steel, unflinching, mechanical terminators who execute each move with robotic precision?

Images of myself tripping over words, concepts, or objections suddenly popped into my head like migraine flashbulbs as I considered the dangers of building a presentation that might actually make me look more inexperienced, nervous, or flat-out incompetent. Would the sellers smirk, wink, or make the dreaded L finger pattern on their forehead as I fished out my three-ring binder with my back to them? Would they hammer me so hard with objections that I would retreat from the house like a wounded animal in a thunderstorm? Would I regret becoming a real estate agent and wonder why, oh why, hadn't I just stayed in the lumber mill and punched a time clock for the rest of my life?

Sitting at my desk a week or so later, still clutching that same number two pencil, I looked down from my contemplative thousand-yard stare to find my answer in a magazine quote from Michael Jordan. He said,

I've missed more than 9000 shots in my career. I've lost almost 300 games. Twenty-six times, I've been trusted to take the game winning shot and missed. I've failed over and over and over again in my life. And that is why I succeed. I've always believed that if you put in the work, the results will come. I don't do things half-heartedly. Because I know if I do, then I can expect half-hearted results.

Amen to that, Michael, I thought to myself with a smile. I can become the agent I want to be if I accept that not everything I do will be perfect, not every presentation will be a success, not every meeting will go as planned. But, of course, that's not the point. The point is that I will have done everything in my power to create a successful meeting, to anticipate challenges, and to give myself the best chance at winning. And so, with the sage advice of an NBA superstar who had no connection whatsoever to real estate, I began the journey of building and using a presentation that would create tens of millions of dollars in real estate sales, create a foundation to build a network of real estate offices, and secure my family's future with millions of dollars in real estate investments.

So what did I learn along the way? One thing that I learned is that a great presentation can change the world.

LEARNING OPPORTUNITIES

Presentations are the flash point where an agent's profitability is determined.

Mastering a persuasive presentation is the key to converting leads generated from prospecting and marketing activities.

The Tokyo Challenge

In the summer of 1950, not too many years after the end of World War II, 21 of Japan's most influential leaders and industrialists met for a private dinner in the heart of Tokyo. The assembled group was beaten down, psychologically bruised, and no doubt somewhat depressed. In the 1950s, Japanese manufacturers were known largely as makers of shoddy, knockoff imitations of their higher-quality American counterparts, and products stamped "Made in Japan" were largely avoided by consumers.

As the dinner concluded, a young, unknown American statistician took the podium. To a skeptical audience, he outlined a plan that would revitalize productivity, create bigger profits, provide more jobs, and bring Japan back to the world stage as an economic powerhouse. The key to opening this door of prosperity, he explained, was the unflinching pursuit of quality. He then carefully outlined a five-year, 14-point plan to make the goal a reality.

His presentation changed the world. Without fanfare, trumpets, or even fireworks, W. Edwards Deming changed the way every company approaches the manufacturing process. As Dr. Deming later recalled, "They surprised me and did it in four years!" Today his ideas are embraced not just in Japan but worldwide.

Growing up on 40 acres of poverty just outside the small town of Powell, Wyoming, Deming probably never would have guessed, during those cold, hungry winters in his parents' tar-paper cabin, that he would someday change the world economy. And yet he did, with one superb presentation.

One superb presentation can change the world, and one superb presentation can certainly change your career. It has changed mine many times, and if you really think about your own career, it will become clear that your successful business is really just an endless string of successful presentations.

My first Million Dollar Presentation was to a friend, which at first blush might make it seem easier, but for me, a kid barely out of high school, it only terrified me more. Bob was an investor, a guy I had known all my life, who had the financial capability to buy an unlimited number of properties, and he was looking, aggressively looking, for new acquisitions. For me this was both terrifying and exhilarating. Land this whale, this high roller, and it would put me on the road to multimillion-dollar sales; lose him, and I would step back down in the trenches and the knife fight of competing for the next big buyer to swim through the shallow waters of my small market.

Like most investors, Bob planned to work with only those agents who could produce properties of interest that fit his narrow needs. For Bob, this meant (in his mind, at least) that he would have every agent in the city looking for new properties for him to purchase. The reality, of course, was that most agents would never lift a finger to do any actual work on his behalf, figuring that the odds of actually closing a deal with him were about as good as finally capturing Bigfoot in the Cascade mountain range, and since most of us had given up on catching Sasquatch (UFOs, after all, are far easier), most agents just ignored Bob altogether. But I had an idea that if I could demonstrate to Bob that I could provide him with a steady stream of properties to consider for his portfolio, perhaps I could convince him to use me as his exclusive agent.

This looked great on paper, but in reality, of course, it was actually akin to finding a piece of hay in a needle stack—very, very painful. The reason for the difficulty was that Bob was after the same investment properties that nearly every other affluent buyer in our market would snap up in a microsecond as well: privately owned farmland. Privately owned farmland in Oregon is sought after because of the profit in harvested agricultural goods (an often controversial topic when it involves timber), but also, and as important, because of the underlying land as well, which in many cases has even higher aesthetic value as a home site.

The challenge was finding these highly sought-after properties, which, short of plugging myself *Matrix* style into the Multiple Listing Service, were almost impossible to find before a swarm of other agents had made full-price offers. I had to find another way. Fortunately, as William Maxwell once said, "If you turn the imagination loose like a hunting dog, it will often return with the bird in its mouth." And so it did. After a few days of pondering the problem, I had an idea: I would go after absentee owners, property owners who lived outside the county. Of course, back in those early computing days, none of this information was available from a title company, or even, believe it or not, from the county itself. Instead, the tax records were kept on old-style microfiche. In short, gathering the names and addresses of all the absentee owners in the county would require that I read every single tax record in the county, then transfer those by hand into my own computer. So I immediately hired an assistant, Jennifer, to do this tedious work for me.

Within a couple of weeks I was sitting with Bob holding a hot potential property for him to review and a presentation. We sat in the back room of my office, which had been commandeered for our mailing program. Stacks of unsent mail were scattered all over the room, along with a computer and a printer that spat out a letter every few seconds. Bob took it all in quietly. A retired builder, he casually wore jeans and a flannel shirt, and, as always, he was armed with a generous smile.

The presentation was simple. I had developed a system for finding his target properties and would be able to provide him first access to viewing and making offers on these properties. In exchange, I would need an exclusive commitment from him in writing that I would become his sole agent, the only one to represent him as a buyer in the county.

"But if I only work with you, Jim, I might miss out on working with other agents who also have properties to show me," Bob said after a long silence. The smile was gone now, replaced with hard concentration.

"That's true, but those agents also won't be bringing you these properties." I held up three more potential leads, leads that I had not yet handed over to him.

Looking back on the conversation, I'm sure I appeared nervous, and maybe my voice shook, but the night before, in thinking about what might be said, I had prepared for this exchange. My confidence rested on the fact that I knew that I could replace Bob, if I was forced to, with any number of other investors. It was at that moment, as Bob considered my offer, that I had something precious, something that I had never had before in a real estate presentation—control.

Within 24 hours, Bob said yes, and we together, investor and agent, went on to make millions of dollars in deals over the next several years. The key to this successful presentation was that I had offered the same thing that Deming had offered to those manufacturing executives in Tokyo 50 years earlier, something that is irresistible to any audience—a solution.

All presentations start with a problem; it's the reason that the client comes to us in the first place. It's the reason clients talk to us, listen to us, or really spend any time with us at all. The better our solution, the more unique, efficient, or effective it is, the better our chances will be of persuading the client to accept our presentation as her solution.

Of course, most agents assume that presentations are built on personality. If they like me, they will list with me. If they like me, they will pay me. If they like me, they won't sue me. Maybe, or maybe not. Maybe a flashy presentation will work, or maybe not; maybe a presentation that includes pictures of your pets will work, or maybe not. Maybe if you cut your commission, clients will commit to you, or maybe they won't. Strong agents don't work in the hazy world of maybes; instead, they cut through the fog of indecision by focusing their presentations on providing clients with a compelling reason to make a decision, to take the next step, to make the commitment. They provide a solution. They know that most clients aren't looking for a new best friend (or a new pet); after all, according to a recent study, the average American spends nearly eight hours a day watching television, so who has the time for new best friends when *CSI* or *Law and Order* might be on?

Deming was right on another topic as well: the importance of quality. Without a high-quality presentation, delivering the right solution may still end in disaster. For instance, imagine that Deming had screwed up his presentation. Maybe he choked, lost his notes, or made some other embarrassing blunder. Where would we all be today? Would some other brave soul have taken up the mantle, or would the idea have rotted and died on the vine? It's an interesting, even scary question to consider, and yet it's extremely important, because without the ability to convey ideas or concepts convincingly in a well-thought-out, high-quality presentation, as Deming was able to do, it's nearly impossible for any salesperson to achieve the success he deserves.

Deming's 14-Point Plan (Applied to Real Estate)

1. *Constancy of purpose.* Decide on a long-range goal.
2. *Adopt a new philosophy.* Become a learning, adaptive company.
3. *Be independent.* Stop relying on others' approval; only the client matters.
4. *Demand quality.* Demand it of yourself and of everyone who is part of your team.
5. *Improve every process.* Search continually for problems and solutions.
6. *Train yourself to win.* Model the best in the industry and commit to training.
7. *Institute leadership.* Lead yourself and others by raising standards.
8. *Drive out fear.* Encourage open communication at every moment.
9. *Break down barriers.* Link your success to the success of everyone around you.
10. *Eliminate exhortations.* Avoid self-praise and focus on improving quality.
11. *Eliminate arbitrary targets.* Every goal should have a driving purpose.
12. *Take pride in your work.* Ensure that every transaction is one you are proud of.
13. *Encourage education.* Educate customers and clients about the process.
14. *Commit to action.* Push every day for advancement in at least one area.

Many agents are still resistant to building—and using—a presentation. Why? Perhaps because they have allowed their business to become market-driven, as opposed to strategy-driven, a key distinction in the coming days of a changing marketplace.

LEARNING OPPORTUNITIES

One superb presentation can change your life and your career.

Wise agents take the time to determine each client's real estate problem.

By offering unique solutions to each client's problem, strong agents are able to take control of client meetings, and their careers.

Market-Driven vs. Strategy-Driven

For anyone who is even loosely connected with the real estate industry (a large number, since nationally 1 in every 266 adults now holds a real estate license), there is little doubt that real estate professionals over the last several years have experienced a near perfect storm of market conditions—interest rates at 45-year lows, an overall strong economy, and buyers and sellers who are ready, willing, and able to trade dollars for deeds. In fact, the numbers are a little scary—double-digit appreciation, cost hikes, buyers stampeding, owners scrambling, and still not enough supply to meet demand (and that's just at the local Starbucks). Residential real estate in the United States went up $2.5 trillion in total value in 2005, to top out at $18.4 trillion.

Like politics, all real estate markets are local, but nationally, according to the 2005 National Association of Realtors Profile of Real Estate Markets, residential real estate increased in value by more than 13 percent in 2005 (see Figure 1-1), with an overall three-year increase of 33 percent (2002–2005). This includes some hot spots where the increase was even higher—areas like Phoenix, Arizona, which had year-over-year gains of 55 percent, and many areas of Florida and California, which had appreciation of between 30 and 40 percent—and some slower markets in the South and Midwest that posted only single-digit gains.

Of course it's easy to find ways to explain away all the hysteria. I'll give you a few talking points for ammunition:

FIGURE 1-1. HOME PRICE APPRECIATION

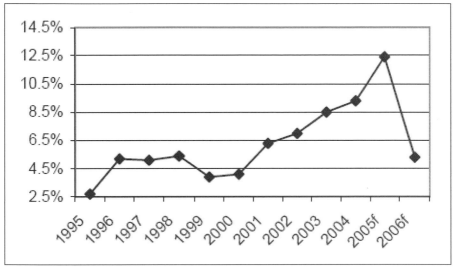

Source: National Association of Realtors.

- Since 1968, when real estate records first began to be kept, most of the country has never experienced even a temporary downturn in home prices, and national median prices have risen every year, even during times of recessions and periods of slower sales. Typically, according to David Lereah, chief economist for the National Association of Realtors, homeowners can expect home appreciation of 1 to 2 percent above overall inflation over the long haul.

- Homeownership is still the cornerstone of wealth for most Americans, and for good reason. According to Harvard University's Joint Center for Housing Studies, a home buyer who puts 10 percent down on her home and holds it for just 3 years will generally receive a 94 percent return on her investment; if she holds the home for 5 years, it ratchets up to 225 percent, and if she hangs on for 10 years, she can expect an infomercial-ready return of 623 percent! How? The return is based on the actual cash invested, not the total purchase price of the property.

- Home prices actually lagged behind income growth for most of the previous two decades. It's only relatively recently that they have been playing catch-up. For example, from 1980 to 2004, incomes rose by 150 percent while home prices increased by 180 percent.

- Home prices are only one way to measure the real cost of home-ownership. Another possibly more accurate way would be to measure housing costs as a percentage of income. As an example, with a 2 percentage point drop in interest rates, a home buyer can afford a 23 percent larger loan, and bingo, you get higher prices.

- A home is more than just an investment; it also offers a tangible benefit to its owners—shelter. You can live inside the darn thing and keep warm. Try doing that with an Enron stock certificate.

Interestingly, the real estate expansion has not just been confined to the United States; it has been a worldwide boom, as the *Economist* magazine stated in June 2005: "Never before have real house prices risen so fast, for so long, in so many countries. Property markets have been frothing from America, Britain and Australia to France, Spain and China."

In a busy real estate market, a high tide floats all boats. Yet, common sense should tell us that when even the worst agent in your office (you know, the guy who couldn't sell his way out of a wet paper bag) sells a couple million dollars of real estate, this should be a red flag to the rest of us that maybe, just maybe, this magic carpet ride won't last forever. As Joseph Kennedy, father of President John F. Kennedy, reputedly told his colleagues in a speech before taking the reins as the first SEC chairman (referring to the stock market crash of 1929), "When your shoeshine boy starts giving you stock tips, it's time to sell." The same might be said about real estate. Yet it is tough—really, really tough—for industry veterans to accept the idea that the market could lose power and parachute softly back down to earth or, worse yet, burn up in the stratosphere. However, great agents are also smart agents; they watch which way the wind is blowing, and the tide is turning against real estate. As Richard DeKaser, chief economist for mortgage banker National City, was quoted, reluctantly, as having said during an interview, "We're coming down the other side of the mountain."

So what does that mean to you and me?

What it should mean is that now is the time to analyze our business practices and make a critical distinction about how we are running our ship. Are we market-driven, or are we strategy-driven? It's an important question, because the answer can determine your fate in the coming market downturn. What's the difference? Let's start with a market-driven agent. A market-driven agent is a person who, by all outside appearances, has done very, very well over the last five years. He has more business than he can handle. He comes in early and goes home late. He wears nice clothes, lives in a nice home, and drives a nice car, and like the rest of us he struggles to keep up with all of his clients, closings, inspections, and minor (and major) problems. These agents are busy people, and they look the part of a successful agent.

But there is a huge problem looming for market-driven agents, an iceberg hidden under the water just off the bow of their business, and they are steaming full speed ahead right toward it. The problem is that they have absolutely no idea where their business comes from. They pretend that they know, and many of them think they know, but they don't. They have no idea what has been fueling the engine of their business; all they know is that it has been cruising nicely and comfortably. As H. G. Bohn once said, "Success makes a fool seem wise." Unfortunately, the engine of their business may soon come to a sputtering stop, and these agents' once-thriving careers may be left red tagged on the side of the real estate superhighway.

So how do you know if you are a market-driven agent? Here is an easy litmus test: If you answer no to any of these three questions, you may have a gremlin lurking in your career's carburetor:

1. Do you know where your clients come from, i.e., floor time, referrals, or prospecting?
2. Do you have a consistent daily system for attracting new potential clients to your business?
3. Looking back at your last three sales, did you actively seek out the clients, or did they just happen to find you?

The market-driven agent is someone who is completely at the mercy of the marketplace. If interest rates go up, her business goes down. If buyers or sellers stop calling, her bank balance drops. More agents enter the business, and she gets a smaller piece of the pie. The economy takes a nosedive and her kids don't go to college. For many of these unfortunate souls, the best years of their career have already come and gone, and it's only downhill from here, unless they decide to make a massive change in the way they view their business, something that's not easy but is

> **Market-Driven Agents**
> Success is tied to the market conditions.
>
> ---
>
> **Strategy-Driven Agents**
> Success is tied to the quality of their plan.

doable. As William Boetcher once said, "There are two ways of meeting difficulties: you alter the difficulties, or you alter yourself to meet them."

This path to progress may lead some to follow the example of many superstars who have embraced a strategy-driven approach to their business. What does this mean? It simply means that strong agents build a strategy to consistently attract new potential customers and clients. They have discovered that the bigger the pool of potential clients they can present their services to, the greater their odds of success. The key difference is that they take control of how and when those potential clients come through the front door of their office. They don't wait for the clients to come to them; they go to the clients. They are not a retail store; instead, they are first and foremost a sales organization. A strategy-driven agent has a predictable pipeline, understands his own business model, and knows how to drive leads to his organization.

At first, this may seem not to be connected to a discussion about building a powerful presentation strategy. But, in fact, it is perhaps the most critical component. Why? Imagine my dilemma if, when I had presented my ideas to Bob the investor, I had had no alternative if he had said no. My position would have been weakened dramatically, to the point that I might never have even had the discussion for fear of losing Bob altogether. But because I had many other investors to turn to should Bob reject my presentation, I was able to retain control of my presentation.

Why is this so important? Take a look at the two agents in Figure 1-2.

Having a predictable pipeline of new customers and clients to present your services to ensures that you can match your solutions to customers and clients who actually have a need for your services. In addition, it gives you the power to become selective when choosing which clients to enter into a professional relationship with. Wise agents build an ideal client model, a picture of the client that they would prefer to work with and for, and then they build their marketing plan around finding those ideal clients.

On the other side of the fence, market-driven agents, especially in a down market cycle, are far more likely to wrap their arms around any potential client they come into contact with. Veterans have seen this before during previous soft markets. Agents are stepping on top of each other to work with anyone and everyone who comes within 500 yards of their SUV: "Unqualified buyers, no problem. I've got a lender who can fix that! Unmotivated, just

FIGURE 1-2. WHICH PROSPECT POOL WOULD YOU RATHER HAVE?

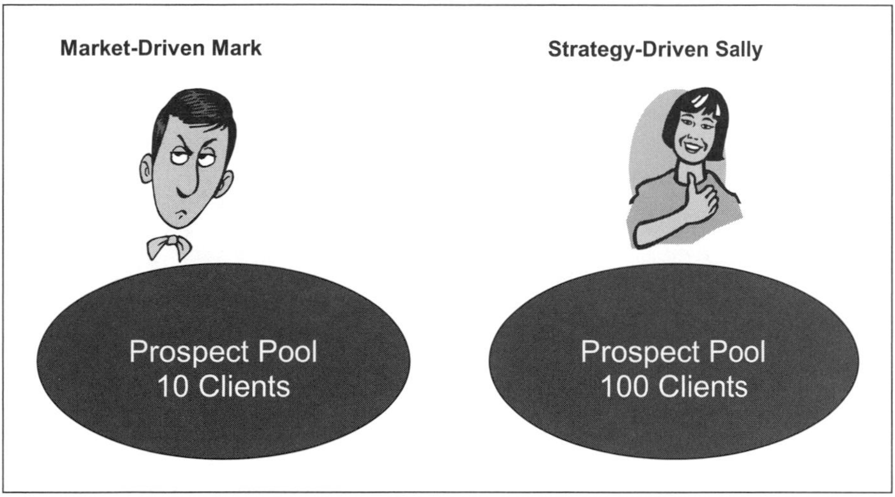

wait till I show you my hot new listing! Unready, well, get ready, partner, because now is the time to sell!"

There is another name for this: creating needs. Weak agents, like vacuum cleaner salesmen, attempt to create needs. They try to fill a void that just isn't there—the people already own a vacuum cleaner, so they don't need another one, or, for that matter, a new house. From a presentation stand-point, these agents are stuck attempting to sell a solution that the client doesn't need or want. They are forever trying to put square pegs in round holes, and they just don't fit (unless you find a really big hammer).

What is the alternative? Strong strategy-driven agents work with large pools of buyers and sellers and present their services only to people who are ready, willing, and able to make a decision, people who have a real estate problem, people who need a—drum roll, please—solution!

So what is your solution, and is it good enough to convince a client to commit to you in writing? If you don't have good answers to these questions, it may be time for you to burn your business to the ground.

LEARNING OPPORTUNITIES

Easy success has led many agents to a market-driven business model. Market-driven agents are at the mercy of the marketplace and are not in control of their career path.

Superstars embrace a strategy-driven approach to their business by building a plan for success; they have a predictable pipeline.

A strategy-driven approach ensures that agents will have a large pool of buyers and sellers to present their solutions to.

Burning Your Business to the Ground

If it ain't broke, don't fix it!

It's easy to think that way; after all, when you're making money so fast that you can't seem find the time to actually deposit your commission checks, it might seem strange to even begin contemplating an overhaul of your presentation strategy, but in reality you may be standing at the threshold of two diverging paths. One leads to continued prosperity even in the face of falling sales and the potential for depreciating home values, and the other path leads to an earnings cliff, where your income drops dangerously out from beneath your feet. The good news is that others have passed this way before. Decision makers like yourself, businessmen and -women who have had to make the tough and in many cases unpopular decision to go against the grain, to choose the less-traveled road, and in some cases to figuratively burn their business to the ground.

General Robert F. Wood was one of these men, a man driven by numbers, statistics, and logistics, a born leader. Such was his talent that he was tapped early in his career to help coordinate one of the most massive building projects in the history of the world—the construction of the Panama Canal. A 50-mile channel of locks, waterways, and dams connecting the Pacific and Atlantic Oceans, it took nine years to build (1904–1913) at a cost of $375 million and involved the management of over 56,000 construction workers. But an even bigger project lay in his future, a project that would help reshape retailing in the United States for decades to come.

After his return from World War I, General Wood noticed something disturbing in the U.S. economy. As historian Richard Tedlow would later write in his book *New and Improved,* he "was one of those fortunate few to whom numbers spoke." His observation: The American farmer was in danger, as agricultural income was dropping precipitously. Conversely, the number of automobile registrations was rising. Disconnected? Not in Wood's mind. These facts, added to the fact that the number of department stores was increasing exponentially (led by retailing maverick J. C. Penney), painted a picture that General Wood could not ignore: The farm economy was dying. Instead, people were buying cars and moving to the cities to find work. For his employer Montgomery Ward, this meant that its once-vaunted catalog business might soon suffer a slow and agonizing death. He said as much in a memo to the top brass at Montgomery Ward headquarters in Chicago: "We can beat the chain stores at their own game," he wrote. "We have four distribution points; we have an organized purchasing system; we have a wonderful name if we choose to take advantage of it." Their answer: Thanks, and oh, by the way—you're fired!

Undaunted, he crossed the retail street and took his conclusions to Montgomery Ward's archrival, Sears Roebuck. The answer there: Let's make it happen! Within four years General Wood had been named president of the company. But changing Sears Roebuck from a catalog operator to a chain store would be no easy task, especially for a company that had never operated brick-and-mortar stores, with managers, locations, marketing, employees, and inventory to suddenly oversee nationwide. In today's world, this might be akin to Amazon.com's jettisoning its Internet portal position and suddenly deciding to open a store in every major city in the country. It was a gamble, a bet-the-company, cross-your-fingers, and hold-your-breath type of wager.

> The price of leadership is unceasing effort; we cannot get smug and self-satisfied, we must always keep learning, we must keep improving our methods, our organization, if we are to retain our leadership.
> —Robert F. Wood

From the beginning, Wood acknowledged that there would be challenges. "Business is like war in one respect," he said. "If its grand strategy is correct, any number of tactical errors can be made." And there would be mistakes, failures, and breakdowns, but as the famous IBM technology manager Fred Brooks was fond of quoting: "Numquam incertus, semper apertus," or, for the rest of us, "Never uncertain, always open." General Wood was certain his decision was correct for the company; he was unwavering, and some might say unsympathetic, but not only was his vision right, it was the only course the company could have taken to ensure survival. However, he was always open to new ideas on how the stated goal might be achieved.

The result: Sears went from being the largest mail-order company in the United States, primarily serving the country's rural population, to becoming the world's largest merchandiser. Montgomery Ward, on the other hand, did not fare as well. Declining sales and a late start putting in more retail outlets led the company, after rejecting a 1950 merger bid by Sears, to declare in 2000 the largest retail bankruptcy liquidation in U.S. history.

So are you ready to burn your business to the ground?

Julie was, but she had problems, and they were hanging all around her. Above her desk, on both sides of her computer, over her office door, they were literally everywhere the eye could see—awards, plaques, certificates, prizes, photos, every accomplishment in her real estate career from her first million-dollar sale to her last record-breaking year, and they were all reminding her of what had worked in the past. So it was hard for Julie, once the envy of every agent in her multiple-listing system, to accept the fact that what had worked so well before might not work again.

"Just lean into your business," her broker had told her. The not so subtle message: Get off your tail and work harder. So she did, prospecting, marketing, and presenting day and night, eight days a week, and nine if she could find the extra time. But still her sales continued to drop. Recognizing a downward spiral, she made a decision. She had to kill what she loved. She had to tear down her old business model and start from scratch. As she later explained to me after I had conducted a seminar for her company, "Successful salespeople aren't built by their last sale but by their next one."

Letting go of past success is the key to future brilliance. For Julie, this meant that she should start with a fresh perspective, a new way of looking at her goals and action plan; in other words, she needed to work on her business and not just in her business. By doing so, she soon realized that volume sales, the push to keep the turnstile of buyers and sellers whizzing through the conference room doors, would not save her or any of her colleagues, who, she had noticed, were also struggling. Of course, the idea that the answer to any business dilemma is just selling more—more products or more services—sounds reasonable. More sales means more profit, right?

The problem is that when everyone wants a piece of that gold-plated pie, it's very easy to reach a saturation point.

> **Commodity:** A term used to describe any product or service that can be sold in mass quantities.

Reviewing the numbers, it wasn't hard for Julie to surmise that in her community, this was exactly what was happening. More and more of the top agents in her community were turning themselves into volume stores, like a Costco or Best Buy, or Sears. More volume can lead to more profits (sometimes even at discounted commission rates). But when too many people in any one market begin using the same approach to selling products or delivering services, there is a name for this in the financial world—commoditization.

When a product or service becomes a commodity—in other words, when you can receive roughly the same services or products from just about any of the competing providers in the marketplace—there can only be one result: Blood will run in the streets as each company or salesperson attempts to undercut the competitors with price discounts, giveaways, and rebates; it can quickly escalate to an all-out no-holds-barred marketing war. Examples from the recent past might include personal computers, Internet service providers, or even travel agencies. As each of these industries experienced a flood of new competitors offering roughly the same products or services, many of the businesses collapsed.

Time Warner's acquisition of America Online and it's subsequent $54 billion writedown (a fancy way of saying loss) in 2002 (roughly equal to the gross domestic product of New Zealand) is a prime example of what can happen to a business when many other players enter the market and begin offering similar services. For AOL, this meant the loss of hundreds of thousands of subscribers. Of course, many would argue that this is great for the consumer, as a competitive market will, in the end, give consumers maximum value for each dollar spent. True, unless to achieve the economies of scale needed to be profitable, the company is forced to cut services or quality.

In any event, after careful consideration, Julie knew that she didn't want to be a commodity player; no top performer would. Top service providers, the most sought after in their chosen profession, never allow themselves to become a commodity. Instead, Julie wanted to build a business that would guarantee that her prospective clients would have to choose her over her competitors, not just because of her terrific marketing or her magnetic personality (or even her trophy husband), but because she had built a company that offered something that her competitors hadn't (yet) commoditized. We might call this building a unique solution.

Her unique solution was to team up with an expert in self-directed IRAs and begin hosting real estate investment seminars, teaching people how they can move their IRA and 401(k) retirement savings from the stock market to the real estate market. Did it work? Yes; within months, both she and her

The Self-Directed IRA

From March 2000 to July 2002, $5.6 trillion in stock market wealth evaporated, along with many families' retirement accounts, college savings, and medical savings. Because of this, many investors decided that instead of placing their money in intangible stock certificates (many of which had dropped dramatically in value overnight), they would be better off investing their retirement dollars in real estate, something that they could see, feel, and drive by every day.

The good news for these new real estate investors is that if they adhere to strict IRS guidelines (www.irs.gov), they can roll over their traditional IRA and 401(k) accounts and use these funds to buy real estate. For more information on using this technique yourself, or to help your own clients, visit www.pensco.com or www.iraplus.com.

expert partner began to see an enormous return on their investment, with both selling in excess of $10 million of product during the next 12 months, far surpassing her previous high-water mark of just under $7 million. The best part, according to Julie: "I don't lose any sleep wondering where my next client will come from, because I know that at each of my seminar presentations I will have at least ten new leads."

Julie burned down her business by rejecting the old-school approach of just trading marketing dollars for clients. She understood that in today's world, if 10 people can do exactly what you can, the only way to win is to stop playing their game. She adopted a new strategy, a strategy that starts with understanding what clients want and delivering a powerful presentation of how you can give it to them.

LEARNING OPPORTUNITIES:

To stay competitive, top producers may need to choose a new business model, and, contrary to what many may believe, volume sales may not be the answer.

Wise agents avoid becoming a commodity, or someone who provides products or services very similar to those provided by their competitors in the marketplace.

To differentiate themselves, superstars build unique solutions for their clients' real estate challenges.

So what do your clients want from you? The answer to this question will become the foundation for building a powerful presentation strategy and the topic of our discussion in Chapter 2, "The People Paradox."

The People Paradox

Real estate buyers and sellers can be odd ducks. Some want what they can't have: "I want $1 million for my single-wide mobile home and not a penny less!" Others demand crazy concessions: "I want this toaster oven but they can keep all the clocks in the house." A few will cook up harebrained schemes: "Let's offer them half what they're asking, and go down from there." Occasionally they hide things: "Bankruptcy? I thought that we took care of that last month." And more clients than you would guess will flat out lie to you: "Fire? No, we just barbeque inside during the winter." As Jim Morrison of The Doors was fond of singing, "People are strange." They are.

A few years ago, a good friend of mine, John, confided to me after a housewarming party he had thrown to celebrate the completion of his 4000 square foot waterfront home, "As nice as this is, I know that in a few months I'll be wishing I had something bigger and better." At first blush, you might say to yourself, "Oh, how sad; the poor devil will never be satisfied." But take a look inward for a moment and ask yourself whether you are completely satisfied with where you live, what you drive, and what clothes you wear. Perhaps we aren't so different from John, with his constant need for more, bigger, and better. This is the people paradox. We always want what we don't, or can't, have. Fulfillment for many of us is never in the here and now; it's just around the bend, over the next hill, just out of reach. Is this a bad thing?

Probably not, as our inner drive, our hard-wired ambition is exactly what allows us to succeed and survive in a highly competitive world.

We need to understand the underlying motivations of each of our clients—why they buy and sell homes. You might think that buying a home is simply a matter of getting a roof over your head or some shelter. Or perhaps you might think that people are looking for safety, because a home provides us with a certain degree of security from the outside world. But in my experience, both answers would be wrong. Why? As one of the fortunate few who live in the richest country in the world, I can say with confidence that very few of us are in danger of losing at least basic shelter. Nearly all of us will have a roof over our heads every night of our lives. So the question isn't whether we will have shelter, but what kind of shelter we will have.

I learned this valuable lesson in the first year of my second marriage. My new bride and I had taken a road trip to visit some family in Washington State, where we had planned to picnic along the Columbia River and enjoy a summer day on the water, fishing and swimming. Unfortunately, after driving several hundred miles up and down the river, I got very lost. (My later defense: It is the largest river in the Pacific Northwest, over 1,200 miles long!) By nightfall we gave up on finding my family.

Frustrated, tired, and irritated, we pulled into a small town along the river that had two hotels. The first was a brand new multistory waterfront hotel. The place was lit up like a Wal-Mart at Christmas, and strangely, after all those hours of driving, searching, fighting, and fatigue, it gave us that same sense of warmth, joy, and euphoria. We couldn't help but smile. Through the window we could see that a fire was blazing in the new lobby, hot coffee was steaming from an oversized pot, and the gleaming white teeth of the cashier beckoned us to come on in. But this is where I made one of the biggest mistakes of my life—I kept on driving. *The place looks expensive,* I thought to myself; *after all, we just need a place to sleep for a few hours.*

"Let's see what's down the road."

What was down the road was my new bride's worst nightmare, an old-fashioned motor lodge. In its day it must have been an incredibly plush hotel, with wood-paneled walls, freestanding ashtrays, and clown-inspired paintings. But now it just looked old and tired (but cheap!). Although the lobby was closed, it did have a night bell, and the flickering sign outside did say "vacancy."

"No," my new wife pronounced. It wasn't a discussion; it was a decision.

I guess as a recent bachelor I just hadn't come full circle yet as to what adequate shelter would mean to my new wife. That night I learned. Four walls and a roof? Not even close to good enough. Fearful of quickly becoming a bachelor once again, I humbly turned the car around and drove back to the first hotel.

To my surprise, there was now a line at the check-in desk. Other lost travelers? As I finally made my way to the front of the line, I learned from the overly friendly receptionist that the last room had just that minute been filled. The retired couple in the elevator had taken the honeymoon suite. She pointed at them and they (mischievously?) smiled as the doors closed. As I slowly made my way across the parking lot, I could feel my wife's eyes boring a hole through my head, past my brain, and into my very soul. Fortunately, there were no blunt instruments within her reach as I opened the door and told her the news—the hotel was sold out.

I am absolutely confident that someday in the distant future, when my wife and I are celebrating our fiftieth wedding anniversary and one of our grandchildren begins talking about taking a vacation or staying in a hotel, she will shake her head in disgust and regale everyone in the room with the story about the night I made her sleep at the motor lodge. Needless to say, today she makes all of our hotel reservations.

For most Americans owning a home isn't about shelter. It's not about staying dry, or staying out of the weather, or keeping the wolves from coming in; it's about something much deeper, something that is beyond physiological needs, and deeply seated in psychological needs. Four walls and a roof do not make a home (or a hotel). Reflect for a moment about your last home purchase or sale. What motivated you to make that life-changing decision? Was it one of the reasons in Figure 2-1?

Like you, each of your clients has a core motivation. But here's the rub: Many of your clients won't themselves realize what it is they are truly seeking. Sure, they know the outside motivations, those surface issues that they present you with as they walk through your office doors, like, "We need a three-car garage," "We want to live in Laurelwood," or "We want to be closer to the center of town." But they haven't yet grasped (and may never grasp) their own inner needs, their core motiva-

Inner Motivations
The core motivation for making a real estate change

Outside Motivations
The surface needs that serve the inner motivation.

FIGURE 2-1. WHY DO PEOPLE MAKE LIFE-CHANGING DECISIONS?

Love/Belonging	Esteem	Actualization
Move closer to family or friends.	Move based on promotion or increased income.	Move to better reflect lifestyle.
Move to accommodate family —size of home.	Move to match self-image change.	Move to accommodate personal growth.
Move to meet needs of family members.	Move to keep up with social circle.	Move to change life direction.

tions for making a real estate change. Instead, these deeper needs remain untapped, repressed, and unspoken. So how do superstars uncover this hidden agenda? Many start by using a simple technique that I call the three-way technique.

The three-way technique is a quick way to diagnose our potential client's core motivations. Not unlike doctors, great presenters evaluate each potential client by probing, narrowing, and exploring the symptoms of what ails their patients. In other words, they quickly find their client's pain. Let's take a look at the three-way technique in action.

The key to this system is to always ask at least three questions during any initial conversation with a new potential buyer or seller client to reveal that client's true motivations and determine if you want to continue building the relationship. For instance:

The Three-Way Technique

> **Buyer:** *Yeah, I'm looking for a three bedroom in the country, around $200,000.*
>
> **Weak Agent:** *Great. I'm not doing anything now. How soon can I pick you up and start showing you homes?*
>
> **Strong Agent:** *Great. Do you mind if I ask you* why *you're looking for a three bedroom and not a four?*

Buyer: *Well, we have a new baby on the way, and we are in a two bedroom now, but we would take a four bedroom if we could find one.*

Strong Agent: *Terrific; and why the country? Did you grow up on a few acres?*

Buyer: *No, but my wife grew up on a ranch, and she wants our new son to grow up on some property.*

Strong Agent: *Great; and do you mind if I ask* how *you decided on looking in the $200,000 range?*

Three questions later and this agent has discovered that this couple's core motivation is to provide a rural environment for their son to grow up in. They're moving because they want to create a loving environment for their son that reminds them of their childhood. This skilled agent knows that she isn't selling bedrooms and bathrooms; she's selling something far more precious—a special place for this couple to raise their new baby. Knowing this, can she now do a better job for her new potential clients? Of course she can. Because in the end, none of us sells square footage; we also don't sell split-levels, condos, ranch-style homes, or ranches. Instead, we sell the way buying or selling real estate makes a person feel. We sell emotions.

Some might say that in order to tap into this hidden agenda with their own clients, they would need the ability to read their clients' minds. They would be right, so let's do that next.

LEARNING OPPORTUNITY

Purchasing a home is a social need.

Inner motivations. The core underlying motivation for making a real estate change is what professional real estate agents work to uncover.

Outside motivations. These are often surface needs that may help to satisfy the greater underlying client motivation. Superstars often use these stated needs as a way to reveal a client's true inner motivation using the three-way technique.

Reading Minds—Uncovering Client Motivations

Odds are that unless you have recently attended one of my seminars, you and I have never met. You are reading this book because you purchased it online or at your local bookstore, or maybe a friend gave it to you as a gift. Nevertheless, I'm going to read your mind. Sound impossible? Let's see how close I can come to hitting the mark. Okay, relax. Go to your mental sanctuary and let me see if I can cross the space-time continuum and tap into your cramped cranium. Take a deep breath and concentrate on something pleasant—like a big commission check.

This may take just a minute, so stay calm and relaxed, with happy thoughts.

Aha, yes, I'm getting you now. I'm receiving you. You're coming in crystal clear. Now let me just make a couple of small adjustments . . . wait there it is . . . I'm reading your innermost thoughts. Interesting . . . um . . . yep . . . oh . . . wow . . . oops! I'd better stop there. I don't want to know too much! Now that I've completed my reading, I'm going to describe you, the real you. Not just the person everyone sees on the outside, but the person underneath your skin, hiding just beneath the surface, the person whom only a few people in your life have ever met. To test my accuracy, I want you to be open and honest to my reading. Okay, here is what I picked up:

> You have a need for other people to like and admire you, and yet you tend to be critical of yourself. While you have some personality weaknesses, you are generally able to compensate for them. You have considerable unused capacity that you have not turned to your advantage. Disciplined and self-controlled on the outside, you tend to be worried and insecure on the inside. At times, you have serious doubts as to whether you have made the right decision or done the right thing. You prefer a certain amount of change and variety and become dissatisfied when you are hemmed in by restrictions and limitations. You also pride yourself on being an independent thinker and do not accept others' statements without satisfactory proof, but you have found it unwise to be too frank in revealing yourself to others. At times you are extroverted, affable, and sociable, while at other times you are introverted, wary, and reserved. Some of your aspirations tend to be unrealistic.

So was it a success? Did I accurately describe the real you? If you're like 95 percent of college students who were given this "cold reading," you would probably rate this description of yourself as good to excellent. How is that possible? It's not. This mind-reading exercise was developed by psychologist Bertram Forer to expose supposed mind-reading psychics as frauds. The reality is that this "reading" applies to the vast majority of the population, and although it sounds specific to the person to whom it's being given, it really isn't. Mystics and so-called psychics often use a number of memorized stock readings and then apply them to their customers as needed.

So should you memorize some stock real estate readings to use with your clients? It's probably not the best idea (unless you can fit a crystal ball into your briefcase), but what we can learn from these so-called clairvoyants is the ability to read people. The skill, as Forer points out, in being a physic or mystic isn't in the divination of voices or thoughts from the great beyond, but the ability to read the subtle feedback given to them by their subjects during a reading. As many of us know, the closer a "hit" that a clairvoyant makes is to the truth, the more "tells" the subject will reveal. A tell is what is often referred to as a sign or signal from one person to another; it's like a flashing neon bulb that says, "I'm trying to tell you something!" but no words are ever spoken. In the psychic's case, if a customer agrees with part of the reading or the client makes an obvious signal that the psychic is on the right track with a tell, the psychic can instantly adjust the message to focus on the obvious hot button.

Why is this important to us as real estate professionals? As many communication experts point out, up to 80 percent of human communication is nonverbal. Instead, it is body language and voice intonation that often clue most of us in to what people are thinking but not saying. For instance, can we feel someone's

> *What's not being said is often more important than what is.*

anger, disappointment, or joy? Of course we can, and often way before we are slapped, yelled at, or hugged. Why? Because before we learn to talk, we learn to interpret facial expressions, voice tones, hand gestures, and many of the other subtle nuances that make up the bulk of nonverbal communication. As children, we did this to avoid spankings and to read our parents for just the right moment to ask for a new toy. As young adults, we did it to fit in with groups and gauge our success (or in my case failure) when talking with the opposite sex, and as adults, we continue to do this every day with our friends, spouses, and coworkers. Unfortunately, we may not be using this intuitive skill with our clients. Yet mastering the art of reading the subtle subtext of a conversation is one way superstars can enhance any presentation. Just like the psychic who hones his reading to appeal to his customers, we can do this when talking with a new potential client. How? Let's look at the Four Ways to Read Minds.

Four Ways to Read Minds

1. *Eye contact and brow movement.* When I teach seminars, students often pose questions about the material; after dealing with their concern, I often follow up my response by asking, "Did that answer your question?" Interestingly, in a group setting many students will say yes, but often their eyes say no. The same can be true when doing a presentation. Here are some behaviors to watch for:

   Acceptance/Agreement
   - *Direct eye contact.* Client is showing interest in your information.
   - *Smiling eyes.* Demonstrate that the client is comfortable.
   - *Relaxed brow.* Shows that the client is open to your discussion points.

   Rejection/Negativity
   - *Head drop.* A client whose head is down is often avoiding a discussion.
   - *Limited eye contact.* This client may want to break off the discussion.
   - *Tension in brow.* The client may be confused, upset, or afraid.

2. *Facial gestures.* Experts in reading body language often study the mouth as a way to determine a subject's acceptance or rejection of a given message. How? Upward turns in the corners of the mouth are often positive indications that the client is engaged and interested, whereas flat lines, downward turns, or pressed lips often can indicate unhappiness or the rejection of a given message.

3. *Upper-body movements.* When someone attempts to throw a swing at you after your presentation, it's a good bet that he has rejected your ideas. But you might have received another, more subtle message much earlier in the conversation if you had just watched for the right cues. For instance, as a general rule of thumb, a closed-off posture means a close-minded attitude; arms crossed, leaning backward, or moving a chair in the opposite direction is not so good. On the flip side, an open

or willing attitude is often inferred by someone who keeps her arms open, leans forward, or nods as you are speaking.

4. *Leg activity.* Although many clients cross their legs for many reasons that have nothing to do with what you are saying, clients who are fidgeting with their feet or legs are often nervous or anxious (or have to go to the bathroom). In either case, it is probably wise to stop talking and ask a question like, "How does that sound?" or "What are your thoughts on that?"

Now, setting all these finer points aside, I think we are already pretty adept at reading minds; we just may not realize it. For instance, I guarantee you that when I walk through the door of my home tonight, I can gauge my wife's demeanor by taking only one quick glance at her face. After all, how many times have you ever heard someone say, "I could cut the tension with a knife?" Think about that statement; how do you sense tension? Can you see it, smell it, or touch it? No, but it's still there, like your weird aunt sitting in the corner staring at everyone. This sixth sense is often attributed to our mind's ability to sense things on a far smaller, more nuanced scale than anyone has yet to comprehend.

Interestingly, computer designers are now chasing the ability to read human emotions. According to Rosalind Picard, professor and founder of the Affective Computing Research Group at Massachusetts Institute of Technology (MIT), the next generation of computers will include the ability to read their users' emotions and respond appropriately. "When people interact with other people who ignore their emotion, who don't empathize with them, who don't look concerned when they are upset, it drives them crazy," Picard pointed out. "And yet technology is full of that." New technology, she explains, will soon be able to measure each user's voice intonations, emotional levels, and user patterns to become more empathetic.

I wonder how long it will take humans to match this upgrade. Think about how many times you have had human interactions where your emotions were ignored, where the salesperson made zero effort to read your body language, demeanor, or emotional state. Anger, confusion, annoyance, interest—ignored. Granted, some people seem to have high-definition extrasensory perception, almost as if they have a pair of beelike antennae waving in the wind trying to catch a whiff of some new disturbance in the force. But many (or most) salespeople never seem to see the pink elephant sitting on the couch no matter how many times he trumpets.

> "It is so much easier to suggest solutions when you don't know too much about the problem."—Malcolm Forbes

Weak agents provide the same solutions to all of their clients, regardless of the client's true motivation level. They use a sort of one-size-fits-all or one-presentation-for-everyone approach. Wise agents, on the other hand, understand that each client is unique, with different needs, questions, and concerns. Clients aren't unisex, interchangeable, or cookie-cutter models. But for some clients, expressing their true motivations, those inner needs, is difficult, sort of like trying to pet a porcupine. They want to, but it really hurts. So it falls to us, the professional real estate practitioners, to unravel the motivation mystery by carefully listening to our clients' verbal and nonverbal communication cues.

LEARNING OPPORTUNITY

Communication. Experts agree that up to 85 percent of communication is nonverbal.

Reading minds. Superstars hone their ability to read their clients' nonverbal communication to better tap into their clients' inner motivations.

The next step in the process is to understand what it is that top producers are looking for when they select potential clients. Wait; don't I mean what *clients* are looking for when they select us? Nope. Great agents enjoy a luxury that mere mortals can only dream of: the power to reject clients who don't meet their ideal client model. This enables them to perform presentations only when they have the best odds of success.

Building an Ideal Client Model

When you picture the average Joe and Jane Buyer or Sue and Sam Seller sitting patiently in your office conference room, what do you see? Not the girl with the clown shoes, or the guy in drag (those are your special clients). I'm talking about your typical, everyday client. According to the 2005 National Association of Realtors Profile of Home Buyers and Sellers, here's what should come to mind:

Joe and Jane Buyer

- Repeat buyers have a median age of 46 and a household income of $83,200.
- They place an average of 21 percent cash down. (Amazingly, 11 percent pay all cash.)
- They pay an average of $235,000 for their home, and 94 percent believe their home is a good investment.
- The typical buyer will walk through nine properties and will spend a total of eight weeks searching for a home.
- On average, they will move 12 miles from their previous residence.
- About 81 percent will use the Internet in their search for a new home.

Sue and Sam Seller

- The typical seller has lived in the home for six years and has previously owned three homes (including the one being sold now).
- The average seller will place the home on the market for four weeks.
- On average, the seller will move 15 miles to the new residence.
- About 61 percent of the market is made up of married couples.
- About 43 percent of sellers choose their agent based on a referral.

One of my favorite classroom exercises is to ask students to describe their ideal client. From top to bottom, head to toe, I instruct them to write it all down. Why? To build a business, you need to understand your target customers, the bread-and-butter clients who will feed your real estate practice today, tomorrow, and for years to come. My specific instructions for each participant are to think back to all of their favorite buyers and sellers, the ones they really enjoyed working with, and then pick out the best traits from each to build their new superclient—a client who is faster, stronger, and better

than those who have gone before her. Why not give it a try yourself? Here
are a few questions to get you started:

The Ideal Client Worksheet

1. What demographic age group does your ideal client fall into?

   _____

   _____

2. Is the client married? Does he have children?

   _____

   _____

3. What income bracket does the client fall into?

   _____

   _____

4. What is his educational background?

   _____

   _____

5. Has he bought or sold a home before?

   _____

   _____

6. What kind of occupation(s) does your client have?

   _____

   _____

7. What is your client's net worth?

   _____

   _____

8. What are your client's hobbies?

   _____

   _____

9. Is your client tech-savvy?

   _____

   _____

10. Does your client own investment real estate or a second home?

    _____

    _____

Many agents will raise their hands at this point and ask, "Why is this
important? I'll work with anyone who pays me!" The funny thing is, they're

right. I think we would all agree that we won't always fall in love with each of our clients, just as a defense attorney won't like all of the clients she defends. Yet we do have the power, as our practice grows, to become more and more selective in choosing with whom we work. So while we may work with a few rough-hewn buyers and sellers in the beginning, as we move up the success ladder, we should be able to graduate to working with clients we might actually be comfortable taking home to our parents (or our broker). But moving up the client food chain requires decision making. After all, take a look around your office and you will probably see a large number of veteran agents who, at any moment, are ready to drop their latte and run like a jackrabbit toward anyone who even whispers the words *real estate* within a hundred-mile radius of the office. Some might call this aggressive, whereas others might find this desperation vaguely pathetic.

How can you avoid the same fate? By building an ideal client model. Wise businesses of all types take the time to build an ideal client model for several reasons. One of the most important is the ability to target their marketing. One truism in the advertising world has always been: You attract the people you advertise to and for. If you place an ad in the penny shopper, you shouldn't really expect a flood of luxury home–buyer calls; on the other hand, advertising a single-wide mobile home in the DuPont Registry will probably also fail to make your cell phone ring. Successful marketing in today's oversaturated, media-rich world requires a narrow target, a window to shoot for. Superstars identify their ideal clients, their target audience, and then market their brand exclusively to this audience.

Also if you know who your audience is before you deliver a presentation, it will become vastly easier to develop a discussion that will be relevant, timely, and interesting. For me, listening to a discussion about the history of Mayan art would put me right to sleep, but for an art history major, I'm sure it would be riveting. Different strokes for different folks. This is exactly why smart marketers often work backward. They first build an ideal client model; then they create a message that they know will appeal to this specific audience.

Having an ideal client model will also enable you to better deliver your services. How? By providing smart agents with the keys to giving their clients exactly what it is they want. A great example of this is how some savvy agents are applying this idea to a new, relatively untapped segment of the market—single women who are buying and selling homes.

The Master Architect's Ideal Client

Architect Donald Rattner understands the power of building an ideal client model. Charged with designing a model home for a new community at the historic Greenbriar Resort in Sulfur Springs, West Virginia, he first set about fleshing out his ideal client. By researching the surrounding area, the economics of the community, and the development he would be building within, he decided that his ideal client would be a family-oriented outdoor lover with the financial ability to purchase a second home. From there, he was able to design a home that would fit this client's lifestyle.

This may be one reason that Greenbriar was listed in 2006 by Forbes.com as "where we want to live!"

To run an efficient business, you must take the time to decide exactly what kind of client you want to attract and work with. Think about your own past experience with buyers and sellers. How many times have you spent days or weeks trying to convince someone to buy or sell a home and received only rejection in return? How did you feel? At your best, ready to tackle the world? I doubt it. Instead you (and probably the potential client) were no doubt frustrated, tired, and irritated by the whole ordeal. So even though your technique and your skills may have been flawless, you still hit a sales wall. What went wrong?

You were efficient but not effective. Great skills are only half the answer to the sales equation. Even though countless books, seminars, and CDs tout the power of sales technique as the answer to all selling challenges, the reality is that even the best skills in the world will take you only halfway to your destination. To get to the Promised Land requires something else—

Emerging Markets—Single Women Buying and Selling Homes

In 2005, 21 percent of homes were sold to single women compared to just 9 percent to single men. In fact, Fannie Mae, the largest secondary mortgage insurer in the United States, estimates that by the year 2010, there will be 31 million women-headed households in the United States, nearly 28 percent of total households. Wisely, some enterprising agents have begun to focus their business on this emerging market by retooling their marketing and presentation styles to better assist their female clients in buying and selling their next home.

As Judy, an agent from the Midwest, points out, "I enjoy helping my women friends buy and sell homes because I think I understand what it is they're looking for in a home." One way she does this is by discussing with her clients the ancillary benefits of homeownership; for instance, the Harvard Joint Center for Housing Studies shows that homeowners are likely to stay in their home longer and to participate more in community and political activities.

effectiveness. As the famous management consultant and author Peter Drucker said years ago, "Efficiency is doing things right; effectiveness is doing the right things." Great agents understand the fundamental business truth that they are effective only when they are presenting their services to qualified buyers and sellers.

But what if a client doesn't fit your ideal model? Do you tell him to go fly a kite?

The short answer is yes; the more pragmatic, realistic answer would be maybe. For most top producers, their ideal client model is not a Polaroid picture; instead, it is more like a mosaic—defined, yes, but able to fit in the odd piece of color here and there. Acceptance or rejection of each client then becomes a business decision, a risk versus reward calculation. Putting this into practice means asking yourself, "How well do these new clients match my business model?" The further the potential client is from your gold standard, the more likely you should be to walk away from the table, chips still in hand. Having the power to push back and say no will help you to become a more powerful and profitable presenter. Now let's look at another technique for unlocking the people paradox: finding more coconuts.

LEARNING OPPORTUNITY

The ideal client model. Superstars build a model of what they are looking for in each new client with whom they work. They then measure each client against this standard.

Three Reasons to Build an Ideal Client Model:

1. Targeted marketing. Wise agents market their services to a targeted audience that they know their message will appeal to.

2. Customized presentations. By building a presentation that focuses on the needs of their ideal client, superstars are far more likely to be successful.

3. Enhanced service delivery. Superstars who provide specialized services will be able to create more client value.

Key question: "How well do these new clients match my business?"

Finding Your Coconut

As a rookie real estate agent, I had the good fortune to spend a day with a true sales professional, a man who had risen through the ranks of a Fortune

500 company to become head of a vast sales department with thousands of employees across the world. While showing him property, I decided to pick his brain for advice, so I asked him what he thought was the greatest lesson he had learned over his long and prosperous career.

Without hesitating, he smiled and said, "Jim, I learned that to succeed in life, you have to be able to find your coconut."

Okay, I thought to myself, that was a little weird. Sensing my confusion, he went on to explain a sales theory that was truly unique and, yeah, a little weird. But weird is fun. So let's have a little fun.

Imagine for a moment that you are the owner of a vast amount of land in Thailand. (I told you it was weird.) You own hundreds of acres of coconut trees, and you must harvest them before the season ends. So to get the job done, you need to hire some employees to do the picking.

The question my client asked me was this: "Whom would you hire?"

My first impulse was to hire local people from the town, but my client quickly shot that down—"They have higher-paying jobs in the cities, so they wouldn't do it."

Digging deeper, I offered another suggestion: "How about bringing in workers from other areas?"

"Too expensive," he explained.

"What about hiring teenagers?"

"It's a full-time job, and they have to go to school," he answered.

Since I was out of suggestions, my client finally revealed what Thai farmers have been doing for generations. They use trained monkeys to climb up the trees to pick the fruits and bring them back down. Why use monkeys? The coconut trees are so tall that it would be too tiring, time-consuming, and even dangerous for farmers to climb up the trees themselves, so they train monkeys to do the job for them.

He went on to explain that a well-trained monkey can pick hundreds of coconuts a day, all for just a few bananas and some affection. What's more, if the Thai farmers were to pay their monkeys based on productivity, most would earn a midlevel salary in Thailand.

"Now, Jim, if that same monkey were earning a midlevel salary here in the United States, he would be beating 95 percent of the salespeople in America, and you know why he would beat them?"

I didn't have a clue, but I have to admit that I was now captivated by this crazy monkey story.

"Because those monkeys have figured out what most salespeople never will—how to earn a banana every day."

It was such a perfectly simple story that I had to think about it for a minute to really grasp what he had just said. So I replayed it again in my mind until I thought I had figured it out.

"So what you're saying is that a great salesperson needs to figure out what he needs to do every day to create a sale and then do those things over and over again, just like those monkeys picking the coconuts."

"Exactly. You see, Jim, most salespeople ignore the fact they there are really just a few simple things that we all need to do every day to create a sale. The bottom line is that salespeople find reasons to do everything else but pick coconuts."

So did you catch the moral of the story? To improve your productivity, you must identify what it is that creates a sale and do that thing over and over again. From a presentation perspective, this means identifying what you're doing right and doing those things over and over again.

But how do you know what is working in your presentation, and what isn't?

It's tough if you're winging it, which is exactly why most agents flounder when it comes to refining and improving their presentation skills. They treat every meeting with a client as unique and unrepeatable, like an artist approaching a canvas. When they do happen to strike creative gold, the process may seem so opaque, unclear, and vague that re-creating the success consistently seems nearly impossible.

For instance, imagine that you do ten seller presentations; five of them end up with you "eating a pavement sandwich," and five turn into signed listings contracts. Reflecting back on those presentations, the big question is: What's the difference? Why did you fail half the time? The easy out is to blame the client, like a surgeon pointing his finger at a corpse. The harder thing to do is to point the finger back at ourselves and assess what we did right or wrong. After all, superstars don't operate on clients who don't need their services. They qualify their clients thoroughly before they ever spend their valuable time and energy on a presentation, but, as we all know, even a thoroughly vetted client can still tell us to hit the bricks if we make a mistake during a presentation. So the question becomes: Are client meetings so unique that our successes really can't be duplicated?

Absolutely not. Rarely do great artists like Rembrandt or Picasso or great photographers like Bernice Abbott or Eugene Atget create only one master-piece; instead, they are able to re-create their success again and again. Not with carbon copies, but with brand new captivating artwork. So even though their individual pieces are uniquely different, their mastery of their art form and the creative process is something that they have learned to duplicate over and over again. The same is true of a real estate presentation. Although every client is different, every home unique, and every situation seemingly incomparable, the way in which the master real estate presenter approaches the appointment is the same. Like an artist who doesn't blame the canvas, or a photographer who won't break his camera after a missed shot, the superstar real estate agent understands that her art is her own responsibility, good or bad, masterpiece or rubbish.

To master your own presentation process, let's take a look at some sim-ple ways you can begin measuring and then improving your performance, starting with the Monthly Presentation Success Chart (Figure 2-2).

FIGURE 2-2.

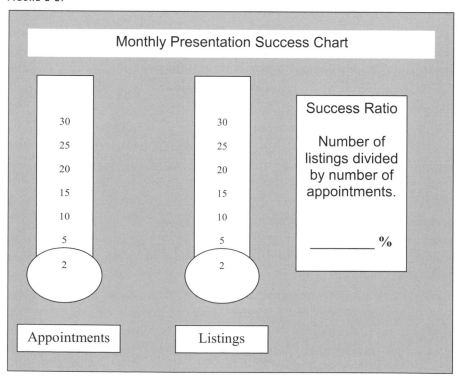

Sherry, a southern California real estate broker, reports, "I find that I can't let myself slip when tracking my presentations. If I do, pretty soon I start getting lazy." If you sensitize yourself to a monthly success ratio, you may find that you will naturally begin to improve your presentation skills by doing nothing more than becoming outcome focused. Sherry uses the Monthly Presentation Success Chart to record how many appointments she goes on and how many actual listings she takes; by doing so, she can quickly determine her success ratio.

Like Sherry, as the president and CEO of your own minicorporation, it is your responsibility to create accountability within your business. So let's tighten the screws just a bit more by using another measurement tool, the Play-by-Play Evaluation.

Even if you're like my wife and hate sports, you no doubt have sat through a broadcast of a professional athletic event or two in your lifetime. During the game, you may have noticed that the announcers often replay the highlights of the game, sometimes to show off mind-blowing field maneuvers like a touchdown or a three-point shot, or in some cases to replay jaw-dropping injuries. This color commentary usually follows the second-by-second action, with some announcers having the ability to freeze and replay the scenes over and over again. Players and coaches use these films to enhance their game and to study their opponent's strengths and weaknesses.

How can we use the same type of system to enhance our own presentation performance? Let's take a look at one Arizona superstar team's technique for reviewing its performance highlights to find out (Figure 2-3).

After each appointment, this team takes just a few minutes and uses the Play-by-Play Evaluation form to quickly rate itself on a scale from 0 to 5, with 5 being the best and 0 the worst. After evaluating each item, the team members add up their numbers and divide by the highest possible total score, in this case 35. This enables them to quickly grade their own performance immediately after every client meeting. For instance, if they are in the 4 to 5 range and they have taken the listing, they have done great; anything below this standard calls for a reexamination of their weak points (even if they have taken the listing).

For agents who are genuinely struggling or brand new agents, a great twist on this idea is to invite a more experienced agent along to complete the Play-by-Play Evaluation on their behalf. This relatively unbiased opinion can reveal listing-blowing mistakes that a rookie agent might not have recognized.

FIGURE 2-3.

Play-by-Play Evaluation	
Task:	**Rating: 0–5**
Qualification	
Asked a series of detailed questions	
Preparation	
Thoroughly prepared for every aspect of the meeting	
Building Rapport and Trust	
Put the client at ease during the meeting	
Presentation	
Reviewed presentation and focused on client needs	
Engaging	
Asked the client involvement questions	
Closing	
Asked the client for the business	
Follow-Up	
Reconnected with the client after the meeting	

Even for the veteran agent, this can be a terrific way to sharpen skills he may have lost over the years. Another way to quickly and dramatically improve any presentation is to create your own highlights reel by recording yourself delivering your presentation.

Of course the ultimate judge and jury of any agent's presentation skills is that agent's audience, buyers and sellers. Strong agents not only rate themselves; they also ask their clients to rate them as well. By doing so, they receive the opinion that really counts, that of the ultimate decision makers. Imagine using this script before beginning any presentation:

Client Evaluation Preparation Script

> *Listen, before we begin talking, I want to let you know that my team always sends out an evaluation form based on my performance today. It takes only about two minutes to complete, and I would really appreciate your thoughts on any way that I can change or improve my presentation. Would that be okay?*

If you were the client, how would you feel about this script? If it were me, I would be impressed by this dialogue for a couple of reasons: First, it would demonstrate to me that this person really cares about self-improvement, and second, it would show me that I'm not working with an egomaniac (not that any real estate agents are egomaniacs).

Now to follow up this discussion point, let's take a look at one Florida agent's actual postmeeting evaluation form.

Meeting Evaluation Form

It was truly a pleasure meeting with you. Because our team is committed to continuous improvement, we ask each of our customers to evaluate our presentation skills. If you could answer this quick questionnaire, it would be greatly appreciated. Thank you.

1. Did you feel that the presentation was well prepared?

2. Did the presentation answer all of your questions and concerns?

3. Was the presentation concise and relevant to your needs?

4. Is there any area of the presentation that can be improved?

5. Overall, what suggestion do you have for our team?

Notice that the questions used here are designed to make the client feel more comfortable about making constructive comments because the focus is on the presentation and not the individual agent. Evaluations that focus on people are rarely answered honestly, if they are answered at all.

So will every client or customer carefully fill out this form? Not a chance. In reality, probably only a small percentage will take the time away from their sitcom reruns to give you any feedback. To improve your odds, you may want to follow the example of many agents who have put the form into an e-mail format, which many clients now prefer as being faster and easier to complete, or, for your technology-challenged consumers, you may consider including a self-addressed stamped envelope for return mail.

Now a final word of caution in using this system: If the vast majority of your evaluations come back positive, but you get that one odd duck that rips out your heart and stomps on it, don't start crying. Evaluations should be looked at based on the totality of the comments, not necessarily on each individual tirade about your mismatched socks or your fancy-dancy shirt. Remember, people are strange. In the professional-speaking business, we are taught to focus on the audience members who are smiling, not on the idiot in the back row who has his arms crossed and hasn't sold a house in 10 years. As superstar presenters, we can't play to the peanut gallery; instead, we must have the discipline to study the bigger picture. Strong agents unemotionally look for trends in their evaluation responses. By looking at trends, they can enhance their presentation by putting each of their client comments into the context of the big picture.

Leaning into your strengths and understanding your weak areas is the mark of the seasoned professional, someone who is confident and understands that every single presentation detail matters. One of the most overlooked details is the power of first contact. Let's dive into this important topic in Chapter 3, "Impact: The Power and Importance of First Contact."

LEARNING OPPORTUNITY

Finding your coconut. Superstars focus on the areas of their business that produce maximum results (like developing presentation skills).

Reproducible results. Although every client is different, every home unique, and every situation seemingly incomparable, the way in which the master real estate presenter approaches each appointment is the same.

Monthly Presentation Success Chart. This measures an agent's rate of conversion of appointments to listings taken.

Play-by-Play Evaluation. This is a self-evaluation of the key aspects of each client meeting to determine areas that can be improved.

Meeting Evaluation Form. This is a form for clients to use when providing feedback on an agent's performance during her presentation.

Impact: The Power and Importance of First Contact

Imagine that your tires are bald. They are so bad that at any moment your vehicle may go careening off the road and into a ditch. So it's time. The duct tape and bubblegum just won't cut it anymore. You're going to have to go to the tire store today and buy some new rubber shoes for your gasoline-guzzling chariot. After walking into the store and waiting in a long line of other procrastinators, you finally reach the clerk, a high-energy kid fresh out of high school. As your eyes meet, he smiles, and then he does something really, really crazy. He bounds over the sales counter, wraps his rubber-stained arms around your new white shirt, and gives you a big, sloppy kiss on the cheek.

"Welcome back!" he exclaims. "It's so great to see you again. We've really missed you around here."

How would you feel at this point—uncomfortable, awkward, or perhaps just a little frightened? For most normal adults, this would be an extremely strange encounter. Why? Because we have no desire to enter into a personal relationship with our service providers (no matter how good-looking they may be). We simply want what we want—in this case, a new set of tires, but it could just as easily be a new television, a car stereo, a cup of coffee, or a new home.

So does this mean that we don't want friendly service? Of course not! We all want our service providers to be affable, courteous, and helpful. We also want them to explain their services thoroughly, be ready to answer our questions, and listen to our problems. But beyond this boundary lies a no-man's-land, a black hole for sales professionals that can lead some unfortunate souls to make a string of potentially career-ending bad first impressions.

The monster under the bed is the tendency of most agents to think that the key to building a good first impression is to "win over" clients with sheer personality. If you blind each new prospect with the power of your great suit, expensive haircut, and bubbly chitchat, those prospects will melt like a small pat of butter on your business pancake, right? Wrong! Wise agents have learned from experience that what clients really crave is a rock-solid professional relationship, an exchange of values, money for service.

Client Relationships
Professionally Based
Based on the client's needs and the services you can offer him.
Personality Based
Based on the client's "liking" you more than your competitor. (What if he doesn't?)

Think about yourself and the tire store example. Going in, what is it that you really want from the clerk? You want professional service, right? In other words, you want to pay a fair price for your new tires; perhaps you want advice on what would be the best tires for your type of vehicle; a guarantee would be good; and, of course, you want the tires put on quickly. To top it off, you probably want someone who asks you detailed questions about your needs and provides concise, easily understood answers.

And herein lies the key to sales excellence. To become a master presenter requires that all client meetings be first and foremost built on a professional relationship. Can a personal relationship follow? You bet. I have become close friends with many of my clients over the years. But the cornerstone of the relationship, the beginning and the end, the alpha and omega, was my professional presentation. Everything else, from my Hollywood good looks to my boyish charm and keen wit (yeah, right!), must always come a distant second.

After all, what if you just don't "click" with every single client? If your career depends on your being the most likable, outgoing, or "on" person in every sales situation, sooner or later you are doomed to failure. Inevitably someone prettier, smarter, funnier, or more magnetic will come along whom the clients like better.

On the other hand, if your sales presentations are based on determining what the client's true needs are and what services you can offer her to satisfy those needs, your likability factor, although still important, is not the determining factor in your being hired. Instead, it becomes a question of who can offer the client the most value per dollar spent. Most value per dollar spent is the basis of every great presentation.

As a consumer, when I perceive that the value of the products or services I am considering exceeds the cost, then, and only then, I begin reaching for my checkbook. I need to be sold. Not on how many compliments a sales clerk can throw my way, or how good a "vibe" I am getting from the car dealer, but on the reasons why this particular purchase will satisfy my personal needs. This is exactly why

> **Value Equation**
>
> Only when the perceived value of a product or service exceeds the perceived cost will a consumer consider a commitment to purchase or proceed.

you may not be willing to spend $5,000 on a Louis Vuitton handbag, but the woman next to you will. The value equation in her mind has been solved; the value of this product to her has exceeded the cost. Once a real estate agent can tip the scale in his favor by offering each and every one of his clients a solution to the value equation, the presentation cards are suddenly stacked overwhelmingly in his favor.

Of course, there is a catch to this logic, because it is very possible that before we even open our mouths to utter a word, a client will have formed an opinion about us and our services just based on how we look, our body language, and our perceived attitude, and, surprisingly, her gut instinct about us will probably be right on the money.

LEARNING OPPORTUNITY

Strong agents strive to build a professional relationship with each of their clients by discovering the client's needs and offering unique solutions.

By solving the value equation, wise agents can help their clients make an informed decision about whom to hire as their next real estate agent.

Judging Books by Their Cover: Mastering First Impressions

Now, I know I just told you that your Hollywood good looks shouldn't matter at all in your presentation, but in the real world, they will have an impact on your ability to make a good first impression and thus will affect your chances of delivering a high-quality presentation. How do we know this? In a first-of-its-kind study published in the November 2004 issue of *Aesthetic Plastic Surgery* from the University of Illinois in Chicago, it was found that a prettier face, natural or man-made, will result in a better first impression. Surprise! "Good-looking" people, it was found, have a tendency to land better jobs, benefits, and rewards than "average-looking" people. (Damn you, Brad Pitt!)

So can you accurately judge a book by its cover? It seems that, contrary to what your mom taught you, yes, you can, with a few added twists, as Dave Kenny, Ph.D., a psychologist at the University of Connecticut and a pioneer in the field of measuring the accuracy of first impressions, has discovered. In his landmark study, which appeared in the *Journal of Personality and Social Psychology*, he studied 250 college students. Each of the students was assigned to a group of three others whom they had never met and had not had a chance to speak with. Armed with nothing more than their first impression, the students were asked to measure each person in the group, including themselves, on five criteria. The results were then compared to the individuals' self-assessments.

Amazingly, the students were able to describe one another's personality traits accurately based on nothing more than their gut instincts. The bottom line: People are extremely good at a mental function that is now known as "thin slicing," a term coined by author Malcolm Gladwell, which means taking huge amounts of data; paring it down to the key elements; and making a conscious, or often unconscious, decision based on this narrow window of knowledge.

If you think about it, we do this all the time. When you meet a friend of a friend for the first time, or perhaps when you meet another parent at your daughter's school, you instantly create a

---

Shake Them Up!

A good handshake is one that conveys self-confidence, trust, and a genuine interest in the other party.

- Always stand, if possible, to shake hands.
- To show trust, move out from behind your desk.
- Make eye contact and smile.
- Grip hand firmly (don't crush).
- Shake for one to three seconds, and then release.

mental snapshot of what you perceive this person to be about. Try not to get a first impression of the next person you meet. It's impossible. You might assume that to achieve this mental feat, our brains are empowered with a phenomenal amount of processing power and memory. You would be right on both counts; in fact, for decades the ability to thin slice large amounts of data was attributed to a large memory, and therefore a higher intelligence level. But in a recent study, Edward Vogel, an assistant professor of cognitive neuroscience at the University of Oregon, found that the brain actually employs a "bouncer"–a neural mechanism that controls what information gets into awareness. The bouncer's job is to assess each piece of information and decide if it gets processed or tossed.

To ensure that we get past the bouncer and have a shot at building a professional relationship, we need to understand the power of making a strong first impression. Many studies, including detailed research from the University of Toledo, suggest that in a sales setting or job interview, we have 30 seconds (or less) to make a lasting first impression. According to these studies, the keys to a great first impression (and the first step to terrific presentation) are based 55 percent on visual appearance (body language, posture, facial expression, and eye contact), 38 percent on voice quality (tone, inflection, and volume), and the remaining 7 percent on the content of your conversation (Figure 3-1).

In building this critical first impression, how you appear to someone visually is the single most important aspect of building a positive impression. One piece of your visual package is your attire. Mike Hasson, a hugely suc-

FIGURE 3-1. IMPACT: THE 30-SECOND CLOCK STARTS NOW!

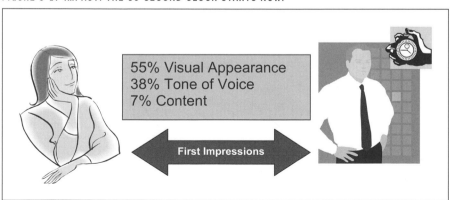

cessful independent broker in Portland, Oregon, believes that dressing for success is essential to building a good first impression. (It is rumored that he has sent home a few agents who did not meet his high office standards.) This may be one reason that, according to *Realtor Magazine,* the Hasson Company's average sales volume per agent of $6.4 million is the highest in the Pacific Northwest and fourth highest in the entire nation.

Within my own firm, we have always encouraged the Million-Dollar Standard, which is the expectation that every agent should, within 10 minutes, be able to meet with a million-dollar buyer or seller. Sure, some agents argue that their clients would prefer them to be more comfortable: "I don't work with millionaires!" But as my friends from the South say, "That dog don't hunt." Consider a truck driver, a mechanic, or a plumber who needs to hire a real estate professional. If he is trusting this person to sell his largest financial asset, does he expect to see someone who dresses the way he does when he walks through the office doors? Of course not. Instead, what clients expect to see, what they deserve to see, and what they are paying to see is someone who is dressed professionally. To become a superstar real estate professional, you need to look the part. (Say good-bye to those sweat pants and T-shirts.)

The client's expectations aside, consider how *you* feel when you dress and look your best. Don't you feel more confident and powerful? You bet you do. This strength is a tangible asset that everyone around you can instantly sense and respect. Try walking into a restaurant, a hotel, or a business meeting looking your best and notice how differently you are treated. What changed? Perception. Perception is reality. People's perception of you changed, and, just as important, the way you view yourself, your own self-image, changed. As Coleman Cox once said, "Keeping your clothes well pressed will keep you from looking hard pressed."

Now, for those of us who won't be making the cover of *GQ* or *Vogue* anytime soon, there is still hope because our visual appearance is only a part of the first impression that we make. Also included in the mix is our tone of voice and the content of our conversation.

What you say is not nearly as important as how you say it!

Consider for a moment what would happen if you closed your eyes in a restaurant and just listened to the voices around you (not the ones in your head). No doubt you would instantly begin forming opinions about each person around you just based on voice quality. It's no wonder, since 38 percent of our first impressions are based entirely on hearing a person's tone of voice. The old adage that what we say is not nearly as important as how we say it is absolutely true.

So are you soprano, tenor, or bass? More important, can you motivate, inspire, and move people to action using just your voice? In the seminar industry, a powerful speaker will use her voice like an instrument to engage, titillate, amuse, and break the hearts of her audience. Within minutes, she can have an audience span the whole range of emotions, from fear and trepidation to tears and laughter, all with just the power of words. Wars have started and ended, democracies formed and crushed, and businesses begun and bankrupted, all through the power of one person's voice.

So how powerful is your voice? In a highly visual culture, it's easy to say little or nothing at all and just let the pictures, graphs, and PowerPoint slides do the talking for us. Yet when we do speak, the sound of our voice can either draw people toward our presentation or repel them from it. Our speaking voice is a very powerful, often unconscious motivator during any presentation, large or small.

We have all been vocalizing since birth—talking, babbling, screaming, singing, ranting, raving, and now selling. Yet rarely do we give our voices a second thought. When we do hear ourselves on a video- or audio-tape babbling like a rhesus monkey about some long-lost banana, we cover our ears and exclaim, "I don't sound like that!" Yes, my furry friend, you do. Unfortunately, most of us haven't taken the time to fully develop our vocal skills. Instead, we fall victim to developing bad speaking habits that can limit the power and persuasive tone of one of our most powerful sales tools.

The good news is that with just a little effort we can all develop a more pleasing voice. One way is by controlling the tempo and volume of your voice. Listening to someone with a flat, monotone voice is like watching a tire deflate: You just want it to be over. Expert speakers modulate their tempo, the speed at which they talk, and the volume of their speech to engage their audience. To inspire buyers and sellers, we also need to perk up their ears by offering variation. By doing so, we can unconsciously force them to stay focused on our discussion points and encourage them to actually listen. Just consider how many ways you can say one word or sentence using the power of variation. This is sometimes known as punching up words to bring attention to the most important areas of a conversation by stressing content words, or words that carry the meaning of the sentence, while giving less attention to structure words, or fillers. To see this demonstrated, watch and listen to any news broadcast and notice how those on camera use the power of their voice to keep audiences "tuned in."

In a business setting, another common mistake among rookie presenters is talking too quickly. It's often been said that the average person speaks at about 100 to 200 words a minute, but an overly excited or nervous presenter can gust up to 500 words a minute. Like a fire hose, they keep gushing information so fast that they drown their listeners. To make our ideas, concepts, and questions resonate, we must pause, slow down, or even stop talking. In fact, the most powerful presenters understand that to really engage a client, they must first ask lots of questions. Think about the next time you are at a business luncheon. When someone new approaches, would she make a better first impression by talking about herself—her hobbies, job title, or shoe size—or would she do better by asking about you—what you do, where you work, your family, and so forth? Our clients and customers are the same way: Their favorite topic is always themselves!

On the phone, where our voice is the only thing that clients will have to base their first impression on, it becomes even more important to develop strong voice and etiquette skills. Take a look at some specialized tips on handling phone inquiries:

Telephone Tactics for Making a Great First Impression

1. *Speak clearly.* Superstars make a point of slowing down on the phone, enunciating clearly, and avoiding the shorthand real estate lingo that can often confuse a real estate client. This shows that they are completely interested and engaged in the conversation.

2. *Smile.* In training real estate agents to prospect, we often use the age-old wisdom of "smiling while you're dialing." Why? Because when you smile, your whole body, posture, voice, and attitude change. Amazingly, you can sense these subtle changes over the phone.

3. *Prepare to take calls.* Real estate agents should expect that they will receive hundreds of calls a month from their listing, marketing, and prospecting activities. Wise agents prepare for these calls by keeping copies of their advertising, prospect inquiry logs, appointment books, and any other necessary tools at their fingertips.

4. *Give them more.* Real estate agents who field calls successfully often find that creating a better first impression is as simple as offering clients more than they asked for. For instance, when talking with buyers about a specific listing, many agents keep a list of similar alternative properties that they can provide information about to prospective buyers.

5. *Take great messages.* In real estate, any phone call can be of critical importance—a deal breaker or a deal maker. Superstars, therefore, take great messages by recording the date and time of each call along with the caller's name, phone number, best time to call, and a brief message. In addition, many superstars now ask callers if they would prefer a call back or an e-mail.

6. *Catch the name.* A client's name is an important piece of information that should always be written down immediately, lest, like me, you forget it five seconds later.

7. *Train your team.* Don't forget that your front office, team members, and assistants can often be a client's first point of contact with your brand. Thus, your front line must be trained on proper phone etiquette.

This brings us full circle to the last critical component of making a great first impression: having strong content. Imagine watching a singer take the stage. He is dressed in a suit and tie; he jokes with the audience, putting it at ease; the band begins to play; and then, like a broken power saw, he begins to sing the most offensive song you could ever imagine. He has perfect pitch, tempo, and volume, but what comes forth from his mouth would make George Carlin, Larry Flynt, and Marilyn Manson queasy. Do you stay and listen? After all, he looks the part. He took the time to engage the audience and build rapport. Most of us would be gone before the second verse, which is why content is still incredibly important. What you say matters.

So what will you say within the few seconds you have to make a lasting first impression? By packaging a standard, clear, and concise sound bite of information, superstars can instantly adapt and customize their dialog to fit any setting. Take a look at these real-world examples:

First Contact Business Meeting

It was a pleasure meeting you. Listen, do you mind if I give you a couple of my business cards? I specialize in selling rural ranch land here in <county name>; in fact, we just started a new marketing campaign <describe>. If you hear of anyone buying or selling ranch land, please give me a ring.

First Contact Phone Call

It's been great talking with you today. You know, I specialize in residential investment properties; in fact, we just closed <name property>. I keep a list of possible investors on my desk at all times for those kinds of hot buys; may I add you to my list?

First Meeting at Client's Home

Listen, before we tour the home, let me give you a couple of my cards. I specialize in real estate relocation for my firm. In fact, my team has already helped 25 families this year buy and sell a home.

Notice that each of these scripts is designed to give the potential client a quick, bite-sized nugget of information that will help the agent stand out from the crowd of other real estate practitioners in his market. "Hello, my name is Bob, and I sell real estate" may be an accurate statement, but it is extremely boring, like a glass of seltzer water—yeah, it satisfies your thirst, but there's no kick, wallop, or buzz to it. How long will someone remember this person? Probably about as long as it takes you to read this sentence. What was that guy's name again?

Take a minute and write down your own first impression sound bite:

_____

_____

_____

Now, although talking with someone in person or on the phone is often how we build a first impression, it's likely, in today's fast-paced world, that our first point of contact with many of our next-generation clients will be in cyberspace. To underscore this, according to the 2005 National Association of Realtors Profile of Home Buyers and Sellers, 77 percent of all buyers used the Internet as their primary information resource. So how do you build a good first impression online? Let's find out.

LEARNING OPPORTUNITY

First impressions are crucial to mastering presentation skills. Superstars work hard to improve their appearance, tone of voice, and content to create a positive first impression.

The Million-Dollar Standard. By being prepared to meet with a million-dollar client at any time, strong agents can improve their confidence level by always looking their best.

Punching up your voice. By using the power of variation, tempo, and timing, wise agents can keep their audience interested and engaged in their presentation.

Content matters. By asking questions that relate to a client's interests and needs, strong agents keep their client excited about building a professional relationship.

The New Internet Interview

Imagine that you aren't a real estate salesperson. Life is treating you pretty good; you have a great job, great benefits, and great friends, but then suddenly your significant other lands a plum job in another state. It's a career-making opportunity that can't be passed up, so unfortunately you will have to sell your home and move.

As a buyer, if you log on to Google, the largest Internet search portal, today, you can find over 355 million webpages that have something to say about the topic of real estate. For real estate professionals specializing in buyer representation, this ease of access to information can provide savvy agents with both a competitive edge and an incredible challenge, as buyers, in order to sift through this literal mountain of available information, become virtual terminators, capable of blasting through websites faster than bolts of greased lightning. In fact, according to researchers at Carleton University in Ottawa, online people are registering their likes and dislikes in as little as a twentieth of a second based on their overall impression of a website's home page. In addition, researchers have discovered a "halo effect" based on that emotional first impression that carries over to cognitive judgments of a website's other characteristics, including usability and credibility.

> **Home Buyers' Use of the Internet**
>
> - **79 percent** of home buyers used the Internet as a source of information.
> - **21 percent** of Internet home buyers found their agent online.
> - **75 percent** of buyers who searched online drove by or looked at a home they first saw online.
>
> Source: The 2005 National Association of Realtors Profile of Home Buyers and Sellers

Welcome to the new Internet interview. where you may be questioned, probed, searched, and discarded without ever knowing that a client has even come into contact with your company. Like shadowy ghosts, these anony- mous Internet-empowered consumers float above your marketing, assessing every aspect of your business before vanishing into a puff of virtual smoke, never to be seen or heard from again.

"It's a constant struggle to move people out from behind a keyboard and through the front door of our offices," says Scot Spalding, managing broker and Webmaster at All State Real Estate (www.allstaterealestate.com) in Roseburg, Oregon. "We constantly have to be improving our website to be competitive."

How many companies have you interviewed online? Hundreds? Thou- sands? Tens of thousands? How many even knew you had evaluated them? Close to none, right? The company had to make a terrific first impression and then offer you something interesting enough for you to take the next step and make contact with it. So how can we do the same for our own website visitors? Often the first step for real estate professionals is knowing what it is buyers want when they visit a website.

According to a study done in 2006 by the California Association of Real- tors, entitled the "Internet vs. Traditional Buyer Study," it was found that buyers primarily visit a real estate website to find information on specific homes and to conduct neighborhood research. Because of this, tech-savvy agents make their property search engine easy to find by placing it front and center on their home page (see Figure 3-2). The importance of this technique is further supported by the 2005 National Association of Realtors Profile of Home Buyers and Sellers, which states that the number one item that buyers want from a real estate professional is help in finding the right home to purchase.

So why wouldn't a buyer just log on to Realtor.com and see virtually every listing in North America? They do. According to the CAR study, 80 percent of Internet buyers who eventually purchase a home visit Realtor.com, but many (73 percent) also visit specific real estate company websites, and 58 percent view individual agents' websites. Interestingly, when asked, In- ternet buyers prefer to deal with local or regional players in their area of interest, most likely because of the perceived value of doing business with someone who knows the intimate details about the local area market condi- tions.

In addition, the CAR study found that the top three items that buyers

FIGURE 3-2.

listed as important on an agent's website were more (and better) photos (78 percent), more detailed descriptions of the properties they had viewed (77 percent), and more virtual tours (47 percent). To stand out in the luxury home market, Roberta Baldwin uses her website, www.njdreamhouses.com, to appeal to all of these buyer requests and much more (Figure 3-3). Likewise, Anthony Marguleas, owner broker of A.M. Realty Inc. in Pacific Palisades and Pasadena, California, has found that having an Internet strategy can pay huge dividends. His team spends $75,000 a year on Internet marketing but yields an impressive $50 million in sales volume per year as a result. He and his 10 sales associates use two virtual assistants to enter Internet leads generated from his website, www.homebuyersonly.com, and other sites into a biweekly e-mail marketing campaign.

FIGURE 3-3. COPYRIGHT © ROBERTA BALDWIN.

What about sellers? For agents who focus on the listing market, a website is still critically important. Consider for a moment the psychology of selling. What is a seller's first step when considering making a real estate change? For many, it would be to start daydreaming about their next home. Because of this, many people begin searching for their ideal replacement property online long before they have placed their home for sale.

As Kellie Jones, a broker-associate with Century 21 Superstars in Santa Margarita, was quoted in Realtor Magazine Online, "If I can get the phone number and a face to face meeting [after the client visits her site at www .kelliejones.com], I can usually get the listing." Strong agents like Kellie are experts at converting buyer leads into seller listings. They have discovered the not-so-secret truth that many buyer leads are in fact seller leads in disguise. An equally important consideration is that many tech-savvy sellers, when considering whom to hire as their listing agent, will first visit a prospective listing agent's website to conduct a virtual "interview." Because of this, Joseph DeLorenzo (www.sellmyhome101.com) uses a unique approach of providing sellers with valuable information through a virtual classroom where sellers can learn about critical aspects of marketing their home and what Joe can offer.

To ensure that your website will make a strong first impression and stand up against even your toughest competitors, follow these simple guidelines from Stanford University based on three years of intensive research, and interviews with over 4,500 people:

Stanford University Guidelines for Website Credibility (Adapted for Real Estate)

1. *Make it easy to verify the accuracy of the information on your site.* Superstars often build their site's credibility by providing third-party support (citations, references, source material, and testimonials) for any information they present. Even if people don't follow these links, you've shown confidence in your material. For example, to find reams of information on housing statistics, check out www.realtor.org, www.nahb .com, or www.census.gov.

2. *Show that there's a real organization behind your site.* Many agents accomplish this by posting a photo of their office location along with driving directions, a map, or even a satellite image of their location. For a quick and easy satellite photo of your office (and your listings), check out www.earth.google.com.

3. *Highlight your expertise.* Wisely, many agents demonstrate their expertise by listing their membership in councils, their accreditations, and their certifications, like ABR, CRS, and GRI. For instance, linking your website to www.rebac.net can highlight your expertise in buyer representation.

4. *Show that you are honest and trustworthy.* To convey a sense of honesty and trustworthiness, many agents use only the highest-quality images and text to describe their services. To add high-quality images to your website, consider using www.gettyimages.com, a website that boasts a database of over a million photographs. In addition, many agents post a brief biography of themselves and each team member.

5. *Make it easy to contact you.* A simple way to boost your site's credibility is by posting contact information in a prominent position on each page

of your website. In addition, many communication companies like www.genutec.com can provide agents with one-stop calling solutions and real-time website client communication platforms to make it even easier for users to find you.

The Stanford study also found that it is helpful to design a site that not only looks professional but is extremely easy to use, as website designers often have a tendency to build sites that may dazzle high-end users but can turn off a typical buyer. The study concluded by recommending that the content within a website be updated often in order to be viewed as credible and timely, with special attention being paid to avoiding errors of all types, including typographical errors and broken links.

These critical components can help create a website that has "flow," a term coined by Dr. Mihaly Csikszentmihalyi in his book of the same title. Andrew King, a respected author and founder of the websites www.web reference.com and www.javascript.com, agrees: "Flow is an 'optimal experience' that is 'intrinsically enjoyable.' Responsive, well-designed websites can induce a flow state in their users."

How can you ensure a sense of flow on your website? One way may be to follow these simple design tips from www.weboptimization.com:

- *Speed and simplicity.* Create web pages that load quickly and easily by using an uncluttered layout. Many agents choose to minimize animation, which can often distract users with a limited attention span.

- *Feedback and clear navigation.* Provide fast feedback for links and site navigation (menus) by including "signposts" such as site maps to help clients find their way around your website.

- *Match the site to the end user.* Many user-friendly websites can adapt to their clients' needs by offering varying download speeds, different font sizes, and even multiple languages.

- *Avoid cutting-edge technology.* Cutting-edge technology often gets in the way of user goals. Research shows that users don't want it; instead, they just want to receive their requested information.

Strong agents actively manage their business brand by carefully orchestrating every aspect of their corporate identity, including their Internet strategy, because they know that at this very minute someone, somewhere has just logged on to Google and is now looking for his next home.

LEARNING OPPORTUNITY

Internet first impressions. Studies have found that our clients can form an impression of our website in as little as a twentieth of a second.

Buyers and sellers. Both use the Internet as a way to "interview" potential agents. By understanding how they use agent websites, we can build a stronger first impression.

Credibility. By following simple guidelines, agents can create a website that helps consumers feel more relaxed and confident about using their services.

Flow. Using simple design principles, any agent can make her website easier to navigate and user friendly, and a website that flows is likely to attract more users.

Building a Brand Presentation

Congratulations, you have just been nominated for your first Oscar! I guess all those acting classes in college finally paid off. Unfortunately, the ceremony is tonight, and you can't make it because you're on location with Vin Diesel in Bangladesh. (Blast!) On such short notice, your agent has informed you that you have only six choices to act as your stand-in to accept the award on your behalf. Your choices are Corey Feldman, Mickey Rourke, Farrah Fawcett, Robin Williams, Tom Hanks, and Susan Sarandon.

So who would you choose to represent you on Oscar night?

In a classroom setting, the overwhelming majority of my students choose either Tom Hanks or Susan Sarandon. Why? They are extremely well respected, likable, and credible actors. They won't embarrass you, make fools of themselves, or run off with your statue. In other words, they would represent you well.

Our clients go through a similar process. This is sometimes known as the ego-driven decision. This ego-driven decision-making process can be influenced by many factors, but it can be boiled down into one sentence: *Your image is a reflection of their image.* And your image is called your brand.

When companies sell a brand name like Gerber, Sony, or iPod, they're really selling what those names represent. Clients buy into a sense of familiarity, trust, and quality when they buy a brand name. This is exactly why movie studios will pay people like Russell Crowe, Reese Witherspoon, or Julia Roberts tens of millions of dollars to star in a new motion picture. They are brand names. Audiences know what to expect, they are comfortable watching them act, and they trust the actor to deliver a good performance.

So if we haven't yet won an Oscar, how do we create a strong professional brand? According to the Small Business Administration (www.sba .gov), there are three aspects to building a successful company identity. The first is understanding the concept of building brand equity, the second is finding a brand personality, and the third is cultivating a brand reputation (see Figure 3-4). Let's take a look at each of these components individually.

Brand Equity

A brand's equity is considered its value or worth. Like other business assets, such as furniture, fixtures, and equipment, a brand name has its own unique valuation. For instance, what would you pay for just the brand names of

FIGURE 3-4. BUILDING A PROFESSIONAL BRAND

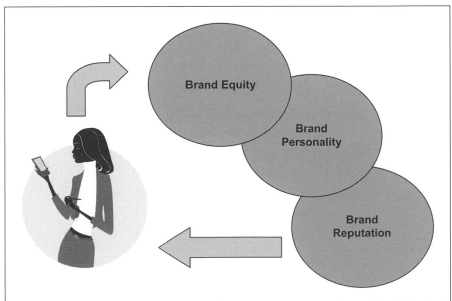

Pepsi, IBM, or Disney? No doubt many wise investors would pay millions of dollars for any of these iconic names. Why? The names themselves have tremendous value.

The importance of branding has become so fundamental to American business that it is often the first consideration when companies fund new ventures. Brands like Joe Boxer, Leapfrog, and Sierra Mist—names that didn't exist 10 to 15 years ago—are now ingrained in our culture and instantly recognizable. How did that happen? With a carefully planned presentation of their product combined with an aggressive marketing plan targeting a very specific audience.

When you use either your own name or a name you have created, such as Judy McCutchin's hugely successful www.dallashomes.com (Figure 3-5) as a brand, the brand must be treated as an asset, perhaps the most valuable company asset you will ever own. Every success adds value to the brand, and every misstep can sharply affect your equity as well. A great example of the power of brand equity is Martha Stewart. Her public company, Omnimedia, worth $2 billion at its peak, saw its share price fall by 60 percent because of an insider-trading scandal involving Martha and her close friends that first emerged in June 2002.

In building your own brand equity, it's always wise to follow the path of

FIGURE 3-5.

companies that have already blazed a trail both inside and outside of the real estate industry because, as has been said many times, *success leaves clues, and failure follows a pattern.*

To determine what superstar brands are worthy of study, Landor Associates, a brand and design consultant in San Francisco, teamed up with Brand-Economics to discover the 10 breakaway brands of the 2000s. To accomplish this feat, they commissioned a study of 9,000 consumers from 2001 to 2004. In asking consumers what they thought of 2,500 U.S. brands, they measured two distinct properties: differentiation and relevance. Differentiation measures how well the brand stands out in a crowded market, and relevance measures whether the product will actually meet the consumer's real needs. For example, a Gulfstream jet has terrific differentiation but very little relevance because most of us don't have the means to buy one (yet); on the other hand, Kleenex is something that almost anyone can use, but a gazillion companies now make facial tissues, so it has very little differentiation. The strongest brands have found ways to give their customers both.

> **Ten Breakaway Brands and Their Value Increase from 2001 to 2004**
>
> - **iPod: $1.3 billion**
> - **DeWalt: $775 million**
> - **Leapfrog: $236 million**
> - **Subway: $1.8 billion**
> - **Gerber: $153 million**
> - **BP: $3.3 billion**
> - **Eggo: $58 million**
> - **Sony Cyber-Shot: $595 million**
> - **Google: $21.3 billion**
> - **Sierra Mist: $131 million**
>
> Source: *Fortune*, October 2005/Landor Study.

So now here are the tough questions: Have you carefully cultivated your services by differentiating them from those of others in your marketplace? Are you demonstrating your relevance to potential clients as an agent who delivers results? Is your brand name recognizable in your community as a result of a consistent, well-thought-out marketing plan?

Strong agents set the stage for presentation success by exposing their potential clients to a quality brand. One way to powerfully influence their decision is by deciding on your brand's personality.

Brand Personality

When I walk through the doors of the Mandalay Bay Casino in Las Vegas, the first thing I do is take a deep breath. Not because I can finally relax, but because the place has a certain smell: tropical, fresh, clean . . . inviting? Honestly, I can't quite put my finger on it, but I can tell you this: I like it. I could go on and on about the other amenities that the hotel offers, like eating at the Russian-themed restaurant Red Square, or listening to music at the House of Blues, or savoring a glass of wine in the huge Romanesque spa. The sandy beach, lazy river, and huge wave pool don't hurt, either. But at the end of the day, when I'm on the plane flying home, the thing that I miss most, and that I long for again, is that smell. Weird, right?

Not really. Great brand managers have found my strange olfactory fascination to be a new beachhead for building consumer loyalty, excitement, and desire—building a brand personality. Contrary to popular belief, many companies have found that the service economy has already peaked. As automation, obsolescence, and offshoring have eroded the value of many products and services within the U.S. economy, it has become all too common to watch once-thriving companies (and whole industries) fall under the weight of commoditization and price-based competition. To fight back, fleet-footed business innovators have embraced a unique solution, known to many advertising executives as experience-based marketing, or just experience marketing. Experience marketing, or building a brand personality, involves surrounding your products and services with experiential value, the key to which is creating a meaningful emotional and sensory experience that a consumer will be excited to have happen again.

For instance, most of us know that Nordstrom's sells fashionable clothing, shoes, and accessories to a market that includes upper-middle-class to affluent customers (a finicky bunch). At the center of the Nordstrom's brand is finding ways to tempt its customers to return to the store. How? One way is by using experience marketing to attract floor traffic, including hiring DJs and hosting cosmetic events, fashion shows, and invitation-only sales. Of-

> **Nordstrom's Experience Marketing**
> - Champagne Receptions
> - Gown Shows
> - Desert Receptions
> - Cocktail Receptions
> - Fragrance Festivals

fering multisensory experiences, Nordstrom's has found, turns shopping from something that many consumers dread into something that they relish. Likewise, according to *USA Today*, Whole Foods grocery stores enjoyed a 15 percent jump in total sales during 2005, whereas the average supermarket grew by just 1 percent. How did Whole Foods do it? One way is by carefully managing its customer experience and its brand personality. At Whole Foods, customers can enjoy a chocolate strawberry fountain, choose from 150 fresh seafood items, and even sample some wine on the way out of the store. Like Nordstrom's, Whole Foods has mastered managing the customer experience. It is these types of companies, the ones that avoid the tendency to homogenize and converge on one boring piece of middle ground, that consumers prefer to do business with.

You might ask, "How can I apply this to building a successful brand personality and building a better real estate presentation?" One start, according to Martin Lindstrom, author of *Brand Sense*, is to ask what feelings or emotions your brand personality evokes when a potential client is exposed to your marketing.

Superstar agents are experts at creating a desire in clients to do business only with their brand. They do this by offering their clients and customers a powerful brand personality, one that rings true throughout

> **Sensory Brand Audit**
>
> **Desire:** Attraction or repulsion
> **Arousal:** Energized or irritated
> **Dominance:** Empowered or inadequate
> **Delight:** Happy or sad
> **Fulfillment:** Contented or anxious
> **Calm:** Peaceful or bored
>
> Martin Lindstrom, *Brand Sense*, 2005.

every "touch" the client has with their microcompany, including a presentation. Check out how Florida real estate agent Patty Willis (www.pattywillis .com), after teaming up with The Agent Design Firm (www.theagentdesign firm.com), successfully created an integrated theme throughout her entire marketing plan (see Figure 3-6). From her business cards to her personal brochures, website, and postcards, she has created a consistent look and feel for her brand. Her brand has a personality.

Looking at Patty's marketing, you might assume that she has been in the real estate business for a long time. Not true. Patty is a relative newcomer to the real estate business, but she has already made her mark in the luxury home market, in part by building a strong brand name. Consider how this will affect her credibility when she is sitting with a client during a presentation. No doubt her clients will get the sense that Patty is committed to a long-term, successful career in the real estate business.

In addition to using traditional print marketing to build a brand personality, many agents are now using technology to enhance their company identity by hosting blogs and broadcasting podcasts. A blog is a cross between a website and a daily diary or log. A great example of a popular real estate blog is www.raincityguide.com. At this blog, a group of dedicated real estate professionals update a constant stream of relevant data about the Seattle real estate market. Potential clients and blog visitors can ask questions, participate in active discussion threads, and review downloadable bits of data, tips, and statistics about the marketplace in real time. Rather than being a static

FIGURE 3-6.

page of marketing information like a website, a blog offers an interactive exchange of information among all the users, with a moderator (you) to help keep the information organized (and appropriate). To start your own blog (for free), check out www.blogspot.com.

Perhaps you're more of a Larry King fan; you enjoy the radio. A podcast is like a radio broadcast, except that instead of sending your signals over the airwaves, you send them through the Internet. Podcasts are made possible through the use of RSS, or Rich Site Summary, an XML format that creates portable audio files that can be distributed in the MP3 format and played by virtually any portable media player and computer on the planet. Yes, for a few dollars a month at host sites like www.audioblog.com, virtually anyone, including you, can start wearing red suspenders and have your very own soapbox. Brad Korn and his team in Kansas City use their regular podcasts to keep their clients up to date on market trends and moving tips (see Figure 3-7).

Brad also uses his podcast as a way to build relationships with customers whom he hasn't even met yet by posting his podcast on his website and his blog. According to Brad, his team receives 15 to 20 quality leads a month, many of which result in a buyer or seller presentation.

So now that you are on your way to building strong brand equity and a unique brand personality, it's time to defend, nurture, and grow your brand's reputation.

Brand Reputation

Have you ever heard the term *soft opening*? It's what happens when a restaurant, hotel, or business opens before it is really ready to do so. The idea is to work out the operational kinks with a limited audience before the "grand opening." The theory is that by sacrificing a few clients early, you can start the cash flow rolling, and down the road, when the business is running

FIGURE 3-7.

1.Kansas City Real Estate Podcast by The Korn Team ⏵play
This month's edition covers Kansas City area market trends, mortgage rate issues, and what people need to know when moving in this area.
Podcast Date: Jan 20, 2006 14:47:36

smoothly, you can overcome any negative press that resulted. This is not unlike the way many real estate agents run their business. They dive headfirst into the deep water and start splashing around in hopes that they can keep their business above water. These agents often take a short-term view of their business and their need to close immediate sales, with no regard for their business horizon or the long-term consequences of their actions.

But is this a wise decision? Probably not, as according to the 2005 National Association of Realtors Profile of Home Buyers and Sellers, it was found that the most important factor by far in choosing a real estate professional was an agent's reputation (41 percent for buyers and 57 percent for sellers). Positive or negative, good or bad, our customers' overall satisfaction is not the result of one great meeting but of the entire history of our professional relationship. It is the cumulative effect of these contact points over a period of time that becomes your brand's reputation. Every interaction, then, that your brand has with a customer is a touch point, holding the potential to carry the brand flag and create either another in a long line of positive interactions with a customer or the place where your business crashes headfirst into the rocks. As Lord Jeffery once said, "A good name, like good will, is got by many actions and lost by one."

On the flip side of this discussion is the realization among veteran agents that just as our clients choose us based on how well we will represent them in the marketplace, the reverse must also be true. This means that strong agents don't accept weak buyers, the ones who will never close a transaction or who consistently make ridiculously low offers, nor, for that matter, do they accept sellers who dramatically overprice their property or who won't cooperate with showings. Why? Because working with weak clients is a bad reflection on a strong agent's brand.

Summing up the importance of managing a real estate agent's brand reputation, NAR (National Association of Realtors) senior economist Paul Bishop had this to say: "Word-of-mouth recommendation is the most common way to learn about real estate professionals. The most important criteria, whether you're buying or selling, are the individual agent's reputation and their knowledge of the local market."

Obviously your brand can and will affect your client's first impression of your company and will directly affect the consumer's choice when she is interviewing you for the position of representing her in the marketplace. Yet even the strongest agents—the superstars who have built tremendous brand equity, a fantastic brand personality, and a great brand reputation—can still blow it by failing to connect with their clients. To avoid becoming the "New Coke" of the real estate world, let's take a look at engaging the client.

LEARNING OPPORTUNITY

Branding. Strong agents strive to create a company identity, a professional brand. A well-managed brand can help clients buy into a sense of familiarity, trust, and quality when buying new products and services.

Three Components of a Strong Brand

1. *Brand equity.* A brand should be treated as a company asset that has tremendous value. Every success and failure can add value to the overall brand or reduce its value.

2. *Brand personality.* Successful brands have their own personality. Strong agents create an integrated marketing approach to show off their signature style.

3. *Brand reputation.* Preserving a high-quality brand reputation is extremely important, as it is the number one reason clients choose an agent.

Engaging the Client

Are you pushing or pulling business?

This question may seem like the beginning of one of those philosophical discussions that may be interesting but really doesn't help you make more money. But if money is the issue, then this may be the most important question you ask yourself all year.

Why? Because one of the biggest companies in the world asked itself this very question a few years back, and it discovered that it had the wrong answer. What's more, to fix the problem would cost time, effort, and energy, and it would shake the company to its very core. The company was Wal-Mart, and the challenge was the age-old problem in retailing of stale inventory.

The challenge for Wal-Mart had always been how to manage inventory so that each store could maximize its profits. Since the dawn of retailing, the sales cycle had virtually remained unchanged. Manufacturers produced products; stores then acquired the products and stocked their shelves in an attempt to sell the items to customers. In effect, then, the manufacturers pushed the products to the stores, and the stores then pushed the products onto the shelves, and hopefully into customers' shopping carts.

Unfortunately, this process has some inherent flaws, the most problematic of which is: What if the customer doesn't want what you're pushing? To deal with this problem, Wal-Mart decided to completely rebuild its sales system. The company began by computerizing its entire distribution system (a massive undertaking that other companies, such as its archrival at the time, Kmart, scoffed at). By computerizing each store, the company could instantly identify exactly which products were selling, how quickly, and for what margins. It also began to ask customers which products they would like to see on the shelves, and which products they didn't really have a need for.

In the end Wal-Mart pioneered the concept of pulling from the customer. By watching for trends, margins, and customer input, Wal-Mart was able to reverse the retailing model. Today Wal-Mart is able to pull from the manufacturer exactly the products that it knows will sell. Instead of buying blind, it works with producers to build products that it knows will have a high likelihood of selling in its stores.

So how does this apply to real estate? How can we reverse the selling cycle?

When you look at most markets, many agents and brokerages are pushing their services. In many cases, these are the same services that have been pushed to real estate consumers for decades. For instance: List your home with me and I'll place your listing in the MLS system, or I'll hold open houses, or I'll have a broker tour. But here is the big question: What is it that your client actually wants from you?

Superstar companies and agents reverse the sales cycle by pulling from the consumer. They discover exactly what it is that buyers and sellers want from them in their market and then deliver on those needs. To lead with the client need, top producers often have to throw out old assumptions and traditions and accept that today's sophisticated buyers and sellers may have a completely different set of priorities from that of their predecessors.

So how can you pull from your customers and clients what they really want? Perhaps the easiest way, and the path used by some of the top companies in America, is to simply ask your clients what it is that they want. Here are five questions to ask your clients before, during, and after a transaction:

1. What services did you find most valuable during the transaction?
2. Can we improve these services in any way?
3. What services should we consider adding?
4. When choosing a real estate professional, what was your biggest motivator?
5. What are three ways in which we can improve.

Imagine for a moment that every client who came into contact with your company was presented with these five questions, by either phone, mail, or e-mail. Would all of them provide meaningful answers? Not a chance. But a few would, and wouldn't that be a powerful first step in pulling from your clients exactly how you can help them best?

Carl, a $7 million producer in San Diego, California, did just that and discovered that what his clients really wanted was more of his time. No surprise there, but when he questioned his clients further, he found that what they were really after was better communication about what was happening (or not happening) each week in the marketing of their home. To address this dilemma, he put together a simple e-mailable form like the one shown in Figure 3-8 to update his clients on all the activity on their home every seven days. He now uses this as a way to differentiate his services when interviewing for new listings. As he puts it, "Clients love the idea of getting constant feedback. I know my closing ratio has gone way up as a result of this one idea."

LEARNING OPPORTUNITIES

Pushing vs. pulling. Strong agents don't push services. Instead, they discover exactly what it is that buyers and sellers want from them in their market and then deliver on those needs.

As many agents have discovered, one of the upgrades that is most requested by consumers is a higher-quality presentation, including a description of what to expect during a transaction, high-quality consultation and advice, and a thorough explanation of the agent's services and fees.

To meet this new standard let's set the stage for success by diving into Chapter 4, "Building a Master-Level Presentation."

FIGURE 3-8.

Marketing Update

Listing ID: 1234567

Listing Address: 1332 Johnson St.

Clien Name: John Smith

Marketing Period: 06/10/06–06/17/06

Website Activity: www.superstar.com (Link Attached)

Page Views: 36
E-mails: 4
Virtual Tours: 12

Additional Websites: www.realtor.com, www.company.com, www.mis.com

Local Print Marketing: *San Diego Daily* (Ad Attached)

Number of Calls: 11
Number of Appts.: 3

Regional Print Marketing: *California Real Estate Guide* (Ad Attached)

Number of Calls: 31
Number of Appts.: 5

Sign Inquiries:

Number of Calls: 12
Number of Appts.: 2
Call Capture: 12
Flyer Box: Restocked
Talking House: Transmitter Working

Open House: *Scheduled: 06/24/06*

Showing Following Up: *22 Showing E-mails Sent/Responses Attached*

Building a Master-Level Presentation

The most important tool in every real estate agent's utility belt should be his listing presentation. Think of it as a universal tool, like a real estate Swiss army knife, that can be used to help buyers and sellers wade through complicated issues, unravel vexing questions, and escape MacGyver style from difficult situations.

For superstars, the real estate presentation is the hub of their conversation with any new client. It keeps them focused, and it enables them to move the presentation forward. The best thing about a strong presentation is its simplicity. Great presentations are never complicated. They are clean, concise, and extremely easy to follow. For a top-producing real estate agent, there are three key elements to every successful seller presentation. To keep it simple I call them the three Ps, otherwise known as price, product, and promotion, as shown in Figure 4-1.

Let's take a look at each of these individually, in order of importance:

- *Price.* The number one reason why a home will or will not sell is its price. This should be the first major discussion point in any listing presentation. Many things contribute to the price of a property, including what terms the sellers are offering, the speed of the sale, and,

FIGURE 4-1. THE THREE Ps OF SELLING A HOME

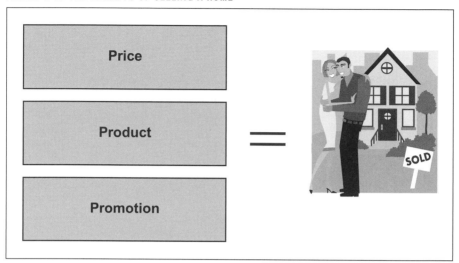

of course, most important, what other homes in the area are selling for.

- *Product.* Every home becomes a product the moment a "For Sale" sign is placed on the lawn. Sellers should be encouraged to improve their home's condition to increase their odds of securing a buyer. Top condition typically equals top price; on the other hand, a home that is in poor condition can have a problem finding a buyer unless the price is discounted to compensate for the needed repairs.

- *Promotion.* This is where a professional real estate agent's job begins. Top producers demonstrate to sellers how they will expose the listing to the widest possible group of buyers in the marketplace.

If you were to strip away all of the frills, the tassels, and the fanfare from your listing presentation, what should be left, standing naked in the breeze, is the three Ps. Without a discussion of these main points, an agent's listing presentation is nothing more than empty calories; sure, it might be fun to eat, but an hour later the client may get hungry and go hunting for something more substantial, like another, more qualified agent. To avoid this fate, check out the three-legged table discussion, and how easy it is to begin a conversation centered on the three Ps.

It sounds easy enough, right? It isn't really. The problem is that agents

---

The Three-Legged Table Discussion

You know, Mr. and Mrs. Seller, the ability to sell any home really rests on three major issues. I call them the three Ps. Imagine a three-legged table, with the ability to sell your home being the top of this table; each of these three Ps represents a leg. If one of these legs is out of alignment, your home may never sell.

The first leg is the *price* you set on your home. This is the number one reason why a home will or will not sell.

The second leg is the *product*, which is the home itself. Your home will be competing with many other listings for a buyer's attention.

The third leg is the *promotion* of the property. This is where I step in to market the property to all of the available buyers in the marketplace.

Can we spend just a few minutes talking about each of these key issues?

---

can talk to a seller for hours and hours about everything from baseball to Venezuelan politics and never get around to discussing the three core reasons why a client's home will either sell or sit like a holiday fruitcake in the back of the real estate market pantry. Whether they're avoiding the tough issues or simply ignorance, agents who fail to discuss the key components of a successful real estate sale are putting their clients' interests at risk and, in my mind at least, perhaps even violating their fiduciary duties. Believe it or not, when agents fail to discuss price, product, and promotion with their sellers, they should be held accountable. *Heresy, you say.* I know it's easier to just blame the dumb client for overpricing the property, or for not cleaning up the front lawn, or for making the property hard to show. But is it the client's fault, or is it yours for not pointing out specifically what it will take to sell the home? Remember, you agreed to take the listing.

Strong agents have strong discussions with their clients about exactly what it will take to sell their home. They use what I like to call gentle brutality, a consultative yet pragmatic approach of explaining to sellers what the realities of the market are and how they can best achieve their real estate goals. As Sandra, an agent from North Dakota, explains, "My clients don't want to be placated or whitewashed. They want me to tell them the straight scoop on what it is going to take to sell their property. No beating around the bush!" This fresh approach to a seller meeting is a key component in something that I call the 100 percent seller solution.

LEARNING OPPORTUNITY

The three Ps of selling a home. The three biggest reasons why a home will or won't sell are price, product, and promotion. Strong agents center their presentation on these key discussion points to ensure that they secure a salable listing.

The 100 Percent Seller Solution

During my second year in the business, I was given a crash course on positioning homes to sell. In that year, I was fortunate enough to take 150 listings in one 12-month period of time. One thing I learned by taking all of those listings was that to succeed in selling all of that inventory I would need to take a different approach to delivering my listing presentation. Showing up with a yellow legal pad, a measuring tape, and my coffee-stained smile just wasn't going to work. Sure, I could almost always get the listing, but, as I quickly learned, getting the listing wasn't good enough, because in 1989, in my market, over half the listings taken would fail to sell the first time they were placed on the Multiple Listing Service (MLS).

> **74 Percent**
> of sellers list their home with the first agent they contact.
>
> 2005 National Association of Realtors Profile of Home Buyers and Sellers.

A 50 percent failure rate should be unacceptable, but surprisingly, many of the training systems at the time encouraged agents to embrace this statistic with open arms as a fact of life. To succeed, they would tell us on tapes and in their books, you just make it up on volume. Expect to take two listings for every one that sells. Work twice as hard for half the money, and you are bound to be successful; after all, it's just a number game. What about all those disappointed clients whose homes didn't sell? Forget about them and prospect harder.

Honestly, I'm not so altruistic that I couldn't live with a few disappointed clients, but half? I just couldn't stomach the thought of wasting half my time, half my energy, half my marketing budget, and half my life failing half my clients. So as I contemplated this dilemma one hot summer day before setting out on yet another listing appointment, I made a decision: My presentation that morning would be different. I would offer these clients something that I came to call the 100 percent seller solution, which is simply the idea that every listing I take should sell (what a concept!). In addition, I further concluded that unless I honestly believed I could sell the home, I should reject the client's listing.

Reject a listing? I know, I know. But don't go running for your defibrillator yet; consider the alternative: I take a listing that I know probably won't sell anyway. For a top producer, it just doesn't make good business sense to take a listing just to take a listing. For strong agents, a stagnant listing, one that has been on the market for what seems like decades, can be extremely embarrassing—it's almost like paying a guy to stand on the lawn of your listing with a bullhorn screaming to every car that drives by, "This agent can't sell this house!" or, "Don't list with Jim Remley because he takes listings but he never sells them!" No, thanks. I prefer to sell listings, not just take them.

How do top producers introduce the 100 percent seller solution? Check out this simple dialogue:

The 100 Percent Seller Script

Listen, you may not be aware of this, but most real estate agents fail about half the time they take a listing. To me, that is just unacceptable; my goal is to sell 100 percent of the listings that I take. In order to accomplish this goal, I have to work quite a bit differently from most agents.

So we can go two ways here: I can tell you what you want to hear, or I can tell you the truth. Which would you prefer?

Follow-up: *Are you sure?*

What would your answer be if you were the seller? As hard as it may be, we all want to hear the truth, which coming from a salesperson can be especially refreshing, and perhaps even unexpected. So assuming that your client has agreed to go behind the woodshed if need be to get the listing sold, what do you do now? Let her enjoy a visual feast.

Creating a Visual Feast

If you visit Fort Ouiatenon in West Lafayette, Indiana, during the fall of every year, you may just stumble upon the annual Feast of the Hunter's Moon, a dramatic re-creation of an event that took place in the year 1717, when French fur traders, Native Americans, and British soldiers gathered along the banks of the Wabash River to enjoy a bountiful harvest festival. During the two-day event, participants can enjoy hearty meals cooked over open fires, try their hand at crafts from the past, cheer on soldiers and military competitors dressed in period costumes, learn lacrosse, and even enjoy some home-made brew. Or instead you could visit the local library in West Lafayette and read about the festival in a book.

Which would you prefer?

It's an easy choice, right? We all want the E-ticket ride, with the big loops, dips, and fast turns. No one wants the lame carousel. This is just human nature. Our clients are the same way. They don't want a boring discourse about local real estate values; they want a visual feast of information, an immersion into the real estate market using an interactive, fun presen-

Edutainer
A person who can both educate and entertain an audience.

tation. To accomplish this goal, many top producers think of themselves as edutainers, people who can educate and entertain a client at the same time. One clear reason for this approach is the fact that attention spans are falling. Many studies have found that the average attention span for an adult in today's fast-paced world is only about 20 minutes of sustained concentration. By keeping a client interested, engaged, and involved in a presentation, moving from one point to the next in a clear, concise manner that is interesting and very specific to the client's needs, wise agents are able to masterfully cover all of the main points of their discussion and walk out of a home with not just a listing but a salable listing.

How do they do it? For many top producers, the first step in designing a powerful client meeting strategy is to embrace presentation software, and by far the most popular presentation software in the world is PowerPoint by Microsoft (www.microsoft.com). One of the advantages of building a presentation using PowerPoint is that you can create a visually appealing, step-by-step discussion of what it will take to successfully market a seller's home; you can then modify, customize, and adapt this presentation to any situation in just a few minutes. Change a photo, add a web file, update statistics—you can do it all with just a click of your mouse (even while you're sitting in the seller's driveway). Check out the ways that many top producers use PowerPoint to enhance their presentation skills:

Five Ways Top Producers Use PowerPoint

1. *On a laptop.* PowerPoint comes with a slide show feature that allows users to advance slides as they are talking about each point in their presentation. In addition, users can link slides to audio and video files, and also to webpages.

2. *As projected images.* Using a compact LCD projector, many agents use their PowerPoint presentation as projected images on a conference room screen, a white wall, or even at the seller's home. To see a catalog of projectors, check out www.infocus.com or www.boxlight.com.

3. *As a printed presentation.* For their low-tech customers, many agents print out their PowerPoint presentations and review a hard copy with their prospective clients, which they can also leave at the seller's home. (That's not a bad idea for a high-tech client as well.)

4. *On a website.* Using third-party software from companies like www .articulate.com or www.pointcaste.com, agents can convert their Power-Point presentations into Flash presentations complete with narration. These files can then be stored on an agent's website and be viewed by virtually any Internet user with a high-speed Internet connection. Of course, it may be wise to provide several teasers in the presentation to give prospective clients a reason to get the presentation live.

5. *On a disk.* PowerPoint comes equipped with the ability to transfer your presentation and narration to a CD. By using this feature, you can hand out your listing presentation to virtually anyone you come into contact with. Superstars are even professionally labeling their presentation disks using relatively inexpensive software and hardware from companies like www.lightscribe.com.

Regardless of what presentation platform you adopt, whether it is a PowerPoint file, a professionally printed booklet, or even just a three-ring binder, the key to success is having a marriage of strong visual design and fantastic content. Just like a professional athlete, not only do you want to look good, but you have to be good.

For some ideas on how you might flesh out your own presentation I've included a sample PowerPoint Presentation that was built using the three cornerstones we discussed earlier: the three Ps of price, product, and promotion (see Figs. 4-2 through 4-14). As you review each slide and the suggested dialogue, take a minute to decide what you might use, reject, modify, or adapt to your own personal style of delivery.

FIGURE 4-2.

Thank you for the tour of your home and for answering all my questions.
Do you mind if I take just a few minutes to show you how I work?

The two top concerns I hear from my clients when they are selling a home is a
desire to sell faster and for top dollar. So I've outlined my top ten ideas to help
sellers accomplish those goals.

FIGURE 4-3.

The number one reason why a home will or won't sell is the price. Because the
average buyer looks at between 12 and 15 homes, if your home is priced too high,
your home may never sell. On the other hand, if your home is priced too low, it may
sell quickly, but at a discount. **At this point, which is most important for you: a
faster sale or a higher sales price?**

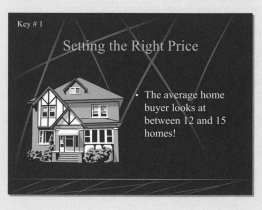

FIGURE 4-4

There are always three prices for every home: what the seller would love to receive, what the buyer would love to pay, and what the home will eventually sell for. One of my jobs as your agent is to provide an in-depth pricing analysis of your home and the entire market. **Would you like me to start that process today?**

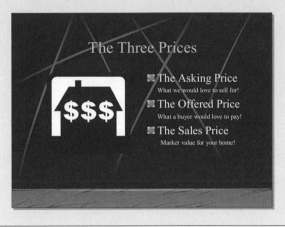

FIGURE 4-5

The real estate market can be influenced by many things: the competition, what homes are selling for and what is for sale, the overall economy and the local housing inventory <add local information>, and the available financing options. **May I have my finance team put together some financing options for your home?**

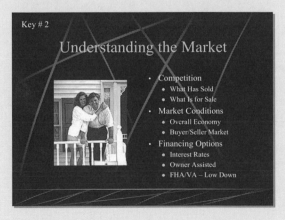

FIGURE 4-6

When your home goes on the market, it becomes a product. To ensure a faster sale and a higher price, many sellers like to have advice on improving their home's condition, including areas like curb appeal, personal items, staging the home, and helping the home tell a story.

FIGURE 4-7

One of my biggest jobs as your agent will be to expose your home to the largest group of buyers possible.

More exposure will lead to a faster sale, a higher price, and fewer hassles. **My company has developed a comprehensive marketing strategy to do just that. In just the last 30 days we've sold these homes. <Provide list.>**

FIGURE 4-8

We cast a wide net in looking for a potential buyer for your home, including a mix of the Internet, print advertising, the MLS system, and e-mail marketing to expose your home to the widest range of buyers possible. ***Do you mind if I show you some specific examples of each of these?***

FIGURE 4-9

In addition, I often use other traditional methods for finding buyers, such as mailings, open houses, signage, and tapping into my sphere of influence. But instead of doing things the old-fashioned way, I like to be more progressive. **Can I show you how my team uses a unique approach to each of these areas?**

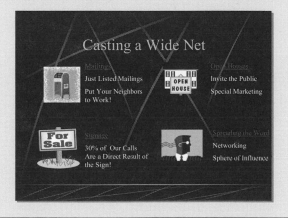

FIGURE 4-10

One of my biggest priorities is making sure that you always know exactly what is happening with your listing. **If we decide to work together, would you prefer a weekly or bimonthly phone call (or e-mail)?** We also send (or e-mail) a regular written activity report to our clients along with all of the advertising copy.

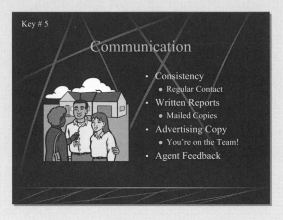

FIGURE 4-11

Staying in control of your home sale is vital. So once we find a buyer, I'll help you manage the entire transaction, including all of the details. <Review> **If you like, I can prepare an estimated net sheet of what to expect as the proceeds from your home sale. How does that sound?**

FIGURE 4-12

One of the reasons I'm able to provide this level of service is that I have a strong company behind me. We have a highly trained and motivated sales team, relocation services, strong ties to the community, a home warranty program, and a great support staff. Plus we provide our clients with a communication guarantee. **Let me show you what that means.**

FIGURE 4-13

A large part of my marketing strategy is to develop an advertising plan specific to your home, including <review list.> **May I show you some samples of plans I have built for other sellers?**

FIGURE 4-14

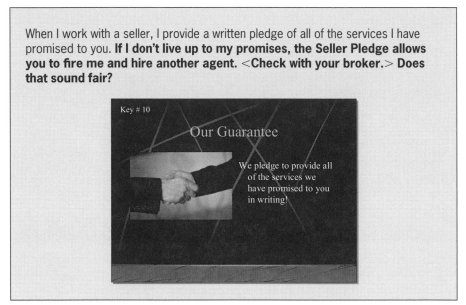

When I work with a seller, I provide a written pledge of all of the services I have promised to you. **If I don't live up to my promises, the Seller Pledge allows you to fire me and hire another agent. <Check with your broker.> Does that sound fair?**

Strong agents use their presentation to organize their discussion and to control the flow of the conversation with the client. Controlling the flow of a meeting can often sound negative; when I hear the word *control*, I think of being pinned to the ground in the fourth grade by a much larger third-grader while he eats my Twinkies. But controlling a meeting in a professional sense simply means that you keep the conversation focused on the client's needs and your solutions. As when you encourage your children to eat their peas and carrots so that they can have a piece of chocolate cake, you control the conversation and the overall direction of your meeting to ensure your client's successful home sale. Terry, a $5 million producer from Tennessee, agrees. "My presentation gives me time to think. I don't have to wonder where the conversation is headed next because I know what's on the next page."

A planned presentation also forces us to anticipate questions, objections, and concerns. For instance, when will a pricing question come up? Obviously, it will no doubt magically appear during the pricing pages. And a question about curb appeal? Probably about the time the seller begins thinking about that stagnating pond in the backyard (which used to be the family swimming pool) during your review of the condition pages. Strong agents encourage these discussions.

Of course, this is sometimes easier said than done. I found this out as a rookie agent during one of my early listing disasters, a presentation to a senior couple in the dining room of their bungalow-style home. As I turned to the last section in my three-ring binder, I finished by asking my one and only question of the morning: "So would you folks like to list your house today?"

"No!" The elderly couple said it in unison, loudly and with conviction, as if the thought of me listing their house was so repugnant that they had to spit it out.

What could I have done differently? Asked more questions. If you look closely at the slide dialogues, you may notice that several pages ask the seller a question. For instance, "May I have my finance team put together some financing options for your home?" These are called *engagement questions*. Engagement questions, sometimes known as trial closes, test the client's thinking process by regularly affirming the client's desire to take the relationship to the next level while also revealing lingering questions or concerns that may prevent a client from moving forward. By learning to ask engagement questions, strong agents can move from a presentation that is centered on their own needs to a presentation that is focused on what the client actually wants to discuss. Take a look at 25 of the engagement questions most asked by top producers:

The Top 25 Engagement Questions

1. How does what I've said so far sound?
2. May I put together a pricing analysis for your home?
3. Tell me, which of these do you prefer?
4. What concerns you the most about selling your home?
5. What is important for you to talk about today?
6. Based on this information, what are your thoughts?
7. What ideally would you like to have happen?
8. May I have my finance team put together a package for your home?
9. Can I do some more research on that question and e-mail it over to you?
10. Would you like me to continue, or do you have any questions?
11. How much time would you need to move after closing?
12. What areas would you like me to focus on?
13. May I take some photos of the home?

14. Do you mind if I do a home warranty inspection?
15. How much notice would you like before a showing?
16. What motivated you to buy this home?
17. What kind of advertising appeals to you?
18. May I put together a sample flyer for you?
19. When ideally would you like to be moved?
20. If what I said makes sense, are you ready to move forward?
21. May I do a curb appeal appraisal?
22. Where would you like a lockbox placed?
23. Where do you see a sign being placed?
24. May I review the paperwork with you?
25. How can I help you?

Having an active, focused conversation about what it will take to sell a home may seem easy for you and me. But for many Americans, who unplug themselves from society at five every evening, turn the TV on, and float free in the warm waves of thoughtless indecision, it can be almost excruciating. By using regular engagement questions, superstars can help snap their seller's attention back to the presentation at hand and get her thinking about what will need to happen if her home is to actually sell. It's also a great time to feed her your presentation cake.

LEARNING OPPORTUNITY

Edutainer. Strong agents seem themselves as edutainers, people who can educate and entertain a client while delivering real estate information.

PowerPoint. Many real estate professionals use PowerPoint from Microsoft to build a visual presentation that can be adapted to many delivery formats.

Planned presentation. A planned presentation provides a client with a well-thought-out, focused outline of information that can help him sell his house quickly and for top dollar.

Engagement questions. Sometimes known as trial closes, these questions test a client's acceptance of an agent's presentation and help to uncover questions or concerns.

Baking a Presentation Cake

During every seminar I deliver that involves the topic of a seller presentation, there is always someone in every audience who will say, "Now wait a minute, Jim, I don't think my sellers really want me to do a presentation."

Yes, they do. According to "Housing Wealth Effects," produced by the Joint Center for Housing Studies at Harvard University and Macroeconomic Advisers, LCC, housing wealth accounts for 36 percent of the nation's tangible assets. With the average American saving only 3 percent a year (down from 8 percent a decade ago), for most Americans a house is more than a home; it is their largest financial investment, their retirement, their nest egg, and their kid's college education. So, yes, they want a professional planned presentation. What clients don't want is a canned presentation, and here is where the fear for most agents lies.

A canned presentation is one in which a salesperson reads from a script verbatim, with no deviations. Like the cookware salesperson at the county fair, she pitches her wares and hopes to get as many customers to the counter as possible.

"Hey, friend, look at the way this knife slices and dices tomatoes. Don't let your wife near this one when she's mad! Right, fellas?" (Wait for laugh.)

Watching anyone recite a canned presentation is painful, and it's no wonder that agents wince when they picture themselves doing any kind of prepared presentation. But a planned presentation is not a canned presentation. The goal of a planned presentation is to tailor the discussion to the specific needs of the individual client. There are no canned speeches, no recitals. I know what you're thinking: But what about the dialogue? The dialogue is simply an outline of what you should cover on each page. Should you memorize it? Yes, just as a doctor must memorize medical terminology, an attorney an opening argument, or a CPA certain sections of the tax code. Professional real estate agents should memorize a professional presentation. But this is not where they stop; this is where they begin. Superstars make their presentation deeper by applying two more layers to their presentation cake:

The Three-Layer Presentation Cake

- *Memorize.* Top producers use a planned presentation that they have taken the time to memorize. Yes, as professionals, we do have to memorize a script. If you want to be paid like a professional, you have to act like a professional.

- *Internalize.* This simply means that you become so familiar with your listing presentation that you know it forward, backward, and in reverse. The presentation becomes an extension of you. Just like a quarterback with a football or a surgeon with a scalpel, you have to know your presentation cold.

- *Personalize.* Because you have the power to personalize the presentation on the fly, you will be able to customize your discussion around the seller's hot buttons and provide the seller with a far more effective and powerful presentation.

Ask any group of superstars what separates them from the rest of the agents in their community who are barely making a living, and the answer may surprise you. They are simply better at the fundamentals, those simple areas of an agent's business that, when overlooked, disregarded, or ignored, can spell disaster. Like professional athletes who go back to spring training every year to get reacquainted with the basics, top producers hone their presentation skills by sticking to the fundamentals. While their competitors hit the snooze button, wait in line for their muffins and coffee, or play just one more game of solitaire, superstars are memorizing, internalizing, and personalizing their presentations. They master the basics, the fundamentals.

So what are you thinking about when you're sitting with a seller? Are you relaxed, focused on the client, and truly listening to both his verbal and his nonverbal cues, or are you in a state of sheer terror and barely hidden panic? Agents who wing every client meeting and don't think they need a planned presentation often fall into the latter group. These agents are often so consumed with trying to think up ways to convince the seller to do business with them that they lose touch with the client himself. Superstars are relaxed, calm, and completely in tune with their clients; they have moved up to subconscious selling.

Subconscious selling is a state in which you don't have to consciously think about your presentation. In the same way that you don't have to consciously think about how to drive a car, ride a bike, or hit a tennis ball, agents operating at a subconscious selling level have their presentations at the tip of their tongue, hard wired. This peak state frees them to personalize their approach to each individual client. Like a chef who can adjust her signature dish for a special guest, top-producing real estate agents are able to personalize their presentation style to best accommodate their individual clients.

Our clients want to feel complete confidence in our abilities—no questions, no second guessing. They want to feel secure about the person to whom they are entrusting their largest financial asset. What breeds confidence? As has often been said, confidence breeds confidence! To help with this endeavor, many superstars have added a new dimension to their presentation, with some even replacing their formal presentation altogether with a success portfolio.

> **Learning Challenge:** Create a planned presentation tailored to your client; then memorize it, internalize it, and personalize it.

Building a Success Portfolio

Once you have mastered your core presentation, you might consider a technique that many agents find helpful: creating a success portfolio. A success portfolio is a pictorial journal of your past success stories. One of the best ways to envision a success portfolio is to imagine yourself interviewing a photographer or an architect. People in both of these professions almost always have a success journal that shows off their talents; for instance, a photographer may include photos of different scenes, lighting, models, and backgrounds, while an architect may include elevations; interior and exterior drawings; and, most important, pictures of completed projects. Likewise, many top real estate agents carry with them a success portfolio, which may include photos of homes they have sold; past flyers and marketing campaigns; pictures of clients in front of the homes they purchased; brochures; website samples; advertising slicks; open house invitations; and, most important, quotes and pictures of satisfied clients.

Some progressive agents even use a success portfolio as their listing presentation. Carolyn, a luxury home specialist from Georgia, says, "I want to impress upon my clients the fact that I get things done. I'm not just talking in a vacuum. When I say something, it happens."

Consider organizing your success portfolio around the same discussion points as your listing presentation. You can then follow the lead of elite agents who use their success portfolio either as a stand-alone tool or to augment their formal listing presentation. Let's take a look at how one superstar introduces the portfolio into his presentation:

Success Portfolio Introduction

If you don't mind, what I would like to do is show you some of the homes I've recently helped families buy and sell here in the area, and some of my most successful marketing pieces. May I show you my portfolio?

Have you ever noticed that you learn faster by listening to a story than when you are just receiving hard facts? This may be one reason why as children we aren't just told not to talk to strangers; we are told the scary story of Little Red Riding Hood and the Big Bad Wolf. Stories are powerful; they resonate, sticking to our long-term memory like a pasta dinner to our ribs. And they aren't just for kids. While attending a recent play with my wife, John Steinbeck's *Of Mice and Men*, I noticed that as the curtain went up, I could still hear a faint rustling and whispering. It was obvious that a number of the audience members were restless, anxious, and perhaps a little nervous. There was a hum, a murmur in the auditorium. But then magically, within just a few short seconds, the room became deathly silent as all eyes focused on a performer who had quietly walked on to the darkened stage and now stood motionless. The story was about to begin.

Master presenters are master storytellers. Statistics, numbers, trend lines, markets, and opinions can be interesting, but when they are wrapped up in a story about real people in real situations, the data come alive and resonate. No longer is the discussion an abstract analysis of what may or may not happen. Instead, it becomes a real-life lesson in what can and will happen, the ups and downs, the triumphs and tragedies that happen to real-world buyers and sellers in the often unforgiving real estate market. Let's take a look at three real-world stories from top agents using their success portfolio as a starting point:

Price

Jeremy, a $6 million producer from Chicago, tells this story while showing a collage of pictures centered on a two-story waterfront home he sold for over a million dollars.

"The couple who sold this home had a tough time, but we eventually were able to get their home sold just before the husband was transferred. The problem was that they decided they wanted to squeeze every nickel they could out of the home, so, against my advice, they priced the home above the top of the market.

"Unfortunately, when the Realtors in the area looked at the property, they pegged it as overpriced, and the home sat on the market for a couple of weeks without any showings.

"So I took the time to call every agent who had seen the home to get their feedback. All of them told me that they felt the home was overpriced. When I took this back to the sellers, after another week of waiting, they adjusted the price.

"Within three days the home was sold."

Product

Sarah, a $9 million producer from northern California, always tells this story while showing pictures to emphasize the importance that improvements in conditions can have for a sale.

"Last year I took a listing that needed some cosmetic work. . . . Here are some photos of the home. The sellers really felt that they could just sell the home 'as is' and let the new buyers pick out the carpet and paint. So we priced the home to sell, and we even threw in a carpet and paint allowance of $5,000 for any full-price offer. After a month, even though we had a ton of showings because of the low price, we received no offers.

"My recommendation to the sellers was that they go ahead and paint the home, which would improve the curb appeal, and carpet the home in an earth-toned color. This is how the home turned out. . . . Take a look at these pictures. . . . The home sold a week later at the same market price but with no allowance."

Promotion

Tony, a veteran from the Florida market who consistently sells over $5 million a year, likes to show off the growth of his marketing campaign over the years he has been in business.

"I've been in the business for a long time, and in the beginning what I thought would sell homes was traditional marketing in the newspaper. . . . Here are a few of my early marketing pieces. They worked, but I like to be more aggressive with my business, so I started doing a tri-fold brochure mailing to my entire service area every three weeks featuring all of my listings, and targeted mailings to families who I know can afford to purchase homes in the area. Tell me what you think of these pieces."

Building a success portfolio will allow you to weave a story into every main point of your presentation. Long after clients have forgotten the percentage of listings sold in their neighborhood, they will remember the story of the lady who refused to budge from her demand to be paid only in gold coins (one of my true stories).

What if you don't have any stories? If you're a new agent who hasn't yet accumulated some anecdotes about your own clients' trials and tribulations, you might consider borrowing some stories from your office mates or your managing broker. Of course, when you present your portfolio, just be sure to point out that each story relates to something that happened within your office, but not necessarily to you.

To ensure that a presentation comes alive for the client and is interesting, captivating, and downright fascinating, strong agents often take out an insurance policy by learning how to anticipate hot buttons.

Learning Challenge: Create a success portfolio with photos of homes you have sold, past flyers and marketing campaigns, pictures of clients in front of homes purchased, brochures, website samples, advertising slicks, open house invitations, and, most importantly, quotes and pictures of satisfied clients.

Anticipating Hot Buttons

Minds are like parachutes—they only function when open.

—Lord Thomas Dewar

Have you ever had the uneasy feeling that your clients weren't paying any attention to you at all? Like wax sculptures, deadeyed and blank, they look past you with a half smile. Many times as I sat across the kitchen table from a seller explaining the benefits of my company and its marketing, I got the distinct impression that I could probably wave my hand within inches of the seller's face and he wouldn't even blink. It's creepy, and it can last for what seems like an eternity until the client magically snaps out of it, as if a spell has been broken, a curse has been lifted, or your presentation is finally over.

So why do some clients turn into barely conscious zombies when you begin discussing the mechanics of selling a home? The easy answer is to say that your presentation is boring (which may or may not be true). But another answer may be that you haven't customized your discussion to fit the needs of this particular client. In other words, you're talking about things she really doesn't care about. For me, this would be like having a long discussion about cooking with tofu. While my dad, a vegetarian, would love to talk about the thousands of ways you can prepare this versatile dish, I would probably nod off about the time you started discussing how to turn the pliable soy into faux hamburger patties (gross!).

To excite a seller client about their services, many wise agents use a preclosing question to better shape their discussion to fit the client's interests. This doesn't mean that they skip the main points, like price, product, and promotion, but it does mean that they focus on topics within those main points that the client is interested in exploring. For instance, some clients may be fascinated with e-mail marketing and want to see all of the ways you tap into this area of advertising, others may be interested in talking about feng shui (an ancient Eastern design philosophy), while still others may want to study the comparable sales in depth. Different strokes for different folks.

Let's take a look at how using preclosing questions can reveal client hot buttons and potential stumbling blocks to taking the listing.

Preclosing Questions

Before I begin my presentation, I want to ask you a couple of questions if you don't mind. First, are there any areas that are of particular interest to you in terms of marketing or preparing your property for sale that you would like me to focus on? And second, if my marketing plan looks like what you are looking for, is there anything holding you back from moving forward today?

Superstars always lead with the client need. I call this process identifying trigger topics. A trigger topic is a presentation leverage point, an issue on which the client's decision to hire you hinges. Strong agents invest their presentation capital on expanding, deepening, and exploring these points of interest. Sure, we could add a bunch of fluff, filler, and perseverance to the mix, but is that what our clients want? Not according to Jan, a luxury home specialist in Seattle, Washington. "My clients are busy, busy people. They aren't going to sit through a lot of nonsense that doesn't relate specifically to getting their home sold and what they want to talk about." I think Jan is right. In today's world of working families, multitasking, and hectic schedules, the vast majority of our clients are just not interested in hearing about anything that does not relate specifically to solving their particular real estate challenge. As my old friend Bob Martin was fond of saying, "They just want the time; they don't want you to build them a clock."

In the second half of the preclosing dialogue, the agent asks another critical question that may reveal many agents' gut-o-meter. Your gut-o-meter is your ability to ask gutsy questions at critical moments. In this case, the agent is determining up front what roadblocks to taking the listing may lie ahead. For example, suppose I ask you, "If my marketing plan looks like what you are looking for, is there anything holding you back from moving forward?" If you reply, "Well, I still need to fix a few things around the house," my approach to the presentation would change to focus more on preparing the product for sale, as this is obviously your hot button. A gutsy question asked in the right way can yield tremendously important information.

Here's a challenge: Take a look at these five gutsy questions and decide which one you could use during your next presentation:

Five Gutsy Questions

1. If the home doesn't sell, are you more likely to give it more time or to adjust the price? Would you like to adjust the price now?
2. May I point out what you may wish to consider upgrading in the home to help you receive better offers?
3. May I show you what an inspector may require to be fixed prior to closing?
4. Many of my clients like to have their home deep cleaned prior to the start of showings. May I refer you to a professional home cleaner?
5. Because many buyers don't smoke, they are very sensitive to the smell of cigarettes. Because of this, many of my sellers use a professional to remove the odor. May I refer you to a company?

Like pulling a rabbit out of a hat, you can often discover hidden thoughts, concerns, and even objections by taking the time to find a client's hot buttons early in the presentation process and, although it may seem a little unnatural at first, asking gutsy questions. The more relaxed you become at asking these questions, the more relaxed your clients will become about answering them.

Learning Challenge: Ask a preclosing question prior to the beginning of a presentation to better shape your discussion to match the interests of each client and better determine his trigger topics. Also try asking a gutsy question at a critical moment.

To take this process further and enjoy a flawless client meeting performance, many agents choose to employ the secret that master illusionists have been using for centuries. Let's explore this together in Chapter 5, "The Magician's Secret."

The Magician's Secret

Eric stood on stage in his signature blue bathing suit. Wiry but strong, he looked out at the crowd that had come to witness his performance. He was pleased. The show was once again sold out, just as it had been at nearly every performance he had given throughout his entire career. Mesmerized by the magician, audience members watched with wonder as two uniformed attendants slowly rolled a heavy riveted metal can toward center stage and then quickly filled it with 22 pails of water.

The tension became palpable. Eric motioned for the heavy lid to be attached to the container along with six spring-loaded locks. After a deep breath and a momentary pause he dropped beneath the water. Water splashed over the sides as the lid was quickly slammed closed, the locks clasped into place, and the milk can along with the magician rolled behind a small curtain.

A drum began to beat slowly. The audience hushed to a whisper. One minute slowly passed, and then, excruciatingly, two. A surge of panic swept the hall. Women began to swoon, and grown men cried out to release the fool. An attendant holding a large axe stepped forward, but just as his arms reached their apex Harry Houdini magically appeared from behind the curtain, his arms raised in triumph, to the relief and thunderous applause of the terrified onlookers.

Eric Weiss, better known worldwide as the world's greatest escape artist and master magician Harry Houdini, had once again done the impossible: He had vanquished death.

So how did he do it?

The secret of the Great Milk Can Escape was a combination of Houdini's superb physical conditioning and his patented tools. Although the trick was extremely dangerous for anyone, including Houdini himself, he minimized the risks through intense preparation. By running and swimming for long periods of time, in addition to holding his breath underwater in his bathtub at home, he trained himself to hold his breath for over three minutes. More important, he designed a special trick milk can with a false lid, completely undetectable under even the closest inspection. By pushing up from beneath the lid, he could bypass all of the locks. Still, with just one miscalculation, the trick could easily have killed him.

Suppose for a minute that the amount of preparation you invested in your next real estate presentation wouldn't just determine your ability to take a listing or make a sale, but would mean your life or death. Would you prepare a little better? Spend a little more time on research and practice? This was Houdini's secret. Everything was on the line during each performance. Escape or die. Now when you and I fail to take a listing, we probably won't keel over dead (although it can often feel that way), but in fact a little piece of our business has died, a piece that can't be resuscitated or saved (not even by the guy with the axe).

For the real estate professional, preparation can mean many things. In the previous chapter, for instance, we worked on some basics, such as creating a visual presentation and building a success portfolio, both of which are tools that you can use with every seller. But to become a master presenter requires more; it requires intensive preparation specific to every individual seller. Just like the performance of a master magician, to your audience, the real estate seller, it should seem that your presentation is effortless, seamless, and incredibly detail oriented. To rise to this master level requires that your tools work flawlessly, your materials be impeccable, and your transitions from one discussion point to the next be superb. To accomplish these goals, let's take a look at how superstars create presentation MAGIC.

Presentation MAGIC

M: Motivate Yourself

Take this quick test: Closely examine all of your presentation materials. What do they say about your motivation level? Do they say that you are completely committed, fired up, and excited about taking a seller's listing, or do they read like standard-issue propaganda pieces? To create a presentation that is powerful enough to motivate a seller to grant you and your firm a percentage of the sales price of his home, you must be able to show him that you are motivated enough to thoroughly prepare for the meeting.

> **Top Producer Tip:** Many agents go the extra mile when preparing for a listing appointment by taking outside photos of the seller's home, which they then insert into sample flyers, web pages, and mailings. Not only can this get sellers excited about your level of motivation, but it may also encourage them to begin visualizing you as their agent. Check out this superstar script:
>
> "This morning my assistant took some quick exterior photos of your home and inserted them into several sample flyers, web pages, and mailing pieces. . . . Looking at these, which style do you find best highlights your home?"

A: Accept Your Limitations

Master presenters accept their own limitations. If they are not tech savvy, they don't pretend to be; if they aren't specialists at explaining home financing, they don't attempt the impossible by trying to describe the APR (annual percentage rate) to their sellers. Instead, they expertly pivot the perceived weakness into a perceived strength. How? Check out this superstar dialogue:

You know, I've chosen not to become a computer person. I'll admit I'm a little technologically challenged, so I hire someone who is an expert to do that work; she works with me every day to make sure our Internet strategy is top flight. Instead, I focus my time on what I do best: finding buyers for my listings. So I'll ask her and find out the answer to your question, but in the meantime let me show you some of the ways I will be working for you.

G: Gain Leverage

To gain leverage on their audience, superstars make a point of knowing more about the local real estate market than their clients do. This may sound easy, but it is becoming increasingly difficult as our sellers gain more and more online resources that let them conduct their own fact-finding missions. To stay competitive and add value to their services, strong agents understand that they must double their knowledge base and extend their research into every possible nook and cranny of the market. Check out how one agent is combating free valuation websites within his market:

> *Many of my clients are doing research on websites like www.zillow .com,* and I have to admit that these are fun places to visit. But when you study the reports that these systems generate, you often find serious flaws in the data. In fact, I have a few examples. . . . Take a look. When my clients are selling their largest financial asset, I feel it's my obligation as a real estate professional to do an in-depth market analysis on each property that I market based on accurate information, which is why I compile data from 10 different sources.*

I: Invest Time and Resources

Winston Churchill, one of the greatest speakers of the last century, reportedly would spend one hour of preparation for every minute of his presentation. Wisely, he understood that to be thought of as a great presenter required the investment of his valuable time and resources. Imagine what would happen if real estate agents made that same commitment.

Building a standard 20-minute presentation would then require 20 hours of preparation, and no doubt a substantial amount of additional time to customize each presentation to meet the needs of a specific client. It's not unthinkable. In fact, Scot, a top-producing broker from Arizona, thinks

---

*One of the latest entrants to the real estate research community is www.zillow.com, founded by Rich Barton and Lloyd Frink, the famous founders of www.expedia.com. They claim that their systems can provide a free home valuation report for nearly every seller in the country without the need to use a pesky Realtor.

Churchill's assessment may be below the mark: "I've invested thousands of dollars and hundreds of hours of time in refining my presentation." This may be one reason Scot makes well over $300,000 a year in commission income.

One way in which some agents ensure that they are thoroughly prepared for every seller meeting is by using a simple seller meeting checklist like the one shown in Figure 5-1.

C: Capitalize on Your Strengths

When conducting an interview to hire employees, I often ask the question, "What is your greatest strength?" It's a tough question. Almost invariably the applicants will smile, fidget, laugh nervously, or stammer as they try to think of something that won't make them sound ridiculously conceited or, worse yet, terribly underqualified.

Why is it so hard to recognize and then communicate our own strong points? One reason is the powerful need to conform, to become a boring part of the crowded masses. Yet master presenters almost always have the ability to separate themselves from the pack and lean into their strengths. They leverage their uniqueness and make it work for them. Take a look at this list of strengths and circle the ones that apply to you:

Acceptance	Assertiveness	Boldness	Balance
Clarity	Confidence	Courage	Creativity
Curiosity	Energy	Enthusiasm	Flexibility
Fortitude	Freedom	Generosity	Gratitude
Harmony	Integrity	Kindness	Learning
Nurturance	Objectivity	Openness	Optimism
Passion	Patience	Persistence	Playfulness
Purpose	Resilience	Simplicity	Stability
Steadfastness	Strength	Vitality	

How well you can convey your own strong points during a presentation may determine how well received and accepted your message is by the seller. She must buy into your story. One way to help guarantee success and set the

FIGURE 5-1.

Seller **Meeting** Checklist

➤ Home Information
   # Customer Service Information
   # Tax Records
   # Zoning
   # CC&Rs (covenants, conditions, and restrictions)

➤ Market Information
   # Comparable Sales 6 Months/12 Months
   # Comparable Listings – Active
   # Average Days on Market
   # List to Sale Price Difference
   # Average Sales Price

➤ Competitive Market Analysis
   # Complete/Incomplete – Need More Info

➤ Marketing Materials
   # Personal Brochure
   # Website Materials/HTML Resaved
   # Referral Book Updated
   # Advertisements – Paper/Magazines
   # Marketing Plan – Updated with Home Information

➤ Prelisting Kit
   # Mailed/Delivered/E-mailed

➤ Samples - Customized
   # Flyers
   # Advertisements
   # Webpages
   # Home Books

➤ Supplies
   # Sign/Lockbox/Listing Kit

stage for a fantastic presentation that focuses on the client's needs is to stack the deck in your favor by using a prelisting kit.

LEARNING OPPORTUNITY

The power of preparation. To become a master presenter requires intensive preparation. To your audience, the seller, it should seem that your presentation is effortless, seamless, and incredibly detail oriented.

Presentation MAGIC:

M: Motivate yourself.
A: Accept your limitations.
G: Gain leverage.
I: Invest time and resources.
C: Capitalize on your strengths.

The Prelisting Kit

Going into a meeting cold can be nerve-racking. As my friend Michael Pappas of the Keyes Company (www.keyes.com), a leader in Florida real estate sales, told me when I was going on stage to do a presentation to his company, "Don't worry, Jim; they'll give you 15 seconds of unconditional love, and then, if you're not good, they'll rip you to shreds." Thanks, Mike!

To ease the pressure when you are sitting in a seller's home, a fantastic tool that many top producers employ is a prelisting kit. A prelisting kit is a packet that is sent or delivered to a seller prior to your arrival at his home that can be a starting point for your initial discussion. Think of it as your warm-up act. A good prelisting kit can do many things; for instance, it can help to build your credibility, demonstrate the quality of your brand, and let the client know what to expect during the meeting. In addition, a well-crafted prelisting kit can serve as a preemptive strike against potential competitors. So what kind of powder do you put into this magic bullet? Let's take a look at what many top producers include in their prelisting kits, and then take a look at a sample kit.

Prelisting Kit Contents

- *Cover letter.* This letter will confirm your listing appointment, provide your contact information, and explain the contents of the entire package.

- *Résumé.* As well as fleshing out an agent's work history, a résumé allows the agent to expand on professional designations. For instance, instead of a long list of letters, like ABR, ALHS, CRS, or GRI, many superstars define what it means to hold each designation by explaining it with a brief sentence or paragraph, such as "Completed the Accredited Luxury Home Specialist Designation program in 2006."

New Agent Tip: Brand new real estate agents may wish to substitute a company résumé, which could include the accomplishments of the company, company history, and a list of differentiation points that sets your company apart from your competitors. Another option is to use a brief biography page (as described later) as a way to highlight your strengths.

- *Personal marketing brochure.* According to *Realtor Magazine,* to build a high-quality personal brochure, you may want to consider these key items:

  An unusual size. Some agents choose to create a brochure that will stand out from others by making it an unusual size. One example is Dan Olague, a salesperson from Puyallup, Washington; his brochures stand out like a head of lettuce at a Krispy Kreme counter. Why? They are six inches square—a weird size.

  A memorable tag line. "The Rancher's Realtor" and "Selling San Diego Skylines" are great examples of tag lines (or, for the buzzword-friendly crowd, positioning statements). Whatever you call them, they are an essential part of a strong agent's marketing strategy.

  Friendly photographs. A mix of professional photographs taken with just the right lighting, background, and colors can make even me (a guy born for radio) look friendly enough to do business with. The secret for many agents is to employ a professional photographer (not their Uncle Jerry). "Consumers today want someone they can relate to," says Greg Herder, a partner in Hobbs Herder Advertising (www.hobbsherder.com).

Testimonials. A satisfied client saying good things about you is always your best advertising. Supercharge your testimonials by making sure they are unedited, specific, and detailed, and include the clients' full names.

Testimonials

June Smith—Home Sold July 1, 2006

Our transaction was an extremely pleasant experience for us, even though the buyer wanted us to spend a fortune on repairs. Sally was able to help us negotiate a fair deal and we were able to close on time! Phone Number 1-541-673-1106

John Thompson—Home Sold April 16, 2006

Sally was able to market our property in a way that attracted a lot of showing; we sold the home in less than four weeks! She stayed right on top of the buyer loan process and we closed three weeks later! Phone number 1-541-672-1159

Jose Cruz—Purchased a Home January 2, 2006

Sally took the time to help us find our dream home. We plan on living in this home the rest of our lives. She really listened to us, and she made recommendations that helped us save a lot of money! Phone number 1-541-672-1559

- *Brief biography.* A professional biography often includes a brief history of your professional career and, for some, an extra helping of personal information as well. Giving a small glimpse of your personal life can help soften your image and personalize your presentation. My personal bio includes this paragraph: "Jim is happily married and has two sons, Michael and Mathew. He currently lives in Sutherlin, Oregon, with his wife, Jessica, where they and the kids enjoy spending time in the garden, camping, and snowboarding in the winter months. Jim is also an active member of his community and contributes his time and energy to many local events and charities."

Top Producer Tip: Many agents include the biographies of the other members of their team, along with photos and contact information. This is wise, as often clients will be speaking with or e-mailing these team members throughout the listing and transaction period.

- *Meeting outline.* Clients are often antsy about their first meeting with a real estate professional for no other reason than they don't know what to expect. You can remove this question mark by providing your new clients with a meeting outline, a step-by-step timeline of what to expect during their initial consultation.

- *Questionnaire.* To gain a huge meeting advantage, many agents ask their clients to fill out a simple questionnaire, which can be sent, faxed, or e-mailed back to the agent prior to his arrival at the client's home. The questions are often the same questions you would ask when you are sitting with a seller for the first time. But knowing the answers ahead of time gives top producers the chance to focus their presentation on hot buttons, as well as anticipate questions in advance.

Top Producer Tip: Some agents find it wise to include a list of questions that the seller may want to consider asking the agent when she arrives at the home. This is also a great tool in multiple-interview situations, as it will arm the seller with tough questions to hammer other agents with (and since they didn't write the questions, answering may be a wee bit tougher for them).

- *Video.* Here's a wild idea (for you wild agents): What if you videotaped yourself delivering your presentation? Just imagine your clients watching with a bowl of popcorn in hand as you walk them through the key points of successfully selling their home. Ralph Roberts, one of the most successful real estate agents in North America, actually sends along a bag of microwavable popcorn with his video. (What, no candy?)

Top Producer Tip: For camera-shy agents, you may prefer to invest in a professionally created video to hand out to sellers. David Knox (www.davidknox.com), a real estate speaker and author, has created two DVDs that may just do the trick: *Pricing Your Home to Sell* and *Preparing Your Home to Sell.* Both are generically designed for agents to hand out or lend to sellers.

- *Press clippings.* If you have been fortunate enough to receive some free press for your accomplishments, why not make copies and keep them as an insert for your prelisting kit? Doing so will expose your potential clients to your status as a living legend without you having to tell them yourself, which would be kind of embarrassing, wouldn't it?

Top Producer Tip: To get your name in the paper, start telling news editors about your professional accomplishments. To learn how to write an effective press release and distribute it free nationwide, visit www.prweb.com.

Now, between you and me, this list could go on forever. But if you give sellers every single shred of information about you, your company, and your services, do they really need to meet with you? After all, why waste an hour talking to you in person when they can make a decision just based on how you look on paper?

My problem is that I don't look so good on paper—5'9, balding, 180 pounds, snores loudly. I look much better in person. So here's a secret that even the most successful agents often miss: What we leave out of a prelisting kit can be just as important as what we put in. A great way to think about your prelisting kit is as a movie trailer. A good movie preview is intriguing;

it grabs you, shakes you, and says, "Come to the movies and watch me! No, no, don't wait for the DVD. Only losers wait for the DVD; you need to see this now!" If you think back to your childhood, you can probably remember the best movie trailers, ones like those for *Jaws*, *Star Wars*, or *Raiders of the Lost Ark*. This is in sharp contrast to some of the extended previews we see today. You know, the ones where you think to yourself: "Wow, they are really giving away a lot of information here. How much longer is this going to last? Why are they showing me all this? Hey, I ate all my popcorn!"

More is not necessarily always better; in fact, sometimes less is more. A strong prelisting kit should entice people to want more, to get them salivating for not just a taste but a whole piece of your presentation cake. So let's put this idea into play by showing a sample prelisting kit. When you review this kit, decide if you would add to or take away from the information, or perhaps completely revise it.

As you read the cover letter (Figure 5-2), notice that this agent refers to the prelisting kit as a premeeting kit. Many agents prefer this softer approach, as it doesn't presume that you will be taking the listing.

She also wisely confirms the appointment and quickly outlines the kit's contents.

Most professional letter writers agree that a sales letter should almost never be more than three paragraphs long. If it's any longer, most readers will instantly disregard the entire letter as too wordy.

In her one-page, no doubt simplified résumé (Figure 5-3), the agent doesn't provide a high school yearbook, a copy of her dissertation, or copies of her designation certificates.

Why not? She knows that her clients are sophisticated enough to recognize the work behind each sentence. She doesn't need to spell it out in crayon.

What's the difference between providing a résumé and providing a biography (Figure 5-4)? It's a good question. A résumé is more or less a list of professional accomplishments, whereas a biography humanizes the agent, making her become more than just a sentence. It tells the agent's professional history and allows the agent to become three-dimensional. This is also a great way for a new agent to show his strengths in areas outside of the real estate business.

A shortcut to re-creating your company history may be to borrow a page from your company's website (Figure 5-5), which often contains either a

FIGURE 5-2.

John and Jane Smith
123 Lakeview Dr.
Portland, OR 97435

RE: Premeeting Kit

<Date>

Dear John and Jane,

It was my pleasure speaking with you today. I'm excited to find out how I may be able to help with your real estate needs. I have you scheduled for an appointment on <Date> at <Time>.

Before the appointment, I thought that you might like to review my premeeting kit. The kit contains many items that many of my clients have found helpful, including:

➢ Résumé
➢ Brief Biography
➢ Company History
➢ Meeting Outline
➢ Seller Questionnaire
➢ Agent Questions
➢ Website Links
➢ Video—Pricing Your Home to Sell
➢ Testimonials

If I can answer any questions before I arrive, please don't hesitate to give me a call or an e-mail. Thank you.

Warmest regards,

Sally Superstar
555-1212

FIGURE 5-3.

Sally Superstar—Resume

Position Objective: My mission is to become your trusted real estate professional.

Educational Background:

- ➢ Graduate Thurston Senior High 1987
- ➢ Graduate University of Oregon 1994—Major in Economics
- ➢ Completed Real Estate Licensing Program 1995
- ➢ Completed Graduate Realtor Institute Training 1997
- ➢ Completed Certified Residential Specialist Training 1999
- ➢ Completed Accredited Buyer Representative Training 1999
- ➢ Completed Accredited Luxury Home Specialist Training 2005

Professional Accomplishments:

- ➢ Bachelor of Science Degree in Economics 1994
- ➢ Currently hold the following real estate designations:
  - ○ GRI, CRS, ABR, ALHS (explained further in kit)
- ➢ Salesperson of the Year 2000 and 2001
- ➢ Multi-Million Dollar Sales Production Since 1996

Memberships:

- ➢ Eugene Association of Realtors
- ➢ Oregon Association of Realtors
- ➢ National Association of Realtors
- ➢ Multiple Listing Service Member
- ➢ Lions Club & Optimist Club

Working History:

- ➢ 1993–1995 OSU Campus Library
- ➢ 1995–1998 ABC Realty
- ➢ 1998–2003 XYZ Real Estate Inc.
- ➢ 2003–2006 All State Real Estate

FIGURE 5-4.

Sally Superstar—Short Bio

Sally is a real estate agent who gets results. A ten-year veteran in the local real estate market, she knows what works and what doesn't to sell homes in Lane County. As a residential specialist, she has developed a completely unique marketing system for her clients. It works! Her system has helped over 500 families achieve their real estate dreams!

Sally is a hometown native who is an avid basketball fan. You can often see her on the sidelines cheering on her favorite teams. Her competitive spirit started early when she began helping her father build a successful carpet installation business while still just a teenager. Working her way through college, she learned to be a self-starter and to manage her time while juggling two jobs and a full schedule of academic classes. Graduating near the top of her class, she carefully researched all of the possible opportunities in her chosen field of study and decided to pursue real estate, a career she had always dreamed of working in.

Sally has gone on to become a respected member of the real estate community. She won Top Salesperson honors within her firm in 2000 and 2001 and has won numerous monthly sales achievement awards. In addition, Sally is one of only a handful of agents in the county to simultaneously hold the ABR, CRS, GRI, and ALHS real estate designations. Her drive to provide her clients with excellent service is one reason her clients keep coming back year after year!

Sally lives just outside of the city limits with her three daughters and husband, Jack, a local builder.

company history or the principal broker's background. Both add depth to the picture of who will be representing the seller's home in the marketplace. (The only caveat to this approach is if you work with a competing broker.)

Providing a meeting outline (Figure 5-6) is sometimes referred to as the "safe island" approach, meaning that we empower the seller by giving her a safe place that we will return to throughout the appointment—the meeting outline.

Also take careful note of the privacy statement, which gives sellers the ability to speak freely without fear of hurting their own interests. Just be sure to check your state's agency laws regarding confidentiality.

FIGURE 5-5.

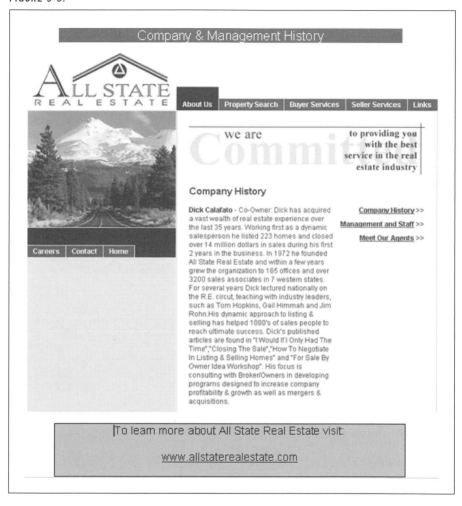

By providing her clients with a preinterview questionnaire (Figure 5-7), this agent is setting herself up for success.

If the client doesn't send the questionnaire back, one of her team members can follow up with a phone call to conduct the interview, or she can use the form during the presentation itself. In either case, she will be in a position to control the flow and tempo of the meeting by focusing on the client's real needs.

By providing the seller with questions that he may wish to ask you upon your arrival (Figure 5-8), you have given yourself a huge sales advantage. Why? Because obviously you should have great answers!

FIGURE 5-6.

Meeting Outline

Arrival at Home & Introduction

Tour of Home:

Interior and Exterior
Landscaping & Systems
Warranty Information

Privacy Statement:
All client discussions are kept
in the strictest confidence.

Review of Property Information:

Square Footage & Lot Size
Tax Statements
Deeds & Recordings
Covenants, Conditions, & Restrictions

Neighborhood Overview:

Schools/Buses
Roads/Access
Neighborhood Condition

Questionnaire Review

Presentation of Available Services:

Pricing Analysis and Competitive Overview
Product Enhancement
Promotional Plan

Success Portfolio:

Sample Marketing Plans

Questions and Answers

When you read these questions, it might be easy to panic. After all, what if you're a new agent or you haven't sold many homes? What then? To overcome these challenges, many agents fall back on the strength of their company. A simple restructuring of the questionnaire can focus the questions on your firm and not on you personally. (Whew!)

Many agents provide their clients with website links (Figure 5-9) as a

FIGURE 5-7.

Seller Questionnaire

By taking the time to answer these questions in advance, you will help me to provide you with a consultation that best fits your needs. You can fax your answers to 555-1212, or if you prefer, you can e-mail my team at sally@allstaterealestate.com. One of my team members may call to follow up on the questionnaire before the meeting.

1. How long have you lived in the home?

2. What have you liked most about living in the home?

3. What attracted you to the home when you bought it?

4. Why are you considering selling?

5. What is your time frame for moving?

6. What improvements have you made to the home?

7. Where are you moving to?

8. What should a new buyer be aware of?

9. What price range do you have in mind?

10. Do you have a loan that needs to be paid off?

11. Would you rather receive top dollar or a faster sale?

12. What items would you like to leave in the home?

13. How much time do you need to move?

14. What kind of marketing are you looking for?

15. What criteria have you set for hiring a real estate professional?

16. What questions can I answer for you?

way to provide additional information without having to add reams of paper to their prelisting kit.

The idea is not to become a Google-like dictionary of websites, but instead to offer a narrow list of the best websites you have found to help your clients research the real estate process.

It's long been said that the best advertisement is a satisfied client. But

FIGURE 5-8.

Agent Questions

When interviewing any agent, including me, to list your home, it's wise to ask questions that will reveal the agent's ability to successfully accomplish your real estate goals. Below is a list of suggested questions:

1) How long have you been selling real estate?

2) How much real estate did you sell last year?

3) How many listings do you currently have?

4) Are you a full-time agent?

5) How many homes have you sold in my area?

6) What do you know about the market in my area?

7) What educational designations have you achieved?

8) What is your average market time vs. the market?

9) What is your list price to sales price ratio vs. the market?

10) How much are you willing to spend on marketing?

11) Do you farm my neighborhood?

12) Will you mail flyers of my home to the public?

13) Will you e-mail top agents about my home?

14) May I see a sample brochure of other listings you have sold?

15) Do you provide a home marketing book for prospects?

16) Do you provide a written report to sellers?

17) Do you have a personal assistant to help with details?

18) May I see your résumé or personal brochure?

FIGURE 5-9.

Website Links

Many of my clients like to do real estate research online. To help, my team has put together a list of sites that may be helpful:

Real Estate:	www.sallysuperstar.com
	www.allstaterealestate.com
Real Estate Agency:	www.rea.state.or.us
Property Searches:	www.oip.net
	www.rmls.com
	www.realtor.com
	www.craiglist.com
Real Estate Guides:	www.realestateoregon.com
Oregon Economy:	www.econ.state.or.us
Mortgage Information:	www.mortgage101.com
Mapping Information:	www.mapquest.com
	www.earth.google.com
Real Estate Info:	www.realtytimes.com
	www.rismedia.com
Demographics:	www.census.gov
Internet Service:	www.broadbandreports.com

---

that's true only if your satisfied clients tell someone about your services. This agent provides not only the names of her satisfied clients but their phone numbers as well (after gaining their written permission). To me, this sends the signal that her clients are so happy with her services that they are willing to provide live testimony to her skills.

So assuming that you run out and build your own kit, how often, realistically, will you send one or have one delivered to your client's doorstep? To be honest, even the most aggressive agents who have every intention of using their carefully crafted prelisting kits often just can't find the time to get them into their clients' hands. To deal with this problem, many agents have taken to delivering their prelisting kits electronically in the form of an e-booklet.

An e-booklet is just a fancy name for a document that is sent or downloaded from the Internet. The advantages to this technique are that it is instantaneous; free; and, most important, far more likely to actually be done.

So now that the prelisting kit is in the mail, we can just put our feet up and wait for the clock to count down to launch, right? Wrong. For top producers, there are still some key ingredients needed to ensure a successful listing appointment.

LEARNING OPPORTUNITY

Prelisting kit. A prelisting kit is a packet sent or delivered to a seller prior to your arrival at his home that can be a starting point for your initial discussion, and later your presentation.

The Due Diligence Inoculation—A 17-Point Research Plan

Okay, here it is—the absolute worst possible thing that can happen to you during a listing appointment. You're sitting with the seller in his spacious kitchen, crunching on a year-old gingersnap and showing off your latest marketing extravaganza, when bam! The seller hits you over the head with a sledgehammer by asking you, "Hey, what did the home across the street sell for?"

Huh? Quickly digging out from underneath a mountain of useless papers, you discover that you don't have the information. The house across the street wasn't a comparable for your competitive market analysis, so it didn't come up in your research. *Dagnabit!* The seller's face drops as you stammer. Quickly you dial your assistant to do an emergency MLS search, but she's gone. All you can get is her voice mail. (It seems that your assistant needs an assistant.) A bead of sweat forms on your palm, then another as the seller's demeanor changes from warm and cuddly to formal and businesslike.

"Don't worry about it," the seller says, no longer looking you in the eye.

It's gone. Your listing just fluttered away like a spindly dandelion puff in a big gust of wind. You could have caught it if you had been fast enough, but instead you tripped and fell face-first in the mud. No flowers for you. And no listing, either. Once again you failed to take the listing because of a lack of knowledge.

Has this happened to you? It's happened to me many, many times. What we failed to do was to complete our due diligence, otherwise known as due care. Due diligence is defined by the online encyclopedia Wikipedia (www .wikipedia.org) as the effort made by an ordinarily prudent or reasonable party to avoid harm to another party. Harm? Yes, harm. When you fail to prepare thoroughly for a client meeting, you can harm your clients by leaving them with unanswered questions or, worse yet, unasked questions. Both can leave the seller feeling anxious and dissatisfied. To inoculate your presentation from potentially lethal mistakes requires vigilant research deep into a home, the surrounding neighborhood, and the local community. This is the kind of due diligence that other agents will scoff at, your broker may discourage, and your assistant may want to lynch you for for even suggesting.

So roll up your sleeves; it's time for your due diligence inoculation. Warning: You may feel a slight burning sensation as you read this list, but don't worry; it's completely normal and should go away within 24 hours.

Seventeen-Point Research Plan

1. *All active, expired, and sold listings in the area.* Sellers are often curious about their neighbor's homes, even when their neighbors have more square footage, an extra bedroom, and a three-car garage. Sellers don't care; they still want to know all the juicy details.

2. *School information.* Detailed school information is available online through many state-sponsored websites, as well as from www.homefair .com, a site owned and operated by REALTOR.com. These sites provide an in-depth look at each school's "report card" and student-teacher ratio, both of which can directly affect a home's value.

3. *For sale by owner list.* A quick drive through the neighborhood should reveal the for sale by owners in the area, and a follow-up phone call or visit can provide you with everything you need to know about each property. Just make sure to follow the federal do-not-call guidelines (www.fcc.gov).

4. *Department of Transportation.* Many local governments and cities provide statistics on road usage, congestion, and upcoming improvements, which can be invaluable when you are attempting to sell a home in a high-traffic location.

5. *Comprehensive plan review.* Many top producers make a point of purchasing their city or county's comprehensive plan. This huge book should provide an outline of the path of progress for your area and provide a red flag when listing homes within these zones.

6. *Farm book.* If you are a farmer, real estate lingo for someone who specializes in a certain demographic or geographic segment of the market, you may already have created a *farm book.* A farm book is a reference book that often includes all of the details about the community you have targeted, including average utility costs, school bus routes, service providers, shopping, and places of worship.

7. *Neighborhood walk-about.* Nothing will put you in touch with a neighborhood faster than just walking around inside it. Taking just 20 minutes to get the feel and flavor of the area can provide insights that you would have missed by just looking at a computer screen.

8. *Satellite image.* Any agent can now view satellite images of every home in her inventory; better yet, she can use the maps as a tool when taking a listing. To pull up a map of your next listing, visit http://earth.google.com.

9. *Competitive market analysis.* Strong agents thoroughly review every comparable sold, expired, and active listing in the neighborhood of their subject property. A word of caution here: Many sellers will ask you if you have actually "seen" these listings. If you haven't, it may be worth a quick drive to at least view the homes from the outside.

Top Producer Tip: Much of the information for items 10 to 17 is generally available for free from your local title company.

10. *Legal owner's name.* This should be confirmed with the seller during the presentation. Often deeds will show deceased parties, divorced parties, children's names, and trusts or corporations, all of which may pose hurdles to taking or closing the listing.

11. *Lot size.* Although we don't pretend to be surveyors, we should have a rough idea of a property's boundary lines before taking the listing. This way, we don't sell someone else's backyard.

12. *Tax record history.* Is the current owner paying her taxes? If she's not, that's not necessarily bad for you. Why? The seller's motivation to sell

may be relatively high, and your likelihood of taking a listing that much greater. (Twisted, right?)

13. *Last deed.* This should show when the seller purchased the home and often (but not always) what he paid for the property. This is a great piece of information to have on hand when going into a listing appointment.

14. *Building permits.* Reviewing these permits can give you a sense of not just the square footage of the property, but what the sellers have done to make the house a home.

15. *Zoning restrictions.* Many agents purchase or keep at their fingertips a list of all of the zonings in their service area. They can then review and photocopy the restrictions for each property that they will be visiting.

16. *Covenants, conditions, and restrictions.* These outline what a seller may do within a subdivision and what she may not do. Watch out for expired CC&Rs that may no longer have any effect.

17. *Homeowner association information.* In many communities, a homeowner association is in place to enforce the CC&Rs, approve new construction, and maintain common areas. New owners may have to be approved by a committee and agree to a monthly assessment for services.

To help with this seemingly monumental task, many agents invest in a virtual assistant. A virtual assistant is a person who helps real estate agents to complete a variety of tasks over the Internet, including research, prospecting, website management, and database management. They are often paid by the hour or by the task, but they rarely come into face-to-face contact with their agent employer. Instead, they are given an assignment and then e-mail their completed work to the agent within a specified time frame. To find a virtual assistant in your area, check out the Real Estate Virtual Assistant Network at www.revanetwork.com.

If you're not quite ready to invest in a live assistant, and a dead one just freaks you out, you may want to consider employing a Web-based research system like www.eneighborhoods.com (Figure 5-10). This system enables agents to choose from a variety of different seller reports that include much of the research data that we listed in our 17-point plan, along with a couple that we didn't, like employment and demographic data sets.

So assuming that you either do the research yourself or have it done professionally, let's do a little *Groundhog Day* reenactment (you know, the

FIGURE 5-10.

movie with Bill Murray where he relives the same day over and over) and see if we can change your fate by deploying our new arsenal of information with your original seller. Ready?

Cue the alarm clock. . . .

"Hey, what did the home across the street sell for?"

"You know, I'm glad you asked, because I went ahead and pulled up every listing that sold in your neighborhood in the last 12 months. Let me show you what I found. . . ."

Yes, yes, yes—all is now right with the universe. By completing your due diligence, you have now taken the first step toward taking a spanking new listing. You should feel at peace and confident that you are at the top of your game, that nothing and no one can stop you. Unless . . . unless the seller pipes up with a statement like this: "So my house should sell for at least twice that, right?"

Sounds like it's time to break out the big gun, the competitive market analysis (CMA). But how do you go about preparing a convincing competitive market analysis? It's a great question and an essential part of the preparation process, so let's take a look at the first step in the process by understanding the overall market.

The Market Grudge Match

Let's be honest, preparing a CMA is something that we in the real estate business like to make a big deal of. We tout CMAs as being objective documents, with numbers, statistics, and trend lines that make them seem infallible, like a Senate briefing or a Tom Clancy novel. But the truth is that most of these documents are about as objective as a rat in a cheese factory.

A competitive pricing analysis is really no more than a pricing opinion. In many cases, it's no different from an appraisal, which by definition is also just an opinion of value. The problem with opinions is that everyone has one, and they are almost always inherently biased by something. (Somewhere I can hear an appraiser screaming.) For example, sellers are biased to want to push the envelope and ask the highest price possible, while buyers are almost always looking for ways to justify a lower price. Agents, on the other hand, have two competing objectives; the first is to take the listing, and the second is to actually sell it. Mixing this all together creates what we in the real estate world call the "market."

The real estate market is the amalgamation of everyone's biases: buyers, sellers, renters, Realtors, lenders, appraisers—everyone's opinion wrapped up like pigs in a blanket into the overall demand for housing. The most pervasive bias wins. Like an emotional grudge match between two bitter rivals, the market is always in flux, moving up and down depending on who's winning the round.

This pushing and pulling, hitting and scratching, biting and kicking is the yin and yang of the real estate market. Like a toilet that won't flush, it always swirls endlessly around the eternal question: Is it a seller's market or a buyer's market (Figure 5-11)? A seller's market is defined as a period when the

FIGURE 5-11. THE MARKET GRUDGE MATCH.

Seller's Market:
High demand for housing, lots of buyers, low inventory.

Buyer's Market:
Low demand for housing, lots of homes, high inventory.

emotional pendulum has swung (or been pushed) to light a fire under buyers to want to own a home, thus creating a high demand for housing. Sellers then have pricing power. They can and do command higher and higher prices as less and less inventory becomes available. In southern California, for instance, during peak buying frenzies, there have been times where the market has had less than one month of available inventory, meaning that if no additional listings were taken, the inventory would be completely sold out in less than 30 days. The flip side of this equation is a buyer's market, an event that many or even most agents operating in North America have yet to experience (but are beginning to). A buyer's market happens when there is an excess of supply and falling demand. This provides buyers with the ability to negotiate lower prices and demand more concessions from sellers.

A home's value, then, is a moving target; its worth is always relative to when the seller decides to begin marketing the home. Contrary to what the tax rolls may indicate, a home doesn't have a static value that moves a certain predictable percentage every year. Instead, it flows like water, following the market's ups and downs until a seller puts a "For Sale" sign in the lawn, and then suddenly, depending on the number of buyers in the marketplace, the home's value solidifies.

So let's talk about pricing a specific home. As a seasoned professional, every time you walk into a new home, you instantly form a price opinion; I call this your gut price. Your gut price is intuitive—it's your brain thin-slicing huge amounts of data, compiling them instantly, and then flicking a switch that says this home is worth X, Y, or Z. Is your gut price always right? Not always. But I'll bet that more often than not, it's pretty darn close to the final sales price.

Unfortunately, many agents don't listen to their intuition; instead, they ignore their gut price and catch a bad case of what I call CMAitis. CMAitis is the need that many agents feel to impress their sellers with hundred-plus-page reports that conclude in a dramatic flurry by predicting, sometimes down to the last penny, what a home will eventually sell for—something like, "Mr. and Mrs. Jones, according to my calculations, your home should sell for $596,325.13."

Sounds impressive, doesn't it? It feels good, too, like you really know what you're talking about. But what if we are competing for the seller's affection with two or three other agents? Who will the seller hire then? Obviously, without anything to go on but the price, most sellers will hire the agent who tells them the highest price. As with an Elvis autograph on eBay, the highest bidder wins. Unfortunately, everyone comes out a loser in a bidding war—the agents who competed and lost, the agent who won the listing but never sells the house, and the seller who never achieves her real estate goals. They all come out losers.

So how can you avoid this fate? The bear trap that snaps the legs of many agents is the tendency to want to name a specific price. Perhaps a seller has asked a specific question like, "Well, now that you have seen the home, what do you think it should sell for?" Watch out! The second you answer that question, you have just slapped a price tag over your mouth that will prevent the seller from hearing another word you say. You will have become the price. Like a cow branded at birth, you will always be tagged as "the bald guy who told us our home was worth only $450,000." (All right, maybe you aren't a bald guy or gal; go ahead and insert your own signature flaw here.) So what's the solution? The solution is to reject the notion that you must become a twenty-first-century Nostradamus and predict to the penny a home's eventual sales price. It's impossible. Instead take a look at this superstar's answer to the question:

Pricing Question Dialogue

> **Seller:** *What do you think the home will sell for?*
>
> **Agent:** *You know, that's the first question that almost every seller asks me, and it's important because price is the number one reason why a home*

will or won't sell. I've put together a competitive pricing analysis that takes the entire market into account, and that'll help answer your question. Do you mind if I show you what I found?

I know what you're thinking. Didn't I just say that a competitive market analysis is a biased document that's almost always prejudiced by an agent's need to take a listing, and also that wise agents shouldn't attempt to predict a specific sales price? Guilty on all counts, but the trick is to not throw the baby out with the bathwater. The data in a solid CMA are incredibly valuable. We absolutely need this information to help the seller price the home accurately, but it's how we present the information that will separate us from the herd. To demonstrate, let's start by filling the client in on the overall market conditions.

Giving the client a sense of what's happening in the overall market is critical to sensitizing him to the big picture. Whether it's good, bad, or even ugly, the client needs to know what's happening at the macro level, before we move down to the micro level of focusing only on his home or neighbor-

FIGURE 5-12.

Overall Market Condition Report			
	July 2005	**July 2006**	**%**
Listings:			
New #	122	135	+10.6
Total #	1321	1421	+ 7.5
Sales:			
Pending #	154	132	−14.2
Closed #	111	109	− 1.8
Average LP	$394,000	$421,000	+6.8
Average SP	$392,000	$412,500	+5.2
LP VS SP	99.5%	98%	− 1.5
DOM	28 Days	39 Days	+39

hood. Take a look at how one of my coaching students, Mark, repackages his MLS data into a very easy to understand one-page report that helps acclimate his clients to the real estate real world (see Figure 5-12).

Now watch as Mark effortlessly breaks down seemingly complicated data into bite-sized pieces of information that his sellers can easily grasp and apply to their own unique real estate challenge.

Sample of Mark's Overall Market Condition Dialogue

Mr. and Mrs. Seller, my team and I put together a report for our clients each month that we think provides an insight into what's happening with the big picture of real estate in our area. We call it our Overall Market Condition Report.

On the top line, we have the number of listings taken last month; this was 135 new listings, which as you can see is over 10 percent more than last year at the same time. This is consistent with the next line, which shows that the total number of listings available in our market is up 7.5 percent to 1,421 listings. A quick calculation tells us that, if no more listings were added to the market, it would take roughly 13 months to sell off that inventory.

The next set of data deals with sales; the top line here is what we call pending sales, or homes that have offers but have not yet closed escrow. As you can see, the number of pending sales last month was down considerably, 14.2 percent, but the actual number of closed sales was down only slightly, to 109 closed transactions.

On the plus side, the average listing price has jumped 6.8 percent and the average sales price is now $412,500, 5.2 percent higher than last year. In addition, sellers in our market who actually sold their home last month received on average 98 percent of their asking price. Also, the average time it took to sell those homes—something we call the DOM, or days on market—was 39 days.

Breaking this down, we see the number of listings is up, so you have more competition, but the number of actual closings is roughly even and sellers are averaging a higher price for their homes.

Do you see anything else that concerns you about these numbers?

Of course, this sample dialogue is specific to the current market conditions; as the market changes, the script changes. Yet regardless of the individual numbers, it's important to notice something very important in the way Mark talks about his statistics: He doesn't take sides. He doesn't spin the information. He isn't saying that the market is a strong market or a weak market, a buyer's market or a seller's market. At this point, he is just stating facts. The numbers should speak for themselves.

By taking sides too early in a client meeting, agents can often take a position that is contrary to a seller's worldview. Our worldview is how we see things from our own unique perspective. It's our worldview that shapes our thoughts, decisions, and actions. It's the reason some people vote Republican, some people vote Democrat, and some people don't vote at all, although we all have access to roughly the same information to make those decisions. For example, looking at these numbers tells me that the market may have peaked; prices may soon level off or even fall, and longer times to market are probably a distinct possibility. This is my worldview. But what if my seller looks at these numbers and decides that what she is seeing is sellers hanging tough on their prices even in a competitive market and still, by and large, getting a higher price than a year before? Is she wrong? No, she's right. Am I wrong? Not from my worldview. We both just have a different way of looking at the same data.

Superstars get in tune with their clients' thinking pattern, their thought process, early in the presentation. By doing so, they will be able to gently guide their clients during the meeting to make informed, reasonable decisions that will benefit their interests. By avoiding taking an early position, agents can remain flexible enough to counteract any crazy thoughts the clients may have without seeming confrontational. For instance, perhaps the seller might reason: "Well, it seems to me that if sellers are getting 98 percent of what they're asking for, we can just ask more and wait for an offer."

An idiotic statement? Yes, but only from your worldview. From the seller's position, it seems perfectly reasonable based on the market data. To counteract this, look at how Mark handles the situation:

"Well, one thing you have to remember about that statistic is that it represents only sellers who actually received offers and closed escrow. Sellers who priced their home over the market and never sold actually received 0 percent of their asking price."

It would be easy to say this with smug, condescending arrogance, like a waiter deciphering a menu in French. But Mark doesn't; instead, he smiles while he talks and states the facts in a kind, warm, engaging manner. He's there to help. He is a consultant, not a friend but an ally, someone to answer questions and wade through mountains of data to make heads or tails of our crazy real estate market.

Now, you might wonder if Mark ever takes a position. Does he ever finally come out and say, "Well, based on these numbers, it's my opinion that . . . "? Yes, but that will come later. First we need to help the seller understand the difference between fantasy and reality.

LEARNING OPPORTUNITY

The market. The real estate market is defined as the overall demand for housing at any given moment; a buyer's market is a high supply–low demand market, and a seller's market is a high demand–low supply market.

The numbers. Wise agents don't spin market information; instead, they allow the market numbers to speak for themselves and get "in tune" with their client's perspective on the market.

Fantasy vs. Reality

Shhh . . . shhh . . . shhh . . . it's supposed to be a secret.

The truth is that real estate agents can actually force a competitive market analysis to come out any darn way they want. It's the reason agents often walk around real estate offices saying, "Hey, what do you think a four-bedroom, three-bath home in Newport Dunes will sell for?" while a chorus of veteran agents sing out numbers like a convention of drunken auctioneers: "$495,000 . . . $475,000 . . . $680,000!"

Sure, we all use sophisticated CMA programs to manipulate and massage the data, but in the end, it is we who finally decide on a recommended price. Like an Enron accountant before an investor conference call, we often spend hours adjusting, tweaking, and bending the numbers to make them come out just the way we want them to. We want to beat expectations and have the sellers buy stock in our presentation.

In preparing your CMA, you will no doubt include all of the usual suspects: a list of all the properties that have sold in the neighborhood, a list of homes that are for sale today, and finally a list of all the homes that were on the market but never sold. It's all neat and tidy. Yet, why is it that if you ask four different real estate agents to do a CMA on the same property you will receive four different answers, sometimes wildly different? The answer is that real estate agents don't set home prices; the market does. We just pretend to.

Wise agents, on the other hand, don't attempt to predict sales prices; instead, they provide their clients with accurate market data and allow their sellers to make informed decisions based on a careful study of the numbers. Yes, it's easier to just give the seller a quick "off the cuff" estimate using what my friend Neil Moffitt calls the PFA, or pulled-from-air, method of pricing. But in doing so, you run the risk of alienating the seller by taking a position she disagrees with or by being just plain wrong.

Wrong? Yes, you can be wrong. To avoid this fate, my friend Rick De-luca, a master CRS instructor, uses the fantasy vs. reality technique. The fantasy vs. reality technique is so deceptively simple that it seems too easy. It shouldn't work. But it does. To use the system, agents build a traditional CMA, but instead of concluding with a traditional price recommendation, they take a different approach: They leave off the suggested price page. Instead, they let the seller decide the price. How do they make this work in the real world? Take a look at this sample dialogue:

Fantasy vs. Reality Dialogue

Mr. and Mrs. Seller, what I have put together for you today is detailed information about properties that have sold and that are comparable to your home—I call these the reality (in other words, what sellers were actually able to sell their homes for in our market)—and a list of properties that are on the market now that haven't yet sold and may never sell—I call these the fantasy.

Ultimately, it's your decision on where you choose to price your home, and then it's just a question of whether the market will accept or reject that price.

What I would recommend is that we look at each of these listings in depth, and then see if we can find a price that you feel comfortable with and that I feel we can successfully market the property for. Does that sound fair?

Top Producer Tip: To defuse competing agents in a multiple-interview situation, consider using the script that Marylyn, an agent from Atlantic City, adds to her pricing discussion. She says this:

You know, there are many agents who will tell you a price just to get a listing, but really, unless an agent is willing to write a check for your home, the number is meaningless.

By using the fantasy vs. reality dialogue instead of entering into a bidding war with other agents, you are able to step into the role of a consultant. Now, to prepare for this pricing conversation, strong agents do more than just pull up MLS printouts; they highlight critical information. Here are three pieces of key information to point out to sellers during your next listing presentation:

1. *Listing feature differences.* Obviously, every home is different. Pointing out the unique features of each property and how it differs from your seller's home is an important consideration. For instance, a home's age and lot size can greatly affect its value, but less obvious factors, like school and taxing districts, utility costs, or even proximity to shopping, are sometimes overlooked.

2. *Starting price and offer-generating price.* Often listings will have been reduced in price a number of times before generating an offer. This is a very important item to point out to sellers, who might think starting high won't be an issue. Strong agents point out that starting at an artificially high price may hurt a seller in the long term, as a home may become stigmatized.

3. *Days on market.* When reviewing both active and sold listings, let sellers know how long each of these properties has been on the market. For instance, a seller may have sold for full price, but perhaps it took six months to secure the offer. Is this seller willing to make a similar sacrifice?

Are there more key points? There are probably hundreds of different things you could point out during a pricing discussion that would be relevant, but although overwhelming the client with data may seem like the right thing to do, it is often the sign of a weak agent. Like a speaker who tries to cover too much information or a book that lingers too long on one topic, sometimes too much is just too much. The wise agent finds a balance between educating her clients and smothering them by paring down mountains of information to a more manageable size, one that the client can act on.

So now that you have done your in-depth research, prepared for a pricing discussion, and sent over your prelisting kit, it's time to roll up your sleeves, bag up the laptop, and head over to the seller's home. Let's explore the nuts and bolts of sitting with a seller in Chapter 6, "Legendary Seller Presentations."

Legendary Seller Presentations

The home offered a view of the lake—a tremendous, breathtaking view that stretched over dark green meadows and rolling hills, and even extended dramatically down into the clear waters of a creek-fed reservoir below.

"Wow, nice view," I said, interrupting myself in midsentence.

The sellers glanced at each other in a knowing way. They were used to a luxury lifestyle. The wife had let me know that they owned three homes and were now building a new lodge-style home in Colorado, as if I would be impressed. I was.

I had already done all of the preliminary work: reviewed the home, sent over a prelisting kit, and asked a series of qualifying questions during the walk-through. It was now time for me to do the actual listing presentation.

"Is there anything you would like to talk about before I start?" I asked.

"Jim, to be honest," the husband replied, "we have already met with three other agents, and my wife has decided on someone she feels could do a great job for us."

Earlier in my career, this answer would have been a sucker punch to the midsection of my presentation. On this day, however, something clicked. It suddenly occurred to me that not only did I still have an excellent shot at taking this listing, but it would be nearly impossible for me not to take it.

My realization was simple: If the couple had been unified in their decision, they would have simply cancelled my appointment. Why waste their time talking with me if they were already sold on another agent? The answer was unmistakable; the husband had just laid it out for me: "My wife has decided on someone she feels could do a great job for us." Yes, his wife was sold on my competitor, but he wasn't.

I started slowly. "To be honest, I guess the biggest difference between me and all the other agents you have talked with is that I don't need your listing."

The couple was momentarily stunned, as if they couldn't decide which emotion to fix on—anger, frustration, jealousy. But this wouldn't last long, so I charged ahead. "Listen, here's where I'm at in my business. I work with only a handful of sellers at a time. Financially, I don't need to take any more listings for the rest of the year, so I can be very selective about the clients and homes that I choose to represent. This allows me to work with clients completely differently from most agents you will meet."

I had the couple's attention. Even the wife seemed to be pondering my statements carefully. Finally she asked, "What do you mean by differently?"

"I mean I don't need to tell sellers what they want to hear just to take a listing. I'll tell you exactly what I think it will take to sell your home and move on with your life, and then I'll leave it in your hands to make the big decisions."

"So what will it take to sell our home?" the husband asked, leaning forward.

"Three things, actually," I replied, turning my laptop around so that the screen faced the couple. "I call them the three Ps."

Bingo, I had them! The home was listed and sold within a month. For me, this magical experience was one of the best sales performances of my career—the kind of presentation that you replay over and over in your head to relive the drama, tension, and excitement of having everything you say come together in one legendary meeting experience. But when I reflect back on that meeting today, I see a serious flaw, a lurking gremlin hidden beneath my success that could easily have torpedoed that presentation and every presentation thereafter. Where was my mistake?

I had failed to follow the mechanics of a perfect meeting by thoroughly qualifying the client. If I had done so, I would have discovered that I was competing for the listing—something that I should have known long before I arrived at the home. Although I got lucky and hit a home run, the meeting could just as easily have imploded. My success had hidden my failure. As one superstar from Seattle taught me years ago, it's not enough to recognize what you're doing right at every client meeting; it's what you're doing wrong that you need to discover and correct. For me this meant relearning the mechanics of a perfect meeting, starting with positioning for success.

LEARNING OPPORTUNITY

An agent's apparent success can hide a serious system failure.

Wise agents take the time to reflect on what they are doing right, and, just as important, what they are doing wrong after each client meeting.

Positioning for Success

As your car idles to a slow stop in front of the home, your heart skips a beat—it's go time. You've done all you can do to prepare. The time has come to stand and deliver your best presentation. An hour or two from now, if you've done a good job, you will step back through the seller's front door, listing in hand, walking on a cloud, unstoppable. But if you make a mistake, slip up, or just plain blow it, you will walk through that same door with your head hung low, frustrated, defeated, and sucked dry of enthusiasm. It's the same door. The only difference is what happens behind it.

What should happen? What are the mechanics of a perfect meeting? I wondered that myself my first couple of months in the real estate business. Like you, I had heard all the motivational stuff—be positive, smile, try to win the sellers over by finding common ground. But that just wasn't enough. What I wanted was a step-by-step, A leads to B . . . B leads to C explanation of exactly what I should be doing from the second I walked through the seller's front door. After a couple of months of pestering, I finally got an answer from an agent in my office, a salty Navy veteran named Tom. Tom agreed to take me with him on a listing appointment to give me an education, a field exercise in how to execute a listing presentation. To my surprise, the lesson began while we were still sitting just outside the seller's home.

"Now, Jim, the second you step outside this car, you have to become an actor," Tom began. "Whatever problems you have going on back at the office or at home, the seller could care less about them. All he cares about is selling his home. So clear your mind of any distractions, and turn off your pager."

This turned out to be great advice. Later, as I went on to coach my own students, I was shocked at what agents would tell potential sellers about their personal lives. Things like: "Last year my son knocked up a girl at school, and yesterday I found out that his brother got kicked out of third grade, so I'm sorry I'm late, but I had to meet with the principal. I'm sure you understand."

No, they don't.

Check your baggage at the door. Sellers don't care about you. They care only about themselves, which was another reason why Tom instructed me to turn off my pager (this was long before cell phones). The worst insult you can give anyone in a meeting is to answer your phone. It says to the person you're sitting with that she is not as important as the person calling. Trust me, I've heard all the arguments before: "Doesn't it make me look busy or in demand?" Nope, it just makes you look like a self-absorbed idiot. Turn it all off.

We started for the door, Tom carrying a leather briefcase and I carrying a stack of papers. As Tom rang the bell, I looked up at a wind chime that had begun to sound, but as I tilted back to get a better view, all of Tom's carefully prepared listing paperwork spilled out of my folder and onto the wet ground. "Crap," Tom snapped. Scrambling, I just had time to scrape up the last piece of paper before the front door opened.

"Good morning," Tom said cheerfully, ignoring my gaff. (He really was a good actor.) "I brought along a friend from the office, Jim. He's new in the business, so he's just here to observe today."

The sellers were a friendly older couple. They graciously ushered us into their small home and carefully locked the door behind us. Standing in the entry, we seemed momentarily at a standstill, not moving forward or back, until Tom took the lead and said, "Do you mind if I drop my briefcase at the kitchen table?" The sellers easily agreed, pointing him in the right direction.

Tom gave me a look that read, "lesson number two." It was obvious to me that the reason he had asked the question was so that he could return to that location later to do his presentation. Tom later explained that instead of attempting to keep up with a conversation that bounces back and forth between a husband and wife, it is always smart to drop your "stuff" in a strategic location, ideally one where you will be able to maintain eye contact and read the body language of both your new clients (Figure 6-1).

Now that Tom had deposited his things on the sellers' well-worn kitchen table, he stopped for a moment to pet the dogs and ask their names. Then, after pulling out a note pad and pen from his suit jacket, he smiled and began his presentation.

"Would you mind giving me a tour of the home?"

I might have expected that Tom would spend more time visiting with the sellers over a cup of coffee or looking for something in the home that he could identify with, like a fishing pole or a picture of a recent vacation, but Tom didn't waste time with fake pleasantries. Instead, he had a unique approach for building rapport and trust with his clients—asking questions.

"Jim, let me ask you a question," Tom explained to me later. "Does your doctor sit and have coffee with you, or chitchat about the weather or local politics?"

Actually, mine did, but this didn't matter to Tom. "Well, mine doesn't, and I prefer it that way. I still have a good relationship with the guy; we talk and joke. But he's there to do a job, not to be my best friend. Jim, the best way to build rapport and trust in a professional setting is to focus on the client's needs."

FIGURE 6-1. POSITIONING FOR A PRESENTATION

Place yourself in a position where you can see all the parties in a meeting or a presentation. This will enable you to maintain eye contact and read body language.

Tom's perspective was interesting. Within the selling universe, the words *trust* and *rapport* are often lumped together to create a catch-all phrase that, roughly translated, means that we need to get clients to like us or identify with us just long enough to sell them something. The actor Jack Lemmon provided a cringe-inducing example of this in the movie version of the play *Glengarry Glen Ross*: As land salesman Shelly Levene, he barges into a prospect's home during dinner and struggles desperately to build trust and rapport with the bewildered family. Did it work? No; they threw him out of the house.

Top producers reject the notion that trust and rapport are joined at the hip. Yes, both are absolutely necessary elements of a successful sales meeting, but, as wise agents know, our clients are perceptive people. They can see straight through a salesperson's vain attempts to build a fake bond or the illusion of common interests. Instead, wise agents break these two topics apart and treat them as separate targets.

The first goal of a superstar presenter should be to establish trust within her new clients. Establishing trust means that a client should feel at ease and be comfortable enough to provide you with honest answers to your questions. Rapport, on the other hand, is the ability to have an easy, free-flowing conversation with your clients without any jerky stops or starts, dead air, or awkward silences. In short, you need to be a good conversationalist.

> **Establishing Trust and Rapport**
>
> **Trust**
> Client is at ease, providing honest answers.
>
> ---
>
> **Rapport**
> Conversation flows easily.

"How do you do that?" I asked Tom, considering his suggestions.

"By asking questions!" Tom chided me.

As we began a tour of the couple's home, I watched in awe as Tom, following his own advice, masterfully built trust and rapport with the couple by using a series of gently probing questions. This simple yet powerful strategy was the first step in a six-step system that I have come to call Tom's Six-Step ACTION Presentation.

LEARNING OPPORTUNITY

Great presenters are great actors; they can completely set aside any negativity and focus completely on the presentation at hand.

> Top producers position themselves where they can see all the parties in a meeting and be able to maintain eye contact and read body language.
>
> Superstar presenters establish trust and rapport with their clients early. Establishing trust means that a client should feel at ease and be comfortable enough to provide you with honest answers. Rapport is the ability to have an easy, free-flowing conversation with a client.

The Six-Step ACTION Presentation

If you were to get the crazy idea of taking up ballroom dancing and you boldly decided to begin your first night by attempting a six-step Viennese waltz in three-quarter time to the music of Johann Strauss, you might soon discover that not only were you born with two left feet, but you seemingly were born with no feet at all.

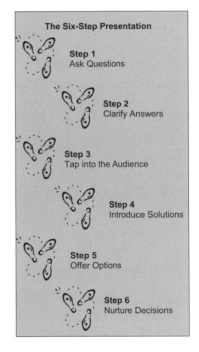

Impossible, painful, embarrassing! These flashes of clarity might detonate in perfect time with each painful connection your backside made with the freshly waxed floor. Because even though it looks easy from the sidelines—*left turn, right turn, quarter turn, dip, right turn, dip (how hard can it really be?)*—it's actually a very intricate sport.

In real estate, our dance floor is our seller's home, and, not unlike the Viennese waltz, our seller presentation includes six key steps that must be committed to memory and practiced rigorously. Our six-step presentation plan (outlined in the sidebar) can be easily remembered by using the ACTION acronym:

A: Ask questions.

C: Clarify answers.

T: Tap into the audience.

I: Introduce solutions.

O: Offer options.

N: Nurture decisions.

Step 1: Ask Questions

Asking questions and letting a client talk is the fastest way to build trust and rapport, as it demonstrates that you are actually interested, engaged, and committed to building a professional relationship. As one top producer explained to me: "When I visit with a seller, I pretend I'm there as a therapist for the first 10 minutes."

How do you get a client to lie down on your real estate couch? Just remember Tom's approach: "Would you mind giving me a tour of the home?"

While he could have sat down with the clients and asked them a series of qualifying questions, Tom, like many top producers, noticed that people tend to be more at ease and willing to answer questions when they are walking around showing off their home. By giving them something else to think about, superstars put their clients at ease while asking them gentle, probing questions. In addition, they don't overwhelm clients with a barrage of rapid-fire queries. Instead, they ask carefully crafted open-ended questions. Open-ended questions are questions that can't easily be answered with just a simple yes or no; instead, they require expository thought.

Take a look at seven open-ended first-step questions that top producers often use during this early meeting phase:

Seven Open-Ended First-Step Questions

1. Where did you move from, and why did you choose this area?
2. What do you like most about living here?
3. Why are you selling?
4. Where will you be moving to, and why?
5. What improvements have you made to the home?
6. What do you see as the home's best features?
7. How well do you like the neighborhood?

Now, you may notice that many of these questions may have already been asked and answered during a premeeting interview or perhaps included in a prelisting questionnaire. If so, any agent can easily modify her questions by making small adjustments. For instance: "I see on your questionnaire that you have lived in the home for five years; what's been the best part of living here?"

While Tom gently peppered his clients with questions, he was also taking copious notes about the home. He had a clipboard in his hand and a pen to record his data. Today many top producers expand on this concept by carrying a digital camera, flashlight, and room measurement device. Others bring along a personal digital assistant, or even use their cell phone to produce a voice recording. Employing these techniques is something that I call using a vesting strategy. Using a vesting strategy

Vesting Strategies
• Take Notes
• Take Pictures
• Measure Room Sizes
• Record Appliance Info
• Test Systems
• Look under the Home
• Look in the Attic
• Locate Property Corners

means that you encourage clients to become invested in a professional relationship by working with them side by side during the interview process. The more information the seller provides and the deeper you dig for details, the more likely the seller is to become vested in your relationship. In fact, some agents go so far as to record appliance serial numbers, test the heating and air-conditioning systems, and even locate property corners during their first appointment.

Now, after all that effort, will the seller want to reset the clock and begin this process again with another agent? The odds are against it. But what happens if a client suddenly turns cold? He clams up, shuts down, or just becomes catatonic? Ideally you will have already qualified the client, but sometimes things change. For instance, a seller who just yesterday was boxing up her Bing Crosby collection may now suddenly appear unmotivated, unready, or unwilling (the three UNs) to market the home. Be very careful here! Many sellers will become unresponsive or appear to have suddenly had a change of heart when the problem is nothing more than a case of nerves or anxiety surfacing. After all, moving is one of the most stressful events in any person's life, and stress can make even normal things seem distorted.

Like doctors, we all wear many different hats. One of these hats is to be a reassuring voice of calm, another is to coax out of our sellers what their true needs are by qualifying their symptoms, and still another is to confirm that what they are telling us is actually accurate. This brings us front and center to the next step in our presentation.

Step 2: Clarify Answers

Have you ever lied to a salesperson? Come on! Yes, you have. We all have; it's natural, and besides, lying to a salesperson isn't really lying, is it? It's more like concealment, self-preservation, survival of the fittest. Why do we do it? What's our underlying motivation? Clients lie to salespeople because the salesperson has failed to establish trust and rapport.

In a real estate setting, this can mean that when you asked the seller why she was moving, when she needed to move, and where she was moving to, she responded by saying, "Oh, I'm moving because my husband has been transferred, and we really need to move up to North Dakota in the next 90 days." The truth is that her husband is in jail and has just been transferred, and she has to sell the house to pay for his next appeal. Unless you clarify her answers, you may never learn this vital information.

So how do you clarify answers? The easiest way is to restate to the client what she has said. This doesn't mean that we parrot the seller; instead, we paraphrase or approximate what she said earlier for clarification. Clients will appreciate this approach because it gives them the opportunity to clear up any question marks and provides them with an easy way to back out of any white lies they may have told you without losing face. Let's take a look at this technique in action:

Clarification Dialogue

> **Agent:** *Ms. Seller, you said earlier that the reason you're selling is . . . , that ideally you would like to be moved by . . . , and that you will be moving to . . . Is that right?*
>
> **Seller:** *Yes, and there's one more thing. . . .*

Clarifying a seller's earlier answers is a master communication tool. While she may have been hesitant in the beginning to confess all her real reasons for selling, by the time you ask this follow-up question, often she will be ready to tell the truth, or at least expand her story. This brings up another question: When do you clarify answers?

Tom's choice was to ask his follow-up questions just as he was making his way back to the kitchen table. This was a good decision, as most top producers make it a point to clarify answers before they begin their formal presentation.

"So, Mr. and Mrs. Seller," Tom began, "it sounds like you are thinking of selling because you would like to be closer to your grandchildren in Ohio, and ideally you would like to be moved in the next three months. Is that right?"

"Yes, that's right," the wife said pleasantly.

Huh? Did we miss a step? Aren't the sellers supposed to come clean by telling us the truth? Yes, but only if they mixed a little bit of fiction into their story in the first place, and the fact is that most of our clients tell the truth, especially if, like Tom, you have done a good job of building trust and rapport. But don't be fooled; even with a strong seller connection, we're not out of the sales woods yet, because now it's time to give your clients a real test.

Step 3: Tap Into the Audience

One of the skills of a master presenter is the ability to involve his audience in the presentation. For a seller, this means that a great real estate presentation is never passive, like sitting down to watch a movie; instead, it's active, like going to a hockey game, where the audience is a vital part of the excitement. After all, without an active, engaged, and often vocal audience, a hockey game would be pretty boring.

Superstars encourage their clients to be vocal, active participants during a presentation, not just passive spectators, which is why it is often wise to give your clients permission to interrupt you, debate you, and even berate you throughout the discussion. Tom's technique for doing this was simply to say, "As we talk today, I want you to know that this is a discussion, so if any questions pop into your head, ask them, and if you disagree with any points or don't quite catch something I've said, please stop me. Okay?"

Once they have their audience engaged, many agents also find it wise to lay out what to expect during the presentation itself. This simple technique gives clients a sense of control and removes any doubts about how the meeting will proceed. Let's take a look at how one superstar explains the process:

Meeting Outline—Discussion

Just to give you an overview of what to expect during our conversation this morning, I'll cover the three main points of selling a home and answer any questions you may have as we go, and then we can review some comparable sales together. The whole presentation shouldn't take any more than 30 minutes. How does that sound?

Now that the clients are primed and ready, it's time to dive headfirst into the most important part of any presentation—introducing solutions.

Step 4: Introduce Solutions

So you're ready to roll out your presentation and introduce your solutions. But how do you do it in a way that is natural? After all, you don't want to look uncomfortable getting out your binder or laptop. This simple challenge, believe it or not, prevents many agents from ever using their presentation. Instead, they leave it inside their briefcase, and there it stays, never to see the light of day.

Tom, on the other hand, didn't have any stage fright; as I sat at the kitchen table, hands folded in my lap, I watched as he approached this dilemma with the practiced calm of a poker player holding a straight flush.

"Do you mind if I just take a minute and show you how I work?" Tom said while pulling back his chair to sit down. Not waiting for an answer, he reached down and brought out a clean three-ring binder, his listing presentation.

"Sure," the couple said nonchalantly.

That was easy. Really, it *is* easy. Although I've seen speakers recommend asking sellers for a glass of water to establish control before beginning a discussion (something I find to be a ridiculous idea), the key to opening a presentation isn't to establish control; it is to maintain trust and rapport. A seller mustn't feel trapped, tricked, or terrified about your beginning your discussion. Instead, he needs to feel at ease and calm, while enjoying the same free-flowing conversation that he had with you earlier. A good presentation, then, should be an extension of your earlier discussion, one that has now simply moved to the kitchen or dining room.

Once the discussion has begun, you can begin to introduce specific solutions on each page of your presentation. One thing to remember when introducing each new concept is the strategy of framing. To frame a discussion means that you take the time to put the subject matter into a context that will benefit the seller, or at the very least pique her interest. To illustrate, let's look at two sample listing presentation pages borrowed from the Luxury Home Council (www.luxuryhomecouncil.com) and use the technique of framing to introduce a solution (Figures 6-2 and 6-3):

FIGURE 6.2.

"When you hire me to represent your home, I will put together a comprehensive marketing plan that will include . . ." (Review list).

"I have over 25 strategies we can use to help get your home sold for top dollar. Just for fun this morning I plugged your home into a couple of sample pieces. Tell me what you think of these. . . ."

FIGURE 6-3.

"When selling a luxury home we are appealing to a very demanding set of buyers. They expect only the highest quality."

"I often help my sellers get top dollar for their homes by providing advice on what areas a buyer might notice that living in the home you may not. You may want to consider (Review list)."

In both cases, this agent successfully framed the discussion as ways in which the seller can benefit from her expertise. She also provided compelling solutions to the challenges of selling a luxury home and receiving top dollar in a very competitive market. Now it's time to offer the seller some options.

Step 5: Offer Options

Would you like French fries or onion rings? A window or an aisle seat? Two queen beds or one king? Options, options, options. Every day it seems as if we, as consumers, have more and more choices to make. Why? Because we like them!

Companies know that because every customer is unique, providing options is a smart way to create products and services that customers will actually be excited to buy. In the old days, we used to call this technique the preference of choice close. Today we just call it a true win-win; the client gets what he wants, and you get what you want: a happy customer.

So how do you provide options to real estate clients? First, look at each page of your real estate presentation and see if you can offer the client any alternatives. At first this may seem like a challenge, but as you begin to review the possibilities, you may discover that there is an almost limitless supply of options to offer your clients. Let's take a look at some user-friendly preference of choice questions:

Preference Questions: Pricing Pages

"Would you like to consider hiring an appraiser, or would you prefer that we take a look at my competitive market analysis? It's free."

"Would you prefer to set a higher price and be willing to wait for a buyer, or would you rather price the home to the market and sell quickly?"

"Would you like to preset a price adjustment 30 days from now, or would you prefer to do that sooner?"

"Would you be willing to help a buyer with closing costs or an interest-rate buydown, which could help you sell quickly, or would you rather wait for a buyer who can pay those costs herself?"

Preference Questions: Product Pages

"Would you like to offer a home warranty that can enhance the marketability of your home at no cost to you unless the home sells?"

"Would you like me to provide you with a list of the best ways to help your home stand out in the marketplace, or would you prefer to sell the home as it is?"

"Would you be willing to begin to pack up nonessentials now, which can help a buyer picture himself in the home, or would you rather wait until we have an offer?"

Preference Questions: Promotion Pages

"Would you like me to do an open house on the property, or would you prefer just a Realtor tour, or both?"

"Would you like to have a flyer box or a talking house on the home, or both?"

"Would you like to feature interior or exterior photos of the home or both in our marketing?"

You might notice that most of these questions assume that whichever way the client answers, you will be listing the property. This technique is called an assumptive close, meaning that just by virtue of the client's answering you have moved closer to listing the property. If you're a rookie or even a veteran who is not used to asking this type of strong question, you can soften this approach by adding a quick preface to each question. For example, some agents add, "If you decide to work with me" or "If we decide to work together" to each question, thus eliminating the assumptive close portion of the question.

Regardless of the semantics, by offering your clients options, choices, and alternatives, you are helping them to take baby steps toward an ultimate decision. This is important because many of our clients have a hard time making decisions, which leads us to step 6.

Step 6: Nurture Decisions

I used to own a small ranch—a ranchette, as they are called in my area. The property was beautiful, lying next to a small stream and adjacent to a historic covered bridge. We loved it.

The first day we moved on to the ranch, my wife had to have chickens.

As an old farm girl, she loved the thought of having animals scurrying around the property. So we promptly drove to the local farmers co-op and picked up some new baby chicks. Not full-size chickens, but little bantam chickens. A banty chicken is like a miniature schnauzer or a toy poodle, but instead of being a small dog, it is a minichicken. Within a few months, our tiny little baby chicks turned into little banty chickens, six hens and a rooster that we named Caesar. The hens made their home in an old barn, and soon each was proudly sitting on top of her little eggs.

Being curious, my son Michael, who was three years old at the time, and I decided to take a peek at the eggs. The problem was that those little hens weren't about to let us get near their babies. As we approached each nest, we talked softly, attempting to coax the hen off of the nest, but to no avail. They sat down harder, covering their eggs protectively. Finally my son, irritated that he couldn't see the eggs, reached under a hen and was rewarded with a peck to the back of his hand. He screamed as if he had been bitten by a viper.

Over the years I have often thought of my clients as being like those hens. They won't be rushed. Colorful and unique, they sit in their home patiently pondering the idea of listing the home. They nurture their decisions. For a real estate agent who wants to take a listing, this can be a frustrating wait, which is exactly why, over the years, I have developed strategies for helping my clients accelerate this agonizingly slow process. Like using a microwave instead of a conventional oven, we can help clients speed up their decision-making process by using four easy strategies:

1. *Don't go big.* Going big means forcing the seller to make a big decision with an ultimatum question like, "Would you like to list your home today?" Going big is like driving to Las Vegas with your life savings and placing it all on red; yes, if you win, you might drive home in a Porsche, but you can just as easily end up hitchhiking home. It's a crapshoot.

2. *Talk them down.* For many clients, making a life-changing decision is like being a first-time bungee jumper. They want to jump, but they really, really don't want to jump. To get them to take that first step into thin air, the positives must outweigh the negatives. Superstars stack up as many positive reasons as possible for their clients to take that leap of faith.

Top Producer Tip: If the client has a negative reason for selling—death, divorce, or financial problems—reframe the negative into a positive. For example: "John, I know that when you sell the home, you aren't going to benefit financially, but on the plus side, your credit will be saved, you will be able to move on with your life, and a huge burden will be lifted from your shoulders."

3. *Employ the cascade effect.* What causes an avalanche to happen? Many scientists ascribe it to something called the cascade effect, where one small push or tipping point causes an unstoppable chain reaction. The same is true in decision making. Top producers use this theory as a sales tool by finding their clients' tipping point, their fulcrum of decision making. They then apply leverage to this point until the client is buried in an irresistible avalanche of reasons to move forward.

Top Producer Tip: Whenever it is to your advantage, use your own personal sales statistics to build creditability and motivation: "From our earlier discussion, it sounds like getting moved before summer is over is your biggest concern. During the last year, my average days on market has been 43 days compared to 69 days for the overall market, which means that on average I sell homes 26 days faster than my competitors. How does that sound to you?"

4. *Gift bag it.* Trying to rip open a gift-wrapped present can be a challenge, which is why many people today use a gift bag. From a selling standpoint, gift bagging means that you make it easy for people to say yes. For example: "Now, if you decide to move forward, I have some space available to do a special feature on your property in the real estate guide next month. How does that sound?"

One question that I get asked at every seminar that I conduct is, "Do I do all of these six steps in one sitting?" It's a great question and the subject of a great debate in the real estate industry.

Top producers use a six-step presentation plan that can be easily remembered by using the ACTION acronym:

A: Ask questions.
C: Clarify answers.
T: Tap into the audience.
I: Introduce solutions.
O: Offer options.
N: Nurture decisions.

One-Stage vs. Two-Stage Appointments

It's an age-old dilemma facing real estate professionals: Do we ask for a kiss on the first date or the second? In other words, do we go for the listing on the same day we meet with the clients, or do we spend more time getting to know the sellers and making them feel more comfortable, and then ask for a commitment?

The good news is that there is no wrong answer. Many multimillion-dollar-producing superstars use a two-stage approach, and an equal or greater number use a one-stage approach (and a few crazies like me alternate between the two styles). Let's take a look at both approaches (see Figure 6-4).

The underlying issue in this quandary is confidence. Do you feel confident enough to ask for the listing after perhaps an hour of talking with the seller, or do you need more time?

During a one-stage listing appointment, all six steps of the presentation are completed during one meeting. The advantage to this approach is that it saves time, both yours and the client's. With a motivated seller, this is definitely the way to go. Why? Because when a seller gives you the signal or says out loud, "We want to list our house," smart agents shut up and list the house. The worst thing you can ever do is talk yourself right back out of a listing, a common occurrence among weak agents.

One of my speaking friends became famous for his one-minute listing presentation in which he simply asked the sellers: "Do you like me? Do you want to list your house with me?" He went big. The downside to this "go

FIGURE 6-4.

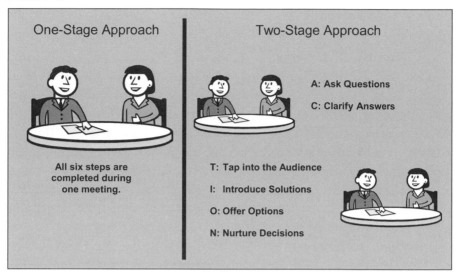

big" style is that the client might not like you, or at least might not like you yet. This is exactly why many agents prefer a two-stage approach.

The two-stage approach to taking a listing means that you complete your listing presentation over two meetings. The first meeting involves a survey of the home, where you build rapport and trust with the seller by asking questions and clarifying answers, and the formal presentation is conducted at the second meeting. The advantage of a two-stage approach is that it allows more time for a seller to warm up to you and your sales style, as well as gives you more time to complete detailed research. One downside, and there are many, is that, as when digging in wet sand, all of the rapport and trust that you worked so hard to build might disappear overnight.

So what's the right answer—one stage or two? Instead of setting a hard-and-fast rule as to which approach you will use with every seller, why not make the decision at the seller's home? How will you know when to pivot from one approach to the other? Take a look at this decision table:

ONE-STAGE APPROACH	TWO-STAGE APPROACH
Seller's motivation high	Seller's motivation low
Competing for listing	No competition

Rapport and trust strong	Confidence low
All decision makers present	Missing a decision maker
Comparable properties accurate	Additional research needed

The first rule of thumb is to always be ready to take the listing. That means that you bring along all of your heavy artillery: listing forms, disclosure statements, and MLS data input sheets. The reasons for attempting a one-stage approach are straightforward: You think you have an excellent shot at taking the listing, all the decision makers are present, the seller's motivation is high, your data are correct, and you have strong rapport and trust with the seller. Or you are being blitzed by a 300-pound center for the competition who will break every bone in your real estate body unless you go for a touchdown.

The reason for considering a two-stage approach might include a little more pragmatic thinking. For instance, perhaps one of the sellers seems unmotivated (not uncommon when you are dealing with a couple) or you are missing a decision maker or there are flaws in your data (you thought it was a one bath and it's a two) or you need to do additional research before talking about pricing or marketing strategy. Any of these items can lead to a low confidence level and be a red flag to schedule a second meeting.

But an agent's lack of confidence may be a warning sign of something far more serious: his inability to deal effectively with objections, questions, and concerns, key ingredients in every seller's decision-making process. To inspire a client's ultimate faith and lead her to entrust her most valuable asset—her home—to you, let's see how top producers deal with these in Chapter 7, "Questions, Concerns, and Objections."

LEARNING OPPORTUNITY

One-stage approach. Agents who practice a one-stage appointment technique complete all six presentation steps during one meeting with a seller.

Two-stage approach. Agents using this approach break up their presentation over two client meetings, giving them more time to do research and find ways to help motivate a seller to list his home.

Questions, Concerns, and Objections

"I'd like a Realtor to explain why I should pay a percentage to sell a house. Do you pay your accountant a percentage of your annual income to do your taxes? Do you pay the guy who washes your car a percentage of the value of your car to wash it? With the Internet (zillow, craigslist, information, and so on), you're being disintermediated right before your eyes. Either you change or you go away. First step: Charge a fee for your services, hourly if you like. But the days of percentages are over."

How would you respond to this challenge? As a contributor to several real estate blogs and forums, I was asked to respond to a very similar post in the largest real estate industry blog (www.realblogging.com). Fortunately, because many of my own clients have voiced similar concerns over the years, I had some experience in handling the objection. My response was the following:

In response to the previous comment, I would say that as a Realtor myself, and someone who charges a percentage for my services, the difference in how I'm paid for my work and the way an accountant or a doctor is paid is that I am paid a "success fee" instead of an hourly fee, meaning that I get paid only if I am successful at doing my job.

Imagine paying your doctor only if he cured you or paying your accountant only if he was able to get you a tax refund. Good luck. Yet, I agree every day to be paid only if the seller receives exactly what he or she wants. Frankly, sometimes I would much prefer to be paid for every hour of my time, because in some cases, even though I have invested thousands of dollars' worth of my time in a project, I never do get paid.

If the majority of clients, like you, prefer an hourly rate, market forces will bring these services to you, and in many markets many of my friends are using an hourly model already. In other markets, some agents are offering clients the option of either a success fee or an hourly fee. The assumption that this will reduce a client's overall costs may or may not be true. What you can count on is that Realtors are powerless in the face of consumer demand. If consumers demand hourly services, they will get them. But be careful what you wish for; the next time you visit a Realtor, he may send you a bill for $400 for taking up an hour of his valuable time.

Do you think I changed his mind? Probably not, but perhaps I got him thinking about his position. Right, wrong, or in between, everyone has a position on just about everything. Your position is your take on the world, how you see things through your life lens.

Unfortunately our perceptions, and therefore our positions, can be dead wrong. As one of my property managers, a former police officer, likes to say, "There is what he said, there is what she said, and then there's the truth." For example, a buyer may not be able to accept the idea that home prices in one area of the country are different from those in another area, or a seller may not be able to accept falling home prices. These false perceptions can give a client some trepidation or outright fear about moving forward with a decision that's contrary to his original position.

There is an appropriate acronym for this type of apprehension: FEAR, or false evidence appearing real. In real estate, our clients come to every meeting with a set of perceptions, their evidence, on everything from commission rates to pricing strategies. Unfortunately, when a client can't or won't accept a new position or new evidence, she often becomes full of this FEAR by allowing old assumptions to override her common sense.

Throughout history, there have been numerous examples of people relying on FEAR to make bad business decisions. One of the biggest examples of this is the story of William Orton and Alexander Graham Bell.

In 1876, Bell had won the race to the patent office (by mere hours, narrowly beating out Elisha Gray) to become the first person to hold a patent on a crazy device called a telephone. But shortly thereafter, when Bell and his new bride left on their long-awaited honeymoon, Gardiner Hubbard, Bell's father-in-law, and another man, George Sanders, the biggest investor in the enterprise, decided to unload the patents for some quick cash. They pitched the patents to communication giant Western Union. The asking price? $100,000!

Western Union's president, William Orton, responded to the proposal by saying, "This 'telephone' has too many shortcomings to be seriously considered as a means of communication. The device is inherently of no value to us." He rejected the offer. His FEAR of something new, a device that would go on to replace the telegraph, clouded his position and his decision.

So how can we overcome this FEAR and gently sway our clients' perceptions on areas where they may have objections, concerns, or questions? The first step is helping them to say no.

LEARNING OPPORTUNITY

Positions. Our clients' positions are formed from their unique worldview. To change their positions, we must change their perceptions.

FEAR. Many times our clients' decision-making process becomes clouded by allowing FEAR to overrule common sense:

F: False
E: Evidence
A: Appearing
R: Real

Teaching Clients to Say No

My partner and mentor in the real estate brokerage business, Dick Calafato, is a legendary sales professional. Working first as a dynamic salesperson, he listed 223 homes and closed over $14 million in sales during his first two years in the business. Then in 1972 he founded All State Real Estate (www .allstaterealestate.com) and grew the organization to 165 offices and over 3,200 sales associates in seven western states.

One of Dick's most famous approaches to working with client questions, concerns, and objections is encouraging clients to say *no*. Sounds strange, right? But Dick spells *no* a little differently from the rest of us; he spells it K-N-O-W (Figure 7-1). So when the rest of us hear an objection or a flat-out no, what he hears is a client saying, "I don't know enough information to say yes." For example, "I don't *know* why I should list with you"; or, "I don't *know* why I should pay you X percent of the purchase price"; or, "I don't *know* why I should give you a three-month listing."

For Dick, hearing the word *no* means that he needs to stop, drop what he is saying, and listen to his clients. He needs to assess what information his clients are basing their decisions on and attempt to influence their position by providing them with additional points of reference. His reasoning is that without a dialogue, a give-and-take, a push and push back, clients often won't move forward with a decision. Do they always come around and agree with him? Obviously not, but by moving toward objections instead of away from them, he has a much better opportunity to convert these clients into closings.

Let's look at five ways superstars, like Dick, encourage objections:

Five Ways to Encourage Objections, Questions, and Concerns

1. "Listen, as we talk today, I want you to feel completely comfortable asking me any questions or voicing any concerns that you may have."

FIGURE 7-1. IS IT A NO OR A KNOW?

2. "Is there anything holding you back from moving forward, any questions or concerns that you may have?"

3. "Based on what we've covered so far, do you have questions I can answer for you?"

4. "Before I begin today, do you have any specific questions or concerns that you would like me to address?"

5. "Have you had any past issues buying or selling real estate that concern you today?"

Superstars don't sell clients on decisions. They don't use fast-talking, slick techniques to manipulate clients into making decisions. Instead, they provide buyers and sellers with a different perspective on each issue, a new way of looking at the world. In some cases, this new information will be enough to motivate a client to take action; in other cases it will be like talking to a pet rock—the client won't budge even when it is in his best interest.

By focusing on how we react and deal with an objection, not on the endgame or outcome, we can free ourselves to focus at all times on the one thing we can always control—our own actions. So what should our first action be when we hear an objection? For many top producers, their first step is to ignore it.

Learning Challenge: Seek out objections by asking for a client's input frequently as a way to move the decision-making process forward. Also assess what information your clients are basing their decisions on and attempt to influence their position by providing them with additional points of reference.

Early Minor Objections

We are taught from birth not to trust salespeople. It's true. As consumers, we often express objections not as a real barrier to working with a salesperson but as a defense against moving too quickly or being pushed into a decision unnecessarily. Why? Most Americans have the ingrained notion that salespeople are out to get them, to steal their money, take their babies, and run off with their spouses (okay, maybe it's not quite that bad). But consider how you react to meeting a new salesperson. Are you filled with feelings of warmth, trust, friendship, and good cheer? Or instead are you immediately consumed by nervousness, distrust, dislike, or even outright hostility?

The bottom line is that, as salespeople, we don't have a lot of built-in goodwill. Instead, we have to earn our clients' trust over time. This is exactly the reason that in the beginning of a new relationship you may run headlong into a thorny hedge of early minor objections.

An early minor objection is simply an objection that you hear over the phone or very early in a client meeting. This first line of defense for a client is meant to push you back, to keep you, the salesperson, at bay until the client decides she is ready to let you into her personal decision-making space.

For example, take a look at this short list of common for-sale-by-owner objections.

"I won't pay a fee."
"If I list, I'm going to list with a friend."
"We've sold many homes by ourselves."

Ring any bells? Be honest; I bet you have been stopped cold by at least one of these statements during your career. You're not alone. These knee-jerk objections stop 95 percent of agents from pursuing a listing any further. Superstars, on the other hand, realize that these early minor objections are nothing more than a conditioned response, like a stuffed animal at a toy store that says, "Hug Me" . . . "Love Me" . . . "Squeeze Me" when a button is pushed. But most agents have a terrible habit: They treat all objections equally, as if each objection, question, or concern is an appointment-killing missile that will explode on impact as soon as it is launched from the client's mouth. This is simply not true. In fact, most objections are just a client's automatic reaction, or conditioned response, and for a top producer, they can amount to nothing more than a minor bump on the road to taking a listing.

So how do you deal with these potentially lethal conversation stoppers? The best way to deal with early minor objections is not to deal with them. Yes, I know; it goes against the grain for most of us not to jump in, roll up our sleeves, and attempt to engage in a verbal dual of wits with a seller, but this approach is very likely doomed to failure. Why? Because the better your offense, the more entrenched and committed the client's defense will become. As when two evenly matched tennis players meet, the verbal volley will continue indefinitely, or at least until the seller walks off the court. To avoid this no-win scenario, strong agents take a unique three-step approach to dealing with early minor objections. Let's take a look:

The Three-Step Method: Early Minor Objections

1. *Listen and empathize: "I understand."* Wise agents give their clients no platform for continuing to object. They are neither offensive nor defensive in their posture. Instead, they listen and empathize with the client's point of view. To achieve this state of swami-like serenity, superstars use the magic words *I understand.* This easy technique can reduce a client's need to shovel himself into a defensive bunker and gives an agent a simple way to neither agree nor disagree with the client's statement.

2. *Sidestep: "At this point . . ."* Don't accept the objection. Like an unexpected gift from your ex-husband, this package can be marked "return to sender." Why? In this case, it's way too early in your new relationship to begin dealing with objections. Wise agents smoothly move past the issue by simply saying, "I understand, but at this point . . ."

3. *Close: "Is today good . . . ?"* Once you have moved past the issue, it's time to move on and either set the appointment over the phone or move into the next topic of conversation at the seller's home. Agents who stand their ground in a vain attempt to win each debate often find themselves left debating which fast food management course looks the most promising.

Now let's put this three-step method to work and take a look at how strong agents deal with early minor objections:

"I won't pay a fee!": "I understand how you feel, but at this point all I would like to do is take a look at your home to see if it would fit any of my buyers' needs. I don't charge anything for stopping by and looking at the home. Could I come by today, or would tomorrow be better?"

"If I list, I'm going to list with a friend": "I understand, and I can certainly respect your loyalty to your friend, but at this point you are trying to sell on your own, right? The information that I have will help you do that, sell on your own without the help of a professional. May I show you my free For Sale by Owner kit?"

"We've sold many homes by ourselves": "I understand that you're trying to sell on your own, and I respect your decision. At this point, what I would like to do is bring you some information that will help you sell on your own, without the help of a professional. Is today good, or would later in the week be better?"

None of these responses deals directly with the stated objection; instead, in a sense, they all ignore the objection by sidestepping it. Interestingly, these seemingly insurmountable objections often don't resurface. They just fade away. How is that possible? Once an agent has successfully built trust and rapport with the client, and then provided an exciting presentation of her services, many of these questions, concerns, and objections disappear.

A terrific quote from one of my mentors years ago is this: "A great presentation closes itself." Think about a time when you experienced a great presentation. What happened next? Did you immediately begin formulating objections, reasons why you shouldn't move forward? Or instead did you become the advocate and begin looking for ways to move ahead?

Yes, great presentations close themselves.

But what if the objection, like bad breath, just won't go away? What if it comes back at the worst possible time, like right when you are concluding your home tour and are warming up for your big dog-and-pony show? Now it's time to move up to dealing with serious or restated objections.

LEARNING OPPORTUNITY

Early minor objections. These are objections that you hear over the phone or very early in a client meeting. In many cases, these objections are nothing more than a filtering device, a smokescreen to prevent agents from becoming too aggressive.

Three-Step Method: Early Minor Objections

1. *Listen and empathize:* "*I understand.*" Let the client know that you care.

2. *Sidestep:* "*At this point . . .*" Smoothly move past the objection.

3. *Close:* "*Is today good . . . ?*" Set the appointment or go on to the next topic.

Serious or Restated Objections

Early in my career, I decided that sellers must have a secret club, an invitation-only back-alley joint where they swap stories on how to avoid working with real estate agents. I came to this conclusion because at almost every interview I went on I heard the same nearly verbatim objections. Inevitably sellers would say something like, "Thanks, Jim, but . . ."

"We're going to wait until spring."

"We have a family member in the business."

"We don't want to pay X percent."

"We had a bad experience with another agent."

Eventually I accepted the idea that I would have to learn how to handle these common seller concerns effectively, because even with a terrific presentation, my business would be doomed to a slow stall and perhaps even a horrific nosedive unless I could learn to answer sellers' objections smoothly. Fortunately, another real estate veteran came to my rescue by explaining his secret to handling every objection using a system that he called the TREAT approach.

You might think of this technique in terms of a surgical procedure. If you have ever had an operation, you know that the highly trained doctors and nurses go through a preoperative routine before beginning any new surgery. Step by step, they prepare the room, the patient, and the tools needed for surgery. They know that if they follow a strict routine they will be less likely to make a mistake that could cost a patient his life. Like these medical professionals, real estate professionals are wise to take a similar approach by using the TREAT approach when dealing with serious or restated objections. Let's take a look at this technique by breaking down the steps:

T: Track

R: Restate

E: Empathize

A: Answer

T: Trial close

Track

The first step in dealing with a major objection is to move toward the objection by getting on the same track as the seller. One of my own agents, Dave Moore, uses an unusual technique to accomplish this goal. When a seller begins to express an objection, he stops talking, listens to the concern, nods his head, and uses a long pause before addressing the issue. Sometimes he may even add a "Hmmmmm . . ." to his pause, for dramatic effect.

Sound a little nutty? Not really. A surprising number of sellers will answer their own objections if they are given ample time and space to do so. This may sound incongruous; after all, why would a seller bring up an objection if he already knows the answer? The answer is that in many cases he feels compelled to do so; for example, take a look at this exchange:

> **Seller (Husband):** *John, we like your presentation, but my cousin is in the real estate business.*
>
> **Agent:** *<Nods his head.> Hmmmmmmmm . . . <pause>.*
>
> **Seller (Wife):** *I wouldn't list our house with your cousin if he were the last man on the planet. The guy is an idiot.*

In this example, the husband felt a moral obligation to at least mention his cousin. But both he and his wife (and I bet his cousin as well) knew that they would never list the house with the guy. The same is true for many sellers; they feel that they must at least ask for something or throw out an objection before moving forward with a big decision. Wise agents don't fall for these red herrings. They give the seller time to answer her own objection or move past it entirely.

But does this technique work with all objections? Of course not, which is why it's so important to learn all the steps in the TREAT approach. Let's look at the next step in this technique.

Restate

Strong communicators are often a little redundant; in other words, they tend to repeat what's just been said before continuing with a conversation. Did you get that? Strong communicators tend to repeat things before continuing with a conversation. Restating an objection may sound like a waste of time to some agents; after all, why would you repeat what a seller has just said? But there are actually a couple of good reasons. First, clarifying a seller's concern before diving in and formulating an answer is a good communication skill because often we may have misunderstood the client. For example, an agent asks a seller, "Did you just say you don't want to market the property until you get more ice cream?" And the seller replies, "No, no, no; I said that we don't want to market the home until we are able to get the home cleaned." Ah, yes, that makes more sense.

But often the communication gaff isn't that you are mishearing the seller but that the seller just isn't making sense. Like a seller who says, "I need to sell quickly, but I need to wait until after Christmas." What? What kind of crazy statement is that? By repeating back to a seller her own wacky comments, it gives her a chance to correct herself: "No, no; I meant to say that we would like to sell soon after Christmas." Ah, yes, obviously so that she can take advantage of that post-Christmas real estate rush.

Another important reason to restate a client's comment is to isolate the objection. Why isolate an objection? Have you ever noticed that when you answer one objection successfully three more can pop up in its place like weeds? Like a merciless track coach, the seller keeps giving you one hurdle after another after another, until finally you end up a bloody mess.

What's the solution? Isolate each objection by making absolutely sure that this is the one and only reason the client is hesitant to move forward. How? Take a look at how one superstar makes this happen in the real world:

Isolating the Objection Script

Mr. and Mrs. Seller, just so I understand you correctly, the only reason you are not comfortable moving forward today is <state objection>. If we set that aside for a moment, is there anything else that's holding you back?

Once the seller has committed himself to one objection (or even several), the agent can move on to the next step in the TREAT approach: empathizing with the client.

Empathize

What's the difference between empathy and sympathy? One of my real estate mentors asked me this early one winter morning before heading out to one of his many appointments. After waiting a full tenth of a second for me to answer, he went on to give me his oddball version of a definition:

> "Jim, I'll tell you the difference. Suppose you were standing on a cruise ship one evening, say out on the poop deck, and you saw a young woman standing near the rail crying. Being the gentleman that you are, you might approach her to ask what was wrong. Now suppose she told you her whole sad life story, and then, just as she was wrapping up, she suddenly jumped overboard. A sympathetic person might get so caught up in the tragedy that he would leap in after her, but an empathetic person would just lean over the railing and wave good-bye!"

It's an interesting analogy—a little kooky, but that's a top producer for you! I think what he was trying to say is that having sympathy for someone means that you have such deep compassion for the other person that you may even begin to share that person's feelings. During my wife's last pregnancy, for instance, I had sympathy pains for her during labor and delivery. In a personal or family setting, this is perfectly acceptable (unless the doctor attempts a C-section). Empathy, though, means that we understand what the other person is experiencing without experiencing it ourselves. We have some distance. This is an important distinction, especially when we are working with a client in a professional relationship.

Great agents are very empathetic. They understand what their clients are going through and attempt to help their clients' real estate transactions go as smoothly as possible. So when she is faced with an objection, a wise agent will often empathize with a seller's dilemma by saying the magic words *I understand.* For example:

> I understand that X percent of the purchase price is a big investment.
>
> I understand that you are loyal to your previous agent.
>
> I understand that you would prefer to wait until spring to get started.

Now, just because you understand the objection doesn't mean that you agree with it; instead, it simply means that you can understand the seller's viewpoint. You can empathize with her situation.

Many top producers find it wise to dig deeper with their clients by explor-

ing other aspects of their clients' thought processes. Check out how they dig
for details:

Digging for Details

> *Encouraging:* "Please tell me more. . . ."
> *Clarifying:* "Explain what you mean by that. . . ."
> *Normalizing:* "I've had other clients who . . . "
> *Soliciting:* "I would like your ideas on that. . . ."
> *Validating:* "I appreciate your willingness. . . ."

Now that you have heard the client's concerns, it's time to answer his
objection. So roll up your sleeves and put your hard hat on; it's time to go to
work.

Answer

Here's the thing. There are about 10 objections that you will hear over and
over again in your career. Sure, you can try to duck and cover, or you can
try to overpower your clients with your dazzling smile, but we both know
that neither of these approaches will work in the real world. Answering an
objection is where the rubber hits the road. Either you have an answer or you
don't. You can't fake your way through it, leapfrog over it, sidestep around it,
or even flat out ignore it. A restated or serious objection is the pink elephant
sitting on the couch next to you; she's not going anywhere, and she's getting
hungry.

So how do you formulate answers for this relatively short list of common
seller concerns? The answer is to become the client and ask yourself: If I
were a real estate seller, what would I say yes to? I call this building a yes-
able answer, something that you would agree to if you were sitting on the
other side of the kitchen table.

Real estate agents are solution driven. They want answers handed to
them gift wrapped, batteries included, so that they can run out and use the
solution instantly. Unfortunately, this can lead some agents to give an answer
to an objection that they would never in a million years buy into if they were
the client. For instance, let me give you an example of an answer that I hear
speakers use all the time that audiences always seem to lap up like cats with
a saucer of milk.

Objection: *I think your commission is too high.*

Speaker's Stage Answer: *Well, I understand what you're saying; the commission is a big investment. But one thing you should understand is that the commission actually covers many services. In fact, let me show you what that fee actually includes <show off a list of services>. Now, if we were to reduce the fee, which of these services would you like me to eliminate?*

Some agents may feel that this is a terrific, yes-able answer, something that would make sense to them if they were the seller. They buy it so that they can sell it. For me, it just doesn't work. In my market, I can just imagine a seller gleefully grabbing that list from my hands, marking off 10 items, and then handing it back to me with a smug smile and a reply of, "Great. Now what will you charge me?"

That being said, I answer that objection before the end of this section, and I also provide you with field-tested answers to 10 additional common seller objections before the end of the chapter. These answers should give you, at the very least, a starting point to begin crafting your own inventory of answers to tough seller questions. Your own unique answers should become an essential part of your selling vernacular, because once you have answered the client's concern, it will be time to take the last step in the TREAT approach—the trial close.

Trial Close

Probably very few of us have ever set foot in a courtroom other than to pay a parking ticket or to bail out our spouse (again!). But I'm sure most of us have watched trials on television. For me, the most interesting part of a court proceeding is the closing arguments, which in many ways are really just a high-stakes game of presenting and answering objections. The prosecution attempts to tear down the defense arguments by appealing to the jury's common sense. The defense, on the other hand, works feverishly to provide alternative explanations, refute the evidence, discredit the expert testimony, and plant seeds of doubt in the jury's mind.

During this process, the best attorneys are the ones who can read the jury. Are the jurors nodding their heads, smiling, engaged, and receptive, or instead are they shaking their heads, arms folded, fists clenched, not at all drawn into the attorney's version of the facts? It's an important skill for an attorney to develop.

Who will win? Typically the side that has done the best job of creating answers that a jury can buy into. Likewise, as real estate agents, we, too, need to develop the ability to read our clients. But unlike attorneys facing a jury, we have a distinct advantage: We can ask our clients direct questions to learn their opinions about our suggested solutions. This process is known as asking trial closing questions.

A trial close is simply a way to test the waters to determine whether a client is buying your explanation, solution, or argument. Typically a trial closing question will come directly after an agent has delivered a potential solution or an answer to an objection. Let's take a look at some ways in which agents might use a trial close to find out if their clients are actually buying what the agents are selling:

Does that sound reasonable?

Does that make sense?

How does that sound to you?

Does that sound fair?

What do you think?

What are your thoughts?

Now, you might imagine that not all of your clients will agree with your newfangled solution. You're right; some might even say, "That's the dumbest idea I've ever heard," or, "I'm still not convinced that moving forward is my best option." What then? Good news; the reason we call this a trial close is that it is first and foremost a test, a trial run of your argument. If it doesn't work out, no problem; you just shift gears and try another answer that may sound more reasonable to the client.

Can you imagine an attorney being able to say to a jury, "Hey, listen, what do you think of this defense? Don't like it? No worries; I've got three more I want to run by you." Now let's see how this might work in a real-world situation by tackling the number one objection in the marketplace—the commission objection.

Handling the Commission Objection

Client: *Listen, we just can't see paying X percent of the price to work with you when other agents charge less.*

Agent: *Hey, listen, I understand how you feel, and to be honest with you, a lot of my clients have felt exactly the same way. But what most of my clients have found is that the most important issue for them hasn't been that they might be able to save 1 percent or even 2 percent with a discount broker; it's been how much they might have to sacrifice to make that happen. You see, the number one service my clients are looking for when they hire me to represent them is my skill as a negotiator. If I can help them make an extra 5, 10, or even 20 percent on the proceeds of their sale, they come out winners. How does that sound?*

And/or

Agent: *I understand that you feel the commission is a big investment. Many of my clients have felt exactly the same way. But let me tell you what a few of them have found after they listed with a discount broker. Generally, when one of these brokers lists your house, he is providing a limited services agreement. One way discount brokers often save money is by offering cooperating brokers less money to sell your home. So imagine you're a real estate agent and you have 10 homes to show; nine of them are offering a full fee, and one is offering a discounted fee. Which home would you show last? <Answer> With fewer buyers looking at their home, sellers often end up taking less money for their home, or even not selling at all. Are you comfortable with your home being the last home shown?*

You might notice that at the end of this objection, we tested the seller's reaction to our argument by using a trial close. In addition, we used another ancient (in the sales world, ancient means 10 years old or older) technique called the feel, felt, found method. The feel, felt, found method can be used with any objection to instantly put a seller at ease because it normalizes a seller's objection by letting her know that other people have shared her concern, as in, "I understand how you *feel*; others have *felt* the same way, but what they *found* was . . ."

Now that we have mastered the TREAT approach, let's take a look at how top producers handle 10 other common seller objections.

LEARNING OPPORTUNITY

To deal with serious or restated objections, many agents use the TREAT approach.

T: Track. Get on the same page as the client by listening to his concerns.

R: Restate. Clarify the client's concern by restating the objection back to him.

E: Empathize. Let the client know that you understand his position.

A: Answer. Formulate a yes-able answer to the objection.

T: Trial close. Test the client's acceptance of your solution.

Answering 10 Common Seller Objections

One of the benefits of becoming part of a profession that has been around since the dawn of carbon copies is that we get to learn from other, more experienced agents what works and what doesn't in the real world of real estate. Because these veteran agents have done the heavy lifting, all we have to do is follow their lead. So let's take a look at how superstars respond to 10 common seller objections, the same ones we all hear day in, day out.

While you're reviewing these answers, take a minute to decide if they are a good fit for your selling approach or how you might modify them to fit your own personality and delivery style.

1. *I have a friend/relative in the business.*

> I can understand that, and I respect your relationship with your relative/friend. Let me ask you, has your relative/friend called you in the last few days about selling your home? <No> Do you think it's possible that he doesn't want to jeopardize your personal relationship by entering into a business relationship? <Pause> After all, it would be tough to ask him to pull the sign out of the lawn, wouldn't it?

> Or

> I can respect your personal relationship with your friend/relative. Setting that aside for just a moment, let me ask you: If it were simply a question of which person offered the most services for the same cost and, more important, who could net you the highest price possible, would you allow me to share what my company can offer you?

2. *I don't want to pay a fee.*

> I can understand how you feel. Many of the For Sale by Owners I talk to about selling have felt exactly the same way, but what many have found is that buyers often ask the seller to reduce the price by the amount of the real estate fee anyway, so the seller often ends up paying the fee whether she uses an agent or not. Let me ask you, though, if I can show you how my marketing plan could actually net you more dollars than you could get on your own, would it be possible to show you how I work?

> Or

> I understand, but what you're really after is the highest amount of net dollars to you after closing, right? <Yes> If I could show you how my marketing plan can expose your home to more buyers, so that you could secure a higher price and net the same amount of money, or actually make a little more, would you allow me to show you how I work?

3. *I'm going to try it on my own for a while and then list.*

> I can understand how you feel. If you sell the home on your own and save the commission, you will be that much further ahead, right? Many of my clients have felt the same way, but what's interesting is that they lost about 40 percent of the market when they attempted to sell by owner. The reason is that statistically 4 out of 10 buyers are out-of-area buyers, meaning that they're coming from another city or state, and those buyers work almost exclusively with real estate agents. How do you feel about that?

> Or

> I can understand your decision. In fact, many of my clients have started out as For Sale by Owners. May I ask how long you plan to market the home yourself before you hire an agent? <Answer> Let me ask you this: If I could demonstrate how I can handle all of the details, decrease your marketing time, and still net you as much as or more than you can get selling by owner, would you consider moving up your timetable?

4. *I had a bad experience with another agent.*

> I'm sorry to hear that. I can understand that you would be hesitant to talk with another agent. Can you tell me what went wrong? <Answer> If I can provide you with some letters of reference from some of my clients who were completely satisfied with my professionalism, would you give me a chance to show you how I work?

> Or

> I understand. One thing that I give all my sellers is a written guarantee of service. If anyone is unhappy with me for any reason, he can fire me and hire another agent. Does that sound fair?*

5. *I can't afford to sell if I have to pay a fee.*

> I can understand your position. In fact, I have had several clients in exactly the same situation. Let me ask you this: If I could secure a higher price for your home than you can on your own, enough to justify my fee, wouldn't it make sense for you to use my services? May I show you how I believe I can make that happen?

> Or

> I understand what you're going through; one of the ways I have helped other sellers in similar situations is to work with their lenders on a short sale agreement, where the lender agrees to take a discount on its fees or loan to facilitate a sale. What's really important is that the home gets sold, you get what you need out of it, and you move on with your life, isn't that right?

6. *We're going to wait until . . .*

> I can understand how you feel. Let me ask you, what was your ideal target date for moving? <Answer> In our area, the average number of days it takes to sell a home is <#>. In

---

*Check with your broker about using a guarantee of service.

addition to that, there is an escrow period of usually <#
days>. So that means, from today's date, you would be looking at <Date> before you would actually be moved. Are you
comfortable with that?

Or (*We're waiting until spring/summer.*)

It's true that spring/summer is one of our peak selling seasons,
so I can understand how you would feel that way. In fact,
many of my sellers have felt the same way you do, but what a
lot of them have found is that because most sellers, like you,
wait until spring/summer to list their home, there are a lot
more homes on the market during those times. More competition for buyers can mean that sellers become more likely to
accept lower prices.

So would you rather wait until spring/summer and com-
pete with everyone, or would you rather start now and get top
dollar for your home?

7. *We're going to list with . . .*

I understand. Let me ask you, is there a specific service that
that company is offering that is helping you to make your decision? <Answer> If it were simply a question of who could
offer you the most services, would you go with the person who
could offer you the most value per dollar spent? <Answer>
May I just take a couple of minutes to show you an apples-to-
apples comparison of our services?

Or

I understand your decision; <Agent name> is a good agent.
Let me ask you this, though: I know that many of my clients
comparison shop before they choose an agent; have you considered allowing someone to give you a second opinion on the
marketing of your home? I know that for many of my clients
selling their home is the largest financial decision of their
lives.

8. *We've decided not to sell.*

I understand. May I ask what your original reason for selling was? <Answer> Has that changed? Let me ask you this: If you were able to receive what you were asking for the home within a reasonable time frame with the least amount of inconvenience possible, would you reconsider your decision?

Or

I understand. Is the reason you are choosing not to sell some frustration you may have had with your previous agent? <Yes> Can you tell me what went wrong? <Answer> What I provide my clients is a 10-point guarantee of service that outlines everything I'll do to market your home if you decide to hire my firm. Does that sound reasonable?*

9. *We have some buyers interested.*

I understand. One way we help sellers like yourself to shake out the real buyers from the tire kickers is by listing the property with a <#>-day exclusion. Here's how it works. Once we have listed the property with your permission, we call the buyers on your behalf and alert them that the property has been listed, but that they have been given an exclusive for <#> days. This means that they have <#> days to make an offer and still buy the property at the prelisting price. Using this method, you can benefit from all your hard work and still get started using our marketing services. Does this sound reasonable to you?

Or

I understand how you feel. You would sure hate to pay a real estate fee if one of those buyers came through, wouldn't you? How long are you prepared to wait for the buyers to make a decision? <Answer> One way I could get started working on your property is by postdating the listing agreement until that date. You could also tell your buyers that if they don't make a

*Check with your broker about using a service pledge.

decision by that time, the home will be on the open market—it might inspire them to make a decision or shake them out if they are just tire kickers. Does that sound like a solution?

10. *I need to talk with . . .*

I understand how you feel. Selling your home is a big decision. Listen, some of my clients are a little hesitant about moving forward because they want to make sure they understand all the facts. Are there any questions or concerns that you have about listing the home that you would like to discuss with me while I'm still here? <Answer> Would you feel comfortable completing the paperwork subject to <Name's> approval within a couple of days?

Or

I understand. Is there a specific concern about listing the property that you need to discuss with <Name> before making a decision? <Answer> How would you feel about completing the paperwork today but then keeping the documents yourself to review with <Name>? If it meets with his or her approval, you can just give me a call to come by and pick up the listing and we can get started.

Now let me guess: You can think of 10 more objections that we could have added to this list, right? Good! Superstars look forward to these challenges; they embrace their sellers' questions, concerns, and objections in the same way a doctor looks forward to a unique patient whom she can help, or an attorney relishes a juicy case.

For a top producer, the ultimate goal is to help each of these clients achieve his real estate goals by gaining his acceptance, something that we will explore in depth in Chapter 8, "Making the Big Decision."

Learning Challenge: Study the various approaches for handling objections and adapt them to your own selling style and personality to create yes-able answers.

Making the Big Decision

The listing agent tracked me down at a business dinner to give me the good news. The decision had been made. I could buy the RV park for $2 million with a down payment of $400,000, and the seller would even agree to take back a note for the balance. The listing agent was giddy with excitement. The seller had just called and given a verbal approval. This would be her largest sale ever!

But sitting at the restaurant with my family and friends, I had a sixth sense. My instincts were telling me that the deal wasn't done. "Can we get it signed tonight?" I asked. To her credit, the listing agent, who had bent over backward to make the deal come together, told me that she would attempt to get the seller's signature that night.

Two hours later, the call came in: "She won't sign it." In a despondent voice, the agent went on to explain that the owner was having second thoughts about accepting such a low down payment. In fact, she had now decided that she needed a $700,000 down payment.

Decisions are often thought of as a final point, the apex of a mountain of smaller choices that, once committed to, are immediately cast and fired into a mold that becomes a person's ultimate verdict. But client decisions aren't immovable mountains; instead, they are more like wide, flowing rivers, stopping and starting, swirling and bending in response to a client's ever-changing mental landscape. At one point the waters can be glassy and clear, with a decision seemingly set in stone; later, even within the same hour, the waters can turn to a churning white froth of dangerous rapids, where clients waffle, turn, and even flip their decisions completely over.

What happens in those few minutes? What changes a seller's mind?

Two major types of issues can come back to haunt even the best real estate agents. I call these two types above-the-water issues and below-the-water issues. Above-the-water issues are outside factors that can suddenly crop up to change a seller's mind about moving forward. Like an iceberg, these floating time bombs arrive at just the wrong moment. Within a real estate presentation, this might be the influence of a client's family, friends, or coworkers. Below-the-water issues are hidden influences that only the sellers are aware of. These might include undisclosed debts or financial obligations, timing problems, spousal disagreements, or even just a bad case of seller's remorse. For example, the RV park owner's decision reversal was the result of a below-the-water influence. She still owed a significant amount of money on the property, something that she hadn't disclosed to her own agent when the property was listed.

To deal with both above- and below-the-water issues, an agent must be proactive. A proactive approach to dealing with decision making ensures that clients will not only make good initial decisions but, more important, stick with them over the long haul. To become proactive, many superstars use the Five-Star Service Technique. This simple approach is shown in Figure 8-1.

FIGURE 8-1. THE FIVE-STAR SERVICE TECHNIQUE

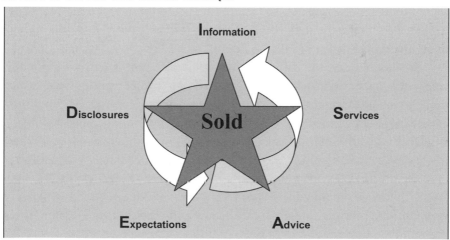

Imagine this graphic as a page in your presentation. As you begin to wrap up your seller meeting, you conclude by using a script similar to the one given here in the Five Star Service Discussion box.

Notice that in just a few short minutes, we can lay the groundwork for future discussions regarding such sensitive issues as price adjustments, condition improvements, motivation issues, family and friend disputes, financial issues, and even seller's remorse.

But we might still have a problem, because this particular seller hasn't decided to list with you. Instead, he's on the fence, straddling the commitment like a six-year-old on his first bike. At times he seems ready to say yes, but then he backslides, putting his feet down and skidding to a dead stop. What next? It may be time to do some decision-making calisthenics to help him build his decision-making muscles.

The Five-Star Service Discussion

Mr. and Mrs. Seller, I am excited that you have considered hiring me to sell your home. I pride myself on helping my clients during every step of the listing and sale process, which is why I've developed my Five-Star Service Technique to ensure a smoother sale.

As you might notice, the first letter of each point spells out the word *IDEAS,* which is good because I think the more ideas, the better! Here's what I think these stand for:

I: *Information.* This means that it's my job to keep you abreast of any new market information that may affect your sale. If you decide to hire me, I would like to set up an in-person meeting with you every 30 days until your home is sold to discuss new market information, along with a weekly conference call. How does that sound? Likewise, if anything changes with your situation, timing, or motivation, please give me a call anytime.

D: *Disclosures.* Part of my job is risk management. If you can think of anything that might affect the sale of your home that I should know about before we get started—unrecorded loans, judgments, or other title issues—please let me know now so that we can work together on solving these issues.

E: *Expectations.* If you see any area where I can improve or enhance my services to meet your expectations, please let me know. Likewise, I will keep you informed of any buyer and agent showing comments. This way, you can stay in control of your home sale by making any listing adjustments you see fit.

A: *Advice.* When you put your home on the market, you may receive advice from family, friends, and neighbors on pricing and marketing strategies. My job is to advise you based on the facts and accurate market data so that you can make informed decisions that are in your best interests.

S: *Services.* My services include more than just marketing your home. I am here to answer any questions and concerns you may have, and to provide you with referrals for support services to help get you moved. If you need anything during the transaction to make your life easier, please call me immediately and I will work hard to make it happen.

How does all that sound? Would you like to get started?

Making the big decision. Clients can often flip-flop when making big decisions for various reasons.

Above-the-water issues. These are outside factors that can suddenly crop up to change a seller's mind about moving forward. They might include the influence of a client's family, friends, or coworkers; an agent's lack of rapport with his client; or even an agent's poor explanation of the listing documents.

Below-the-water issues. These are hidden influences that only the sellers are aware of; they might include undisclosed debts or financial obligations, timing problems, spousal disagreements, or even just a bad case of seller's remorse.

Agents often help their clients move past these issues by using *IDEAS:*

I: Information
D: Disclosures
E: Expectations
A: Advice
S: Services

Building a Client's Decision-Making Muscle

Look around at the people in your life—not your friends and family (they're perfect), but the people at the periphery, the ones you see in the coffee shop, or at the doctor's office, or in line at FedEx. Don't some of them seem a little dazed and confused, like they're just going through the motions in a state of zombie-like semiconsciousness?

For instance, look at the cashier. How many more mochas will she serve today? Does she really care? Now imagine her being asked to make a real estate decision that will affect the rest of her life and shape her financial future for decades to come. Would she be able to rise to the occasion, take command of the moment, and make a quick judgment call? No way. Or at least not without a triple shot of espresso.

I know, you're not selling homes to kids behind a coffee counter, right? Or are you? Today's Generation X, young adults born between 1965 and 1978, are moving up to their second and even third home, while their younger cohorts, the infamous Generation Y, born between 1979 and 1994, are fast on their heals. Interestingly, a groundbreaking study by Century 21 Real Estate LLC and International Communication Research (ICR) found that these two generations move through homeownership differently from older age groups. For instance, both Generation X and Generation Y tend to be motivated to purchase and keep homes as investments, rather than as a family sanctuary; they are also willing to spend more than older generations on housing (on average up to 25 percent of their household income), and they hold on to their homes for shorter periods than their parents.

But contrary to popular assumptions, the same study also found that both Generation X and Generation Y seem to suffer from a mild case of decision-making paralysis when they attempt to purchase a new home. In fact, these seemingly quick-talking, fast-moving, cell phone–loving "kids" took as much as a full month longer to decide on a home to buy than their older counterparts, even while using the Internet as their primary source of information.

So for many of our younger clients (and a few of our older ones as well), making a decision is difficult, and making a big decision is extremely difficult. Fortunately, the study of neuroeconomics sheds some light on this decision-making quandary. This relatively new field explores such phenomena as how the brain tends to release a pleasure-inducing chemical when it anticipates big financial rewards and how emotions influence thinking. For instance, experts point out that when it comes to making big decisions (including housing-related ones), most people are incapable of being objective. Instead, they tend to consider abstract, unrelated, or emotional pieces of information by giving them too much weight, with the result that they often make poor choices or no choice at all. For this reason, many of our clients may suffer from a condition known as mental atrophy, or the wasting away of their figurative decision-making muscle.

Consider the big real estate decisions you have pondered over during your life. Have you ever allowed rumor, speculation, or past experience to cloud your decision-making process?

I can't live on a street with a dead end; it's too spooky.

We can't sell our house in July; that month has only four letters.

My mom sold her house 10 years ago for a bundle of money, so our house should be worth over a million bucks, right?

Crazy ideas, disconnected thoughts, unrelated data—they can all come flowing through our brains like a broken sewer line when we attempt to focus on a big real estate decision. Our sellers are the same way; they often fall victim to overthinking the next step.

So how can we rebuild our clients' decision-making muscle and help them make good "big picture" real estate decisions? For many top producers, the answer is to provide their clients with a decision touchstone. In ancient times, a touchstone was a literal stone, such as jasper or basalt, that was often used to test the quality of gold or silver. Today we can use a decision touchstone to help our clients measure their real estate decisions against their real estate goals.

Let's take a look at how one agent applies this simple technique:

The Decision Touchstone Discussion

Agent: *Listen, I know that making a decision to market your home is an important step, so I want to ask you a really simple question. At the end of the day, what would you ideally like to see happen with your home sale?*

What are your real estate goals?

Client: *<Answer>*

Agent: *I understand. If you don't mind, as we review my presentation, I might ask you if you think that the services I'm proposing would help you make that happen. Would that be okay?*

Client: *Yes.*

Amazingly many agents can meet with a couple, build trust and rapport, provide a great presentation, and even list a home without ever finding out why their clients are selling or what their real estate goals are. If they know their clients' ideal endgame, the result they are looking for from the sale of their home, wise agents can use this as a decision touchstone throughout their presentation.

For instance let's check back in with this same agent as he wraps up a page on e mail marketing:

Agent: *As you can see, my team uses the Internet not only as a way to stay in contact with our existing customers, but also as a way to constantly cross-*

sell every listing in our inventory. Can you see how this might help you find a buyer faster and meet your goal of selling the home by August?

Notice how the agent is now encouraging the sellers to measure his presentation, piece by piece, against their real estate goals. By using minor agreements, superstars give their clients the ability to make a series of smaller decisions before ramping up to the big one. But, believe it or not, we can make it even easier for our clients to make that last leap of faith by employing the oldest closing technique in the book of sales—the old-fashioned assumptive close.

LEARNING OPPORTUNITY

Decision touchstone. To help clients rebuild their decision-making muscle and help them make big picture decisions, many top producers use a decision touchstone. A decision touchstone is a reference point against which all choices can be measured.

The Assumptive Close

Years ago, there was a television series called *The Odd Couple*, based on the Neil Simon play. The television series starred Tony Randall as Felix Unger, the uptight neatnik, and Jack Klugman as Oscar Madison, the obnoxious, unkempt sportswriter. In one of the most famous lines in television history, Tony Randall yells at his costar, "You should never assume. Because when you assume, you make an ass out of U and ME!"

That may be true, Felix, but not in real estate. Why? For many agents, the most successful technique is the assumptive close, which means that after receiving enough positive-feedback, minor agreements from a seller, the agent moves straight into completing the listing paperwork. Yes, you read it right. These gutsy agents don't get down on one knee or stop and ask a big closing question; instead, they just start filling out the listing paperwork. I know what you're thinking: Isn't this presumptive and potentially offensive to some clients?

Yes, it certainly can be, which is why superstars use this technique only after careful consideration. Here are five key points to consider before moving into an assumptive close:

1. Do I have strong rapport and trust built with this client?
2. Have I built a decision touchstone and used it throughout my presentation?
3. Has my client provided positive feedback to my presentation?
4. Is it in my client's best interests to move forward?
5. Am I confident that the client is ready to move forward?

If you answered yes to all of these questions, it may be time to consider using the assumptive close, and believe me, it's one of the easiest things you will ever do in sales. How is that possible? Because the assumptive close starts with asking simple assumptive closing questions, questions that gently guide a client from being a passive presentation participant to being an active, engaged decision maker. Let's take a look at 10 real-world assumptive closing questions that you can use today:

Ten Assumptive Closes

1. *Sign placement.* "Now, where would you like to place the sign, near the driveway or closer to the road?"
2. *Lockbox placement.* "I've brought along a lockbox. Where would you prefer to have this, on the front door, or perhaps on the faucet, where it is less visible?"
3. *Flyer design.* "I can have my assistant create a flyer this afternoon; which design style do you prefer?"
4. *Advertising.* "I can submit advertising to the newspaper this afternoon. What features of the home would you like me to focus on in the advertising?"
5. *Website promotion.* "I can have the listing posted online later today, but I'll need to take some photos. Do you have any preferences on what angles you would like me to feature?"
6. *Paperwork.* "To begin the paperwork, I like to start with the disclosure statement. It outlines to a buyer everything he needs to know about the home."
7. *Flyer box.* "I like to use a flyer box on my listings, but I'll need your help to keep the box full. Would you mind refilling the box every week? I'll have my assistant stop by later and drop off a hundred to get us started."

8. *Talking House.* "I like to use a Talking House on my listings. A Talking House broadcasts a constant 90-second radio message about your home to anyone driving by. I just need a place to plug the unit in. Do you have a good spot near a front window?"

9. *Top producer e-mail.* "When I list a home, the first thing I like to do is to e-mail all of my top producer colleagues; I have a list of every agent who closed over $3 million in sales last year. As soon as we complete the paperwork today, I can send that out immediately. How does that sound?"

10. *Showing instructions.* "Are there any times of the day that you would prefer the home not to be shown or any special showing instructions that I should note on the paperwork?"

You might notice, in reading these dialogues, that by answering just one of these questions the seller is indicating that she plans to move forward. In order to stop this forward motion, a seller has to put on the brakes and say, "Hey, wait! I haven't even decided to list my house yet!" To be honest, some unethical agents use a seller's reluctance to take such a strong stand as a way to rack up bigger listing numbers. Their attitude is that the more cavalier they are, the bigger their odds of success, but obviously clients who feel that they were unfairly manipulated will find a way to back out of the listing, so in the end the agent will have gained nothing. Strong ethical agents, on the other hand, use the assumptive close as a way to help clients who have already shown a strong indication that they would like to move forward. These agents take the burden off of clients who may have a hard time confronting a big decision by giving them an easy out.

But what if the assumptive close just doesn't feel right? Trust your instincts and consider using the if–then close.

LEARNING OPPORTUNITY

The assumptive close. The assumptive close simply means that after receiving enough positive feedback from a seller, many agents choose to move straight into completing the listing paperwork without stopping to ask the seller a big closing question.

The If–Then Close

My son Michael is a master negotiator, capable, I'm sure, of negotiating with world leaders, heads of state, and rogue nations if necessary to gain something he wants—like an Xbox, Playstation, or Nintendo video game. As a student in the art of closing, he is shrewd, crafty, and diligent in his quests. He is so good, in fact, that occasionally I get the feeling that a no is what he really wants, perhaps as part of some higher-order negotiating gambit, so I fake him out with a yes, just to show him who's boss.

In studying Michael's technique over the years, I have noticed that he has developed a sophisticated closing strategy that I call the if-then close. The magic in his technique is that it is literally endless. A no in Michael's world is never final; it is simply a minor delay. Interestingly, I have noticed that not only does Michael use this technique, but all great negotiators do as well. In other arenas it's referred to by different names, but I'll always refer to it as Michael's if-then close, and here's how it works:

> **Michael:** *Hey, Dad, can I get Mario Party 19 for my Game Cube?*
>
> **Dad:** *Nope.*
>
> **Michael:** *I understand.* <Yes, he actually says I understand!> *Well, if I clean my room, then would you get it for me?*
>
> **Dad:** *Nope.*
>
> **Michael:** *Okay. . . . How about if I clean my room and mow the lawn; then would you buy it?*

You can see where this is going, right? No matter how many times I say no, it doesn't matter, because he doesn't give up. He just keeps coming back with a different approach. The key for Michael is to know when to move ahead and when to back off. So he watches and listens, all the time attempting to diagnose when he can push forward with another proposal and when he is risking life and limb. Like a supercomputer, he endlessly crunches possible solutions, often while eating Cap'n Crunch cereal and watching *Tom and Jerry*, until finally, with a slurp and a smile, he arrives at a new ingenious approach.

In the world of real estate the if-then close can be a terrific tool for clients who need a little extra help in making a decision. Obviously we can't go through endless scenarios with our clients; besides, they couldn't possibly have that much Cap'n Crunch on hand. Instead, we need to choose our proposals carefully.

Let's take a look at five real-world if–then closes:

Five If–Then Closes

1. "Let me ask you this: *If* we could still get your property in the upcoming real estate guide, *then* how would feel about moving forward this evening?"

2. "Perhaps *if* we went ahead and filled out the paperwork today, I could *then* begin putting together all of the marketing pieces while you're preparing the home to be shown. How does that sound?"

3. "I know you're a little hesitant to move forward because the numbers look a little tight. Perhaps *if* we can go ahead and list the property but remain firm on the price, *then* you can still hit your goals. How does that sound?"

4. "Listen, *if* I agree to list the house at the price you have in mind, which based on the market numbers is a stretch, *then* would you agree to a price adjustment in two weeks if we have had no offers?"

5. "I understand your reluctance to sign a long-term listing. Let me ask you this: *If* I agreed to provide you with an easy out, meaning a no-questions-asked exit strategy, *then* how would you feel about moving forward?"

By providing clients with alternatives, choices, and easy ways to say yes, strong agents are able to help clients move past their indecision and toward fulfilling their real estate goals. During this process, it's important to recognize the importance of ego and the danger of putting a client in a position of losing face, something that humans, like all animals, will almost never do willingly.

LEARNING OPPORTUNITY

The if–then close. The if–then close is a closing technique used by skilled negotiators who are attempting to provide their clients with possible alternatives, choices, and options. By using this technique, strong agents are able to help clients move past indecision and toward fulfilling their real estate goals.

"Facing" Your Clients

Walking into the seller's home, one of my students, Carl, a broker from Idaho, found himself him in a dilemma. The home featured a giant illustration of the solar system, not a small one but a huge one, almost life-sized, extending from the kitchen to the living room. With the sellers watching proudly, Carl traced his way from Earth to Mars and back again. "Wow, interesting wallpaper."

"Do you like it?"

Oops. Carl froze in midflight. "Houston, I think we have a problem." If Carl said he didn't like it, his clients would be embarrassed, and having a red-faced client is never a good way to start a listing presentation. On the other hand, if he said he did like it, the clients might not be willing to do anything about it when preparing the home to sell.

Brilliantly, Carl, in a clutch moment of inspiration, blurted out, "It's unbelievable!"

Carl, like many of us working in the real estate field, was faced with a common quandary: How do we talk to clients about sensitive issues or help them make big decisions when we may end up causing them to lose face?

Sarah Rosenburg, a political science expert and member of the University of Colorado Conflict Research Consortium, has this to say about the term *face*:

> *Face* is a multi-faceted term, and its meaning is inextricably linked with culture and other terms such as honor and its opposite, humiliation. Saving face or giving face has different levels of importance, depending on the culture or society with which one is dealing. Perhaps the most familiar term to many is "saving face," which we understand simply to mean not being disrespectful to others in public, or taking preventive actions so that we will not appear to lose face in the eyes of others. Some will immediately associate the term "face" with Sino-Japanese cultures, but it would be a mistake to think that those are the only cases where face issues are important.

In helping our clients make big real estate decisions, losing face often becomes a central issue. Let's take a look at four ways in which the risk of the client losing face may affect your ability to take a salable listing:

1. The seller's opinion of price differs from your information.
2. The seller has relatives whose opinion has no basis in reality.
3. The condition of the seller's home is less than acceptable.
4. The seller has unreasonable marketing expectations.

In the end, no matter how strong your logic, services, or sales record may be, clients won't list their home with you unless you continue to foster feelings of rapport and trust. Once these crucial connections are lost, the listing is lost. To deal with these issues and still be able to take the listing, strong presenters use three strategies to avoid the flight-or-fight response that losing face can trigger.

Strategy 1: Don't Take a Personal Position

Sellers love to pigeonhole agents by asking questions like, "What do you think my home will sell for?" If you answer this question, you can easily become the price, meaning, in essence, that the seller now looks at you as a walking representation of your opinion. That's great if she agrees with you, but it can be a disaster if she doesn't. Presentation experts avoid this trap by redirecting this type of question to the ultimate source of pricing answers—the market. Take a look at the way some superstars deflect this question:

Client: *What do you think my home will sell for?*

Agent: *You know, my opinion doesn't really matter; what matters is what's happening in the market. Let me show you the comparables I've found.*
Or
I think the home should sell for $5 million, but unfortunately I'm not buying it. Let's take a look at the market numbers.

This same tactic will work for many types of similar issues. For instance, let's take a look at a seller with unrealistic marketing expectations:

Client: *I'd like to see my home advertised in the* Wall Street Journal *every weekend. Don't you think you can find more buyers that way?*

Agent: *Well, I can certainly understand what you're saying, and honestly I've had similar requests from other clients. But in conducting our after-sale survey, something we do with every client on the day of closing, we've found that when buyers are shopping for a home locally their number one source of information was the local real estate guide, and second to that was the Internet.*

Or

You know, my motivation is to get your home sold for top dollar in the shortest amount of time possible. Based on the 2005 National Association of Realtors Profile of Home Buyers and Sellers, a survey sent to 90,000 consumers across the country, the number one answer for how buyers learned about their home was from a real estate agent, the next was through the Internet, and the third was through a yard sign. I've brought along a copy–take a look. <Show graph.> I would consider all of these to be local sources of information.

Strategy 2: Don't Question the Reasoning

Clients often come up with all kinds of bizarre reasoning to justify their positions. Unfortunately, the second you question a seller's crazy ideas, you may fall victim to becoming viewed as an adversary instead of an ally. To avoid this fate, many agents have learned to stutter step around these sensitive issues by not questioning a seller's absurd ideas; instead, they focus on unbiased market data. For instance, let's take a look at how one agent deals with a client whose nutty relative has suddenly become an overnight real estate expert:

Client: *My uncle Bob says the house should be worth $20,000 more than our neighbors' because it has a porch swing. What do you think?*

Agent: *You know, ultimately the market takes every aspect of a home into consideration. Let's do this: Let's take a really hard look at all the amenities that each comparable home is offering and see what homes are actually selling for, and then you can decide for yourself what you think.*

Or

I understand. Actually, in addition to the market data and comparable sales that we have already reviewed, I've brought along the National Association of Realtors Cost vs. Value report, which highlights home amenities and their relative value to buyers. Let's take a look.

We can also use this strategy when dealing with clients who can't understand that their home isn't in show-ready condition without offending them. Check out how one agent makes this happen:

Client: *Hey, we just like to live comfortably. Can't buyers understand that?*

Agent: *Well, I can certainly understand it, but buyers may not. What happens is that you're competing with other homes for a buyer's attention, and if* *you look at the homes that have sold over the last six months, you'll see that most of them have been in top condition, and the two that weren't sold for a discounted price. How do you feel about a discounted price?*

Or

Really, I can understand it, but one thing to consider is that condition and price are always linked. Just like when you buy a car or a piece of furniture, the better the condition, the higher the price. So really it comes down to your decision: Do you want top dollar, or are you willing to accept a lower price?

Strategy 3: Don't Allow Sellers to Argue in Front of You

If you can think back far enough to remember when you were a kid, you may be able to recall your parents fighting. Afterward you may have noticed that one party or the other was generally the winner. But did this dynamic change when an audience was present? In many cases, when we have an audience, whether it is during a friendly debate or a knock-down, drag-out brawl, our potential for losing face raises the stakes dramatically. Where once we might have settled down and even accepted a common-sense resolution to an argument, now, with others watching, we might pound the table with the self-righteous indignation of the innocently accused, even if we are dead wrong and guilty as sin.

Our real estate clients are the same way. When one party wants to sell more than the other does, as is often the case, this can lead to serious disagreements that can spill over into a listing presentation. To solve this challenge, wise agents never allow clients to argue in front of them. Instead, they excuse themselves from the conversation. Take a look at how one top producer handles this tough situation delicately:

Client: *<Arguing>*

Agent: *You know, if you don't mind, I'm going to return a couple of phone calls while you two discuss this issue.*

Or

Listen, either way you decide to go, I'll support your decision. Why don't I start taking some photos of the outside and let you two discuss this in private?

So what happened to Carl? Wisely, he waited until after he had the listing signed to explain to his clients that to receive top dollar for the home, they might wish to consider removing their precious wall art. Reluctantly, they did, but not until he had tipped the scales in his favor.

LEARNING OPPORTUNITY

Face. In helping our clients to make big real estate decisions, losing face often becomes a central issue. To avoid having their clients fall into this awkward dilemma, many agents use three strategies:

1. *Don't take a personal position.* Wisely, whenever possible, many agents avoid taking a position on topics that can later lead to an adversarial discussion.
2. *Don't question the reasoning.* Instead of attacking a client's thought process, top producers default to a discussion centered on facts.
3. *Don't allow sellers to argue in front of you.* Excusing yourself from an argument between sellers allows them to hash out their disagreements in private.

Tipping the Scales

If you were a Viking living in 920 A.D. (and who wouldn't want to be a Viking—with those horns on their helmets, big swords, and cool boats?), it's not likely you would have carried paper money with you as you pillaged and conquered your neighbors. Instead, the Viking economy was a bullion economy; traders carried small scales that could measure the weight of their customers' gold and silver very accurately. For the Vikings, then, the more metals they carried in their purse, the better their chances of getting what they wanted. Likewise, today we can tip the scales in our favor during a real estate presentation by always carrying a full purse of benefits that outweigh our client's reluctance or objections to moving forward. The more reasons we can pile on the decision-making scale, the more likely it is that it will tip in our favor, and we will be rewarded with our prize: the seller's listing.

Now you might think, "Didn't I already do that when I reviewed my listing presentation?" Yes, you did show the client your list of services, but at that moment it wasn't being measured against his reluctance or objections to moving forward; at that point, he was probably just taking it all in. Like a jury watching a trial, your client heard all of the testimony, saw all of the evidence, and listened to the eyewitnesses. But he still needs to be convinced. In real estate, as in all sales, we often engage in this type of moment marketing, where our entire presentation comes down to a handful of seconds during which the client is weighing his options. What clients need is a closing argument. Trials are won and lost on closing arguments, and the same can be true of real estate listings. The more powerful the argument, the more likely an agent will be to take a listing.

Take a look at how one agent uses his closing argument to stack the presentation deck in his favor:

The Closing Argument Discussion

> **Client:** *You know, I think we need to sleep on this before we make a decision.*
> **Agent:** *I understand, and I certainly want you to be comfortable moving forward. Now just to review the benefits I can offer you, I've prepared a bulleted list of my services. <Review list.> Let me ask you, is there anything that's not on the list that you would like me to add that would make you feel more comfortable about moving ahead this evening?*

Using this kind of closing argument obviously requires that you take the time to build an overview of your real estate services, one that doesn't attempt to rehash your entire presentation, but rather covers the high points. By doing so, wise agents load up their client's decision-making scale with their precious cargo of services.

Take a look at the sample overview of services in Figure 8-2.

There is an old adage concerning writing, speaking, and presenting information: First you tell your audience what you're going to tell them, then you tell them, and then you tell them what you told them. The same is true of a real estate presentation. By using a simple overview, you can tell your clients what you told them by reminding them that if they hire you, they will be getting not only your winning personality and expensive wardrobe, but a raft of incredibly valuable services to boot.

So now that we have completely sold the client on our services and she is ready to sign the listing agreement, have we forgotten anything? Yes, we have. We have forgotten to plant some early seeds, a critical component in repositioning a listing that fails to sell right out of the gate. Let's take a look at this critical step in Chapter 9, "A Superstar's Guide to Salable Listings."

FIGURE 8-2.

Overview of Services

- Competitive Market Evaluation
- Overall Market Review
- 30-Day Market Updates
- Financing Strategy Report
- Curb Appeal Review
- Home-Staging Support
- First-Class Signage
- Dedicated Webpage
- Showing Follow-Up Reports
- Exclusive Open House program
- Communication Guarantee
- 30-Day Written Marketing Reports
- Color Real Estate Guide Advertising
- Local Newspaper Marketing
- Call and Inquiry Tracking
- Offer Review and Recommendations
- Counteroffer Preparation
- Inspection Management
- Transaction Management
- Closing Follow-Up
- Relocation Assistance
- Postclosing Services

I want to earn your business!

LEARNING OPPORTUNITY

The closing argument. At the end of a presentation, it is often wise for agents to do a quick review of what they covered during the meeting. Many accomplish this by creating a visual overview of their services.

A Superstar's Guide to Salable Listings

Just like our clients, we often create arbitrary boundaries, guidelines, and standards that probably have nothing to do with our true needs, but instead keep us anchored in a warm bubble of what we consider to be safe. Our decision making, then, is often skewed by this compulsion to stay within our own comfort zone. For instance, we often don't want to offend a seller by telling her that it's possible that she will have to adjust her price or the condition of her home in order to achieve her desired real estate goals. Yet superstars must move beyond these self-imposed barriers to move up to creating real estate presentations that make millions.

For instance, somewhere in the country, or maybe in your own city, town, or even office, there is a top listing agent, an agent who really rips through new listings, prospects hard core every day, uses her sphere of influence to the full, and always asks for new business. But as successful as this agent seems to be, she may also face a huge problem: the cost of supporting all those listings! Why? Taking a listing isn't free; it costs real money. In fact, after factoring in the cost of signs, advertising, labor, flyers, Internet posting fees, and lockboxes, many industry veterans claim that they spend $500 to $1,000 or more for each new home they list.

Because of this staggering investment, an agent who is taking overpriced listings, listings that are in poor condition, or listings with unfavorable terms may be sitting on a huge pile of costs. Like a clothing store that is trying to sell winter clothes in the summer, these agents can easily suffer from stale, unappealing inventory. And as we all know, taking a listing means that you have to market the listing, and when you market a listing that has little or no chance of selling, you have created a monster. This monster must be fed, and what is it being fed? Your time and money.

The good news is that if you understand the age-old dilemma that has faced buyers and sellers since the dawn of private property rights, you can turn this dilemma on its head by taking back control of your inventory. Believe it or not, this conundrum underlies and controls every seller's decision to sell and every buyer's need to complete a purchase.

What is this great, often hidden motivator that is lurking in the dark corners of your clients' gray matter? For sellers, it is the need either to sell within a set time frame or instead to hold out for the best possible price, and, as you might guess, for buyers, it's the need either to buy within a set time frame or to purchase a home for the lowest possible price.

Looking at Figure 9-1, you can quickly see that a seller who would like to sell for top dollar should be prepared to potentially wait longer for a buyer who is willing to pay a premium price. Like someone who is trying to sell ice during December, a seller might have to give the stuff away just to get rid of it, but if he waits long enough, say until mid-August, when temperatures rise

FIGURE 9-1. THE PRICE VS. TIME SOLUTION

Sellers	Higher Price Longer Time	Lower Price Shorter Time
Buyers	Higher Price Shorter Time	Lower Price Longer Time
	Motivation	

to crest over 100 degrees, that same ice can suddenly have real value. On the flip side, a seller who needs to sell quickly and doesn't have time to wait should expect to have to discount her price somewhat because of the limited time she has to expose her home to the market.

What's the difference? Timing.

By having a price vs. time discussion with your clients, you can help frame the seller's decision making in real-world terms that he can instantly relate to. How? Let's take a quick look at how one superstar incorporates these concepts into her listing presentation:

Price vs. Time Discussion: Round One

> **Agent:** *One item to consider when pricing your home is timing. As they say, timing is everything, and that is certainly true in real estate.*
>
> *In general, the higher the price of your home, the longer it will take to sell. The more competitive the price, the faster your home will sell.*
>
> *So what do you feel is your highest priority—selling quickly or selling for a higher price?*

You might guess that many of your clients will smile coyly when you pose this question and answer, "I want both!" The funny thing is that they aren't kidding.

This sticky situation often reminds me of one of my first jobs after graduating from high school, which was working the graveyard shift at a local lumber mill. Like clockwork every night, the foreman would come by to monitor my production. We called him Perry, which could have been his last name or his first name, because he never clarified it. Over the roar of the machinery, Perry would cup his hands together and yell, "You need to put out more wood!" Finally, after an especially tough day, I looked him in the eye and yelled back, "Do you want quantity or quality?" Throwing his yellow hard hat down on the concrete floor and then kicking it for emphasis, he snarled back, "I want both!"

Like Perry, most of our clients want their cake with the icing generously slathered on top. Not only that, but they want it with a glass of milk, and yeah, maybe a little bit of ice cream, too. They want it all.

But as much as they hate to admit it, the truth is that sellers are almost always motivated by either a need to sell quickly or a need to get top dollar. Sure, they aren't going to make it easy for you, just as Perry wasn't about to make it easy for me. Instead, they'll attempt to put the responsibility back on your shoulders. If this happens, take a look at how one smooth operator hands their gift back to them by using a simple follow-up question.

Price vs. Time Discussion: Round Two

Seller: *I want both.*

Agent: *I understand, and believe me, it's my goal to get you both, but let me ask you this: If we should get to the end of the listing period and the home hasn't yet sold at this price, do you think you would be more likely to give it a little more time or adjust the price?*

This is not, as you might think, a gotcha question; we're not trying to trap the seller into committing himself to an immediate price adjustment or a change in the listing terms. Instead, we are framing the ability to sell the home through a timing question. We want the seller to understand that receiving top dollar may require a longer period of time, and if he wants to sell quickly, then a price adjustment may be the fastest way to accomplish this goal. It boils down to motivation. Top producers have learned that it is imperative to help sellers thoroughly understand the difference between these two key motivations.

Why is this so critical? Take a look at this same listing a few months down the line. The seller is pacing the floor; the home hasn't sold, and he is on pins and needles waiting for an offer to come in. Let's take a look at how an agent might follow up her earlier price vs. time discussion:

Price vs. Time Follow-Up

Agent: *You know, when I took the listing, I asked you a very important question: I asked you what was more important to you, selling quickly or selling for a higher price.*

At this point, we can continue to try to find a buyer at the listing price we started at, which may take more time, or we could make a price adjustment so that you can secure a buyer faster. Which would you prefer?

Notice that this approach shifts the responsibility of securing a buyer back to where it should be—on the seller's shoulders. The seller decides how long he is willing to hold out for top dollar and when he is ready to make a price adjustment. Depending on his motivation, he can choose to wait for the market to catch up to his price, or he can choose to take control of his home sale by adjusting the price.

Of course, this isn't a one-way decision. A listing contract is a bilateral agreement, meaning that you have some choices in this matter as well, the biggest of which is, do you really want to take the listing? So how can you and the seller really know if you have a listing that has a reasonable shot at actually selling?

Many agents have found that one of the easiest ways is to use a home-scoring system.

LEARNING OPPORTUNITY

Price vs. time. Sellers are almost always motivated by either a need to sell quickly or a need to get top dollar. Top producers have learned that it is imperative to help sellers thoroughly understand the difference between these two key motivations.

The Home-Scoring System

Okay, so you took the listing. It was overpriced, and you knew it, but you didn't argue too much because you really needed a listing, and besides, the seller was really pushy. Two days later, when you're sitting at the morning breakfast meeting, while each of your colleagues dives headfirst into an oversized banana nut muffin, your mind races to find a way to explain your pricing mistake. Heart pounding, sweat beading, stomach fluttering, you watch nervously as the team leader finally makes her way to your seat, and then asks with a smile, "Any new listings this week?"

"Yeah," you begin nonchalantly. "Uh . . . this one is owner priced. . . ."

Smooth.

How many times have you heard an agent begin a listing pitch to other Realtors with this opening? Countless, right? As an agent sitting on the other side of the conference room table, what do you do next? Do you sit rapt with anticipation, pen at the ready, or do you instantly move on to thinking about how your pet hamster didn't seem quite so spunky this morning?

Saying that a listing is owner priced is like waving a red flag that says,

"I'm a weak agent," or, "This listing is a waste of your time." But that's not the worst of it; what happens next is far more painful—some would say bordering on torturous. What could that be? The seller blames you for not selling her overpriced home. Even more outrageously, she demands that you find a way to produce a buyer or she will fire you and hire another agent (often at a lower price).

You might think that, as highly paid real estate professionals, we would scoff at this treatment and calmly explain to the seller that, in fact, she was responsible for overpricing the property (we just filled out the paperwork). But by and large we don't. Instead we meekly accept responsibility for the failure. You don't believe me? Take a look at how most of these conversations go down, and see if you have ever had a similar experience:

> **Seller:** *Why hasn't my home sold yet?*
>
> **Agent:** *Umm, well, we have been getting a lot of calls. . . . It just takes that one right buyer.*
>
> <And the crowd screams, "Here we go, defense, here we go!">
>
> **Seller:** *Yeah, but don't we need showings to get offers? Where are you advertising?*
>
> **Agent:** *Well, we do have your home in the newspaper this week. What if I do a bigger, color ad in the upcoming real estate guide, or how about an open house this weekend? How does that sound?*

Sad isn't it? This poor sap of an agent is now stuck spending more money on a dog of a listing that will probably never sell. Why? To keep the seller at bay long enough so that maybe, just maybe, a Hail Mary buyer will arrive— you know, a buyer who falls off the pumpkin wagon and is willing to buy any home, no matter how overpriced it is or what condition it's in. And it gets worse. Short of winning the lottery, this agent is going to have to face this same seller not once but over and over again to explain why he just can't seem to pull his head out of his Aston Martin long enough to sell her home. Guess what? Most agents just can't deal with this pressure. So within weeks they begin to duck the seller's calls. They become invisible, shielding themselves behind e-mail reports and handwritten notes while pretending that the problem will just go away. It doesn't.

So what's the solution? For many agents, the answer is a home-scoring system. Many top producers around the country use a home-scoring system to reverse the communication dilemma we just encountered. Here's how it works: When you take the listing for the first time, you announce to the seller that as part of your services you provide each of your listings with a home score. This score will determine how salable the home is. For instance, if the home scores low, it may never sell; if it scores in the midrange, it has an average chance of selling; and if it scores high, it has a terrific chance of selling. Take a look at the sample in Figure 9-2.

During the listing presentation, a home-scoring system allows a strong agent to enter into a discussion of the key elements necessary to put the seller's home into a realistic position for selling. It's a pragmatic, realistic approach to getting homes sold quickly and for top dollar. No more pie in the sky, hoping for the best, or wishing upon a star. Instead, a home score is a score; it's an unemotional, clinical evaluation. Can a seller disagree with your assessment of an item—for instance, the overall condition? Absolutely, but that's the beauty of the system. It front-loads these discussions at the beginning of your relationship instead of waiting for the middle or the end.

FIGURE 9-2.

Your Exclusive Home Score

		Circle #			Circle #
1. Home Protection Plan		3	10. Property Condition	Poor	0
				Good	1
				Excellent	4
2. Financing Terms	Conv. Only	1	11. Market Area	Outer	0
	FHA/VA	2		MLS Zone	2
	Owner Assist	3			
3. Terms of Listing	120 Days	1	12. Average DOM	Over 120	0
	180 Days	2		60–120	1
	210 Days	3		60 or less	3
4. Percent Above Expected Price	6–10%	2	13. Competition in the Area	Strong	0
	1–5%	3		Average	1
	Market	5		Weak	3
5. Activity in Price Range	Weak	0	14. Function and Use	Poor	0
	Average	1		Good	1
	Strong	3		Excellent	2
6. Yard Sign Allowed	No	0	15. Easy Access for Showing	No	0
	Yes	2		Yes	1
7. Immediate Possession	No	0	16. Available for Open House	No	0
	Yes	1		Yes	1
8. Preordered Appraisal	No	0	17. Strategically Priced	No	0
	Yes	4		Yes	1
			Total Score =		
9. Contingencies	Yes	0			
	No	1	Home Score Rating		
			35–42 = A 20–30 = C		
			30–34 = B 15–20 = D		

This particular home-scoring system has 17 points, each covering an important aspect of creating a product that has a reasonable shot at selling. By completing the worksheet and tallying up the overall score, any agent can rate a home's ability to sell. It's easy. For instance, in using a similar form myself, I have found that any home that is rated A, meaning in this case a home that has received 35 points or more, has sold. Because of this, I can truthfully say to a seller, "If you want to sell, I can tell you that 100 percent of the homes I have represented that scored a 35 or better have sold." That's a powerful statement to make to a seller.

Now you might wonder how a form can predict a home's ability to sell. It can't, but common sense can. Take a minute to study the form. For example, take a look at the first topic, a home protection plan. A home protection plan, otherwise known as a home warranty, protects a buyer against any unexpected mechanical system breakdowns after closing. Buyers love these plans because they take the mystery out of buying an unfamiliar home. Because of this, on this particular agent's home-scoring system, if the seller offers a home warranty as an inclusion in the sale, the home gets 3 points. Naturally, some sellers may ask a question as you're reviewing the form, like, "Hey wait, what if I don't want to pay for a home warranty or a preappraisal. You're telling me that my home is less likely to sell?"

The short answer is yes. The long answer, the one you say slowly and with empathy, is that the form is simply a way to compare competitiveness. Sure, by itself, offering a home warranty or a preappraisal may or may not cause a home to sell, but the cumulative effect of these 17 selling points can certainly have an effect on a home's overall competitiveness.

From an agent's perspective, using a home-scoring system allows you to open up discussions on items that may have been missed or overlooked during the listing presentation. But that's not even the best part. The best part about using a home score is your ability to take back control over your seller interactions after you have taken the listing.

Check out how your follow-up calls might change when you use a home-scoring system as a tool:

Home-Scoring System: First Follow-Up Call

Agent: *Good morning, John. I'm just doing my regular follow-up on your listing. Let me give you an update on what we've done so far. . . . Now, I*

have to be honest; I'm a little concerned about the amount of activity we
have had. By this time we should have had more showings.
  Do you remember the home-scoring sheet we did together?

Client: *Yes.*

Agent: *Great. I've got your home's profile here in front of me. I noticed that*
when we took the listing, the deck still needed some repair, so we gave the
home only a good instead of an excellent on the condition. At this point,
would you prefer to work on the deck, or would you like to make a price
adjustment?

Client: *I'll work on the deck.*

Remember that the seller controls both the price of the home and the product; you as the agent control only the promotion. By giving the seller the ability to make changes to his listing, you empower him to take control of his home sale. What's more, you force him to come to grips with the fact that he can either take action and move forward with his home sale or not, but it's his choice, not yours.

Check out how this agent continues the dialogue a couple of weeks later:

Home-Scoring System: Second Follow-Up Call

Agent: *Good morning, John. I'm just doing my regular follow-up on your*
listing. Let me give you an update on what we've done so far. . . . As you
know, we still haven't received an offer on the home, and frankly, I'm
concerned about the amount of activity we're having. Do you have a
minute?

Client: *Yes.*

Agent: *Great. Listen, first, I want to thank you for fixing the deck; I think that*
did help us generate some more interest, but I want your home sold, and
I know you do as well. Looking back on the home-scoring sheet, I noticed
that we offered only conventional financing as an option. What do you
think now? Should we go ahead and open it up to VA and FHA buyers, or
would you rather adjust the price?

So who will be ducking whose call now? Feels good, doesn't it?

By taking control of the communication dilemma and turning the tables on the person who is ultimately responsible for a home's selling (the seller), you can actually help sellers to realize that selling a home is less about who can do the most open houses or pile on the most signage, and more about which seller is willing to offer the best product to the marketplace at the best possible price. The seller who can turn up the heat and make her home—yeah, I'll say it—the sexiest home on the block is often the first one to have buyers knocking down the doors to get inside.

To turn on the charm even more, let's take a look at some other creative techniques to make a seller's home stand out.

LEARNING OPPORTUNITY

Home-scoring system. Many top producers around the country use a home-scoring system to reverse the communication dilemma that many agents encounter by helping a seller to understand how to make his home more competitive in the marketplace.

The Sexy House

Your sellers want top dollar for their home (hey, who doesn't, right?). So how can you help your clients secure the highest possible price for their home in the shortest amount of time? Use the strategy that professional marketing executives have known for years: Make the product sexy. How in the world do you make a house sexy? you might ask. That's a great question. Let's take a look at several ways to make your listing the most attractive house in the neighborhood.

Dress Up the House

The home's curb appeal will create an instant and irreversible first impression on every buyer. According to Ellen Boettcher, president of Staging by Design, real estate professionals should assess several factors when listing a home for sale, the first of which is: "How bad is the place?" "Maybe the general appearance of the property is dated, worn, or unattractive," says Boettcher. Use this checklist to make sure your listing is dressed for success:

- Paint the trim and front door.
- Plant flowers and pull weeds.
- Clean the downspouts and gutters.

The Psychology of Color

The first impression on prospective buyers should be a lasting and positive one. Researcher Debbie Zimmer of the paint manufacturer Rohm & Haas says that there is a psychology of color that sellers can use to help make a good impression on buyers. According to Zimmer, these colors have a special impact on people:

Red. The color red can increase blood pressure, heartbeat, and energy in most people. It instills feelings of intimacy and passion, and it increases appetite. Red is often a good choice for a formal dining room.

Orange. This color works well in living rooms and family rooms because it can warm up a room in a friendly way. Sellers often experiment with various tints and shades to find the best match for their tastes.

Yellow. Yellow is warm and welcoming, but it is more of an attention getter than either red or orange. It is a good color for poorly lit foyers or dark hallways.

Blue. This color makes most people feel tranquil and at ease, which is why it is ideal for use in bedrooms. Blue has also been shown to be an appetite suppressant, so it is not a good option for a dining room.

Green. This is also a relaxing color that many find more versatile than blue. Light greens are ideal for bedrooms and living rooms; midtones are good for kitchens and dining rooms. It is often used in hospitals, workspaces, and schools.

Violet. Many adults dislike purples but are fond of the rose family, which can work in many rooms. Young children, on the other hand, seem to like violet, so this color can be used successfully in children's bedrooms and play areas.

- Clean the screens and windows.
- Pressure wash the sidewalk and driveway.
- Mow the grass and apply new bark mulch.
- Replace outside lightbulbs.
- Wash the house's exterior, or paint it if needed.
- Clean or replace house numbers.
- Remove all cobwebs and spray for pests.

Create a Warm Environment

Every home should offer the potential buyer a warm, friendly experience, especially during the first showing. What greets the buyer on the other side of the seller's front door? Things to consider:

- Consider the smell of the home—candles and vanilla can help.
- Replace lightbulbs; clean drapes, blinds, and windows.
- Professionally clean carpets; replace if needed.

First Impression Home Study Findings

A recent study conducted by the Canadian firm Royal LePage showed that

- 53 percent of buyers said that strong odors, such as pet or cigarette smells, had a bigger impact on their impression of a home than the overall tidiness and cleanliness.

- 41 percent of men stated that they would pay more for a home with updated décor, while only 30 percent of women said that they would pay a premium.

- 79 percent of buyers said that they would be willing to pay more for a home with a renovated kitchen.

- Paint or wash walls.
- Clean doors, cabinets, and closets.
- Dust the home; remove cobwebs.
- Clean appliances.
- Paint or clean baseboards.
- Recaulk bathtubs and showers.
- Replace cracked or damaged outlet covers.

Remove Barriers from the Relationship

Buyers need to build an emotional bond with a home before they can make a decision to purchase the home. Help them by removing potential barriers:

- Pack and store seasonal clothing.
- Remove unused furniture.
- Remove personal photo clutter.
- Secure pets before each showing.
- Remove and replace fixtures that are not included with the sale.
- Leave the home during showings.

Tell a Story and Be Interesting

Buyers want a home that stands out from the competition. To help, many agents recommend to clients during the listing presentation that they employ the services of a professional home stager or, if they have been trained to provide the services themselves, offer their own staging recommendations. Jeanne Gardner, owner of First Impressions by Gardner, agrees: "Your listing presentation should incorporate a comprehensive marketing strategy—one that includes a consultation with a home stager."

Here are a few top producer suggestions for staging your next listing:

- Set the kitchen table.
- Turn down the master bed and place a book on the nightstand.
- Display an open game in the kids' room.
- Turn on the fireplace in the living room.
- Turn on soft music.
- Display a family DVD near the entertainment center.

Use Accessories

The smallest items can often turn the buyer on to your listing. For instance, many agents use a home book as a tool to organize a mix of critical information that the buyer may need in order to move forward with a purchase. Examples that superstars include are:

- Copies of the public MLS information
- Disclosure statements (if required)
- Flyers of the home
- Plot maps and tax information
- Financing and payment sheets
- Average utility costs
- A local service provider list
- Warranty information
- A letter from the seller entitled, "Why We Love This Home"
- Photos of the home at different seasons
- An offer form

Open Up the Dark Areas

Buyers want to know everything about a home before they decide to move forward. In most cases, this means that they want to view every area of the home. By making this easier, you may be able to position your listing as the most appealing match to the buyer's needs. For example:

- Unlock and open all areas of the home.
- Clean the garage—sweep and pressure wash.
- Unlock outside buildings, including shops.
- Clean out the closets and pantry.
- Provide access to the crawl space or cellar
- Provide access to the attic.

Offer Protection

Buyers want to feel secure in the purchase of their new home. One way to help them feel more secure is by removing the fear of added repair costs after closing. You can accomplish this by simply offering the buyer a home warranty. The cost of the warranty can generally be paid at closing. For more information on home warranties, go to www.ahs.com.

Offer Incentives

According to the 2005 National Association of Realtors Home Buyers and Sellers Report (www.realtor.org), the average buyer will look at nine homes over eight weeks before making a purchase. How can you make your listing stand out from the crowd? One way is to offer the buyer an incentive to purchase your listing. Here are some examples of incentives that could be offered:

- Buy down the interest rate or pay points.
- Pay for limited closing costs.
- Pay for inspections or compliance work.

Incentives on the Horizon

According to Kemba J. Dunham and Ruth Simon of the *Wall Street Journal Online*, as the market has begun to slow down, many builders are beginning to pile on the incentives to keep their homes moving.

In a recent posting, they noted, "One developer is offering as much as $10,000 toward closing costs, while another home builder is throwing in golf-club memberships. Some incentives are available to any buyer, while others are tied to the buyer making use of a builder's preferred mortgage lender."

Builders also are paying higher commissions or special bonuses to real estate agents. Other deals are more creative: A Miami developer is offering to buy back its condo-hotel units at a premium after 18 months. Another builder, taking a cue from last summer's automakers' deals, is offering "employee pricing" discounts in certain markets.

- Provide an allowance for upgrades.
- Provide a home warranty.
- Provide a selling agent bonus (broker approval required).

Prepare for the Sale

What would happen if a buyer decided he wanted to purchase your listing and close within a short period of time? Prepare for success by taking care of the details of the sale in advance. Top producers' suggestions for their sellers include the following:

- Presale inspections done for pest and dry rot for the whole house
- Pre-preliminary title reports done to remove clouds on title
- Net sheet check prepared based on estimated sales price
- Moving and storage companies researched
- Utility company list compiled for switchover
- Packing boxes ordered
- All keys and garage door openers located
- Loan numbers and estimated balances obtained
- Relocation research started
- Alternative short-term housing researched

Follow Up

It's not always love at first sight for buyers. In many cases, buyers need added information or an extra push to help them make that big decision. Smart sellers and great agents team up to ensure that buyers are never left without all the information they need to make an informed decision.

- Establish a communication plan—seller and agent.
- Follow up with potential buyers and agents after price adjustments.
- Follow up with all showing agents to learn their thoughts.
- Follow up with all open house attendees to learn their thoughts.
- Follow up with MLS and tour attendees to learn their thoughts.

So there you have it—10 ways to make your home sexier even in a hot market. Taken separately, each item may seem insignificant and barely worth mentioning, but taken as a whole, this list may be just the ticket for attracting a high-quality suitor for your next listing. Ah, but what if the buyer doesn't even make it to the front door?

Often buyers don't see every home that may have fit their needs because listing agents fail to recognize the power of strategic pricing.

LEARNING OPPORTUNITY

The sexy house. Superstars explore ways in which sellers can make their home stand out in the marketplace and appeal to the largest number of buyers possible. They do this in many ways, including recommending ways to stage the home for showings, encouraging the seller to prepare for a sale, removing barriers that keep buyers from building a bond with a home, offering incentives for a buyer to make a purchase, and helping the home tell a story.

Strategic Pricing

Here is a conversation you almost never hear in a real estate office:

"Okay, folks, you mentioned earlier that you have a price range in mind based on your lender's recommendations. Staying within those guidelines, I've gone ahead and set our search pattern to look for homes priced between $332,000 and $308,500."

Does anything strike you as odd in this statement—like a price range of between $332,000 and $308,500? For whatever reason, buyers and agents almost always look in price ranges in $10,000 or $5,000 increments. For instance, a more likely price range for this agent would have been to look at homes priced between $330,000 and $310,000. Because of this psychological oddity, wise agents use what I call price points as a way to gain the maximum exposure for their client's home.

Let's take a look at how top agents use this simple technique:

SELLER PRICE	STRATEGIC PRICE POINT	MAJOR PRICE POINT
$307,000	$305,000 or $310,000	$300,000
$283,500	$280,000 or $285,000	$275,000

| $196,000 | $200,000 or $195,000 | $200,000 |
| $512,000 | $510,000 or $515,000 | $500,000 |

By slightly adjusting a seller's price to a more strategic price, agents can greatly increase the chances that the home will come up during a buyer search. For instance, take a look at the first example of a seller who wishes to price her home at $307,000. A buyer looking for homes probably isn't going to say, "Let's look for homes from $292,000 to $308,000." So pricing a home at $307,000 doesn't make a lot of sense. Instead, a strategic price for this home would be either $305,000 or $310,000. By making this simple adjustment, agents can help keep their listings in the sweet spot for buyer searches.

You might notice that there is another category for this home as well, called the major price point. A major price point is a $25,000 pricing increment. Major price points are important to recognize because these are generally the diving boards that buyers and agents spring their home searches from initially and then slowly ratchet up from later. To stay with our first example, a buyer probably wouldn't start a search by looking at homes that are priced at $305,000 or $310,000. Instead, most buyers, at least in the beginning, would say, "Let's look at homes priced at $300,000 and under." Because of this, a seller who wants to secure a sale quickly may consider adjusting his price down to the nearest major price point.

Now for something really controversial. How many times have you heard the urban legend about a seller who after unsuccessfully marketing her home actually increased her price and then, bingo, sold the home? I know; whenever I hear a seller begin one of these tales, I always think, "Yeah, right." But the truth is, it can happen. How? The seller probably hit a more active price range. By researching which price ranges in your market are the most active, you can help your sellers fish for buyers in the best market holes.

For instance, take a look at these sample data:

PRICE RANGE	NUMBER OF SALES, JANUARY–JUNE
$200,000–$225,000	162
$225,000–$250,000	97

$250,000–$275,000	104
$275,000–$300,000	173

Obviously, the most active price range for this particular market is the $275,000–$300,000 price range. Now, I know this goes against the grain of traditionalist thinking, which says that you should always price a home based on its individual merits compared to other similar homes. But this often ignores the overall market reality. For instance, might it be wise for a seller who was considering pricing his home at $270,000 to move up to the next major price point of $275,000? It makes sense to me if there are significantly more sales in that price range. Of course, this works both ways; for instance, a seller who was considering a strategic price of $230,000 may be wise to move down a category and price her home at $225,000. Why? For the same reason: It's a better pricing strategy.

So let's assume for a minute that you miss the mark with pricing, because inevitably you sometimes will, and the home just sits. No showings, no calls, no activity, nothing but dead air, silence. Now may be the perfect time to consider a price adjustment.

LEARNING OPPORTUNITY

Price points. Most buyers and agents conduct MLS searches by searching for properties in $10,000 and $5,000 increments. Because of this, many agents find it wise to price their listing at these strategic price points.

Major price points. A major price point is any $25,000 pricing increment. Major price points are important to recognize because this is often where a buyer begins a search for her next home.

Price range research. By understanding the most active price ranges within a neighborhood, agents can better counsel their sellers on how to find the highest concentration of buyers.

Price Adjustments—Planting an Early Seed

In sales, we are often told that what you do today will affect your income tomorrow. It's a classic scientific theory: causality, cause and effect, actions create results. But what we often fail to consider is what happens when we take the wrong actions. A classic example of this is spending a tremendous amount of energy and effort listing a home and then watching helplessly as the home sits, like a cement slab, at the bottom of the market ocean because of a pricing mistake. Thankfully, there are steps that all of us can take during the listing presentation to ensure that we end up with the result that the seller hired us to make happen: getting the home sold.

One simple action we can all take to make this happen more frequently is to have the no-showing discussion. The key to this technique is planting an early pricing seed during your initial consultation. Planting an early seed simply means that we give our clients ideas to consider early in a relationship, preferably during the initial consultation, that may help later if it is necessary to reposition the listing because it has failed to sell.

Let's take a look at the no-showing discussion in action:

Agent: *I'm very excited about getting to work on marketing your home, but one thing I would like to talk about before we begin the process is what can happen when we begin advertising and promoting the listing.*

It doesn't happen often, but it's certainly a possibility to be aware of. You see, on average, it takes about 12 to 15 showings to produce an offer. So if we find that the home isn't attracting buyers, even with my extensive marketing plan in place, what that is signaling is that the market is rejecting the price, and no matter how much advertising I do, I can't overcome that.

If that happens, we may need to consider a price adjustment.

Now you might think, "Well, that's a big buzz kill. Do I really want to say that right after I have taken the seller's listing?" For many top producers, the answer is yes. The reason is that if you wait and attempt to have this discussion later, say when the home is not being shown and the seller's time deadline is ticking down to zero, the seller may not buy into your statements. At that point, she may think that you're just trying to cover your tracks. Instead, superstars, like Boy Scouts, come prepared. During the listing presentation, they talk about things that may help them later.

Another powerful strategy for planting early seeds is to employ the price adjustment letter technique. This user-friendly approach ensures that should you and the seller misfire when you aim your pricing gun at the market you will be able to reload and try again at a more competitive price. When using this technique, you simply explain to the seller that as a normal part of your sales process, your team mails out a price adjustment letter every 30 days to any listing in your inventory that has not yet received an offer.

Take a look at how one superstar employs this powerful technique:

Price Adjustment Letter Discussion

I want to thank you for this listing. I'm very excited to begin marketing the property. I want to take just a couple of minutes and talk about the follow-up process. Would that be okay?

One of the things that my team does is mail out a price adjustment letter every 30 days to all of our listings that have not yet received an offer. I don't want you to be offended by this; we do it with every seller. You can do one of several with the letter: You can throw it away or you can save it in case you might want to use it in the future or you can just fill in the price adjustment and mail it back in. If you do adjust your price, let me tell you what will happen then . . .

Notice that this agent explains that these price adjustment letters are part of her SOP, her standard operating procedure. In other words, she does this with every client, not just this particular seller. She is not singling this client out, so there is no reason for him to be offended. This is a powerful technique. Like a dripping faucet, this strategy forces the seller to consider, every month, the fact that the reason his home isn't selling may be at least partially because it is overpriced.

One key item to notice in the dialogue is that the agent discusses not only the price adjustment letter itself, but makes the transition into what will happen should the seller decide to go forward with a reduction. For most agents, this will mean a minimarketing blitz that will reenergize the listing and reintroduce it to the marketplace. This added enticement may be just enough to motivate a seller to consider sending the form back in.

Let's take a quick look at a sample price adjustment letter:

Mr. and Mrs. <Seller>
123 Any Street
Any Town, Any City, Zip

Dear <Seller>,

As a service to my sellers, I provide a monthly opportunity to consider a price adjustment.

Price is the number one reason why homes sell in any market, and it's my firm commitment to help you sell your home for top dollar.

If you think now may be the right time to make an adjustment in your price strategy, please fill out the enclosed form and mail it back to my office. Rest assured that we will immediately market your new adjusted price aggressively through every medium available to our firm.

If you would like to talk to me personally about this important issue, please call me at your earliest convenience.

Warmest Regards,

Jim Remley
Broker

You might notice that the key words *price adjustment* rather than *price reduction* are used in the body of the letter. Why? In many sellers' minds, the words *price reduction* can have a negative connotation, as if they are actually giving up money that they might have eventually received. In fact, I've often heard sellers later say, "Yeah, well, I came down from X," or, "Well, tell the buyers I started at X." Using the words *price adjustment* may help sellers make the mental leap needed to realize that they aren't really giving up anything; after all, it could take years for the market to catch up with an over-priced listing. Instead, they are simply tweaking their current price by making a small adjustment toward an offer-generating price range.

But there could be a flip side to this coin that many agents never prepare their client to face, which is a home that generates loads of showings but still produces no offers.

Condition Adjustments—Planting Early Seeds

You would think this would be a rare event: A home is priced right—in other words, the market loves the price, so it generates lots of showings—yet mysteriously it still fails to generate offers. Amazingly, this is a relatively common occurrence; what's uncommon is to find agents who understand what's actually going on.

The answer is that the market is rejecting the home, the product. There is something inside the home that is turning buyers off. Thankfully, we can prepare our clients for this possibility by planting another early seed at the outset of the listing, during the initial presentation.

Take a look at how one agent tactfully covers this ground:

Condition Feedback Discussion

Agent: *Earlier we talked about the possibility of having no showings of the home and the need to consider a price adjustment if that happens, but on the other side, it's also possible to have a lot of showings on a home but still receive no offers.*

In that case, what's happening is that there is something about the home itself that is preventing buyers from moving forward. Part of my job will be to talk to everyone who tours your home to get their feedback. Good or bad, I'll report this information back to you. How does that sound?

No one likes to be rejected, which is why even the most jaded sellers will often be spurred to action by this discussion, even before the first showing takes place. This discussion also creates a great starting point for an early price adjustment or allowance should the seller still be unwilling to make a condition improvement and prefer to sell "as is."

So how do you track the feedback on showings? Many agents simply instruct their clients to alert them when a showing takes place so that they can then follow up with the agent who showed the home. Some agents use technology to help them speed this process along. For instance, Figure 9-3 shows a sample follow-up form that many agents use after completing an open house.

Personally, I think five questions is the maximum; any more and you may scare off your potential client. Will everyone respond? Nope. But a surprising number will. Once you have received the results, you can strip off the client's e-mail address and any potential confidential information, and forward this unbiased, unfiltered information directly to a seller. Like it or not, the seller will get a glimpse of what real-world buyers are saying and thinking about his home. Sometimes the truth both hurts and helps.

Many agents who really want to streamline this process are turning to

FIGURE 9-3.

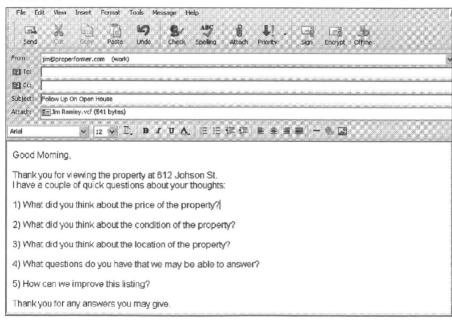

outside vendors like www.homefeedback.com that can provide automated solutions for customer feedback tracking.

LEARNING OPPORTUNITY

Condition feedback discussion. This discussion creates a great starting point for agents to explore the importance of keeping a home in top condition if the seller expects to receive top dollar.

Powerful listing agents gently open their client's eyes to the importance of creating a competitive product, an important consideration in a constantly changing real estate environment. These superstars have learned how to master the game, something that we cover in depth in Chapter 10, "Mastering the Game."

Mastering the Game

Some people just seem to be naturals. They are born to win, fearless leaders who are, I think, genetically predisposed to success. Within my own real estate company, I can think of many top producers who by all appearances slipped into the real estate business as if they were putting on a pair of their favorite sneakers—agents like Kelley Forney, a successful entrepreneur who before entering the real estate business had built a successful chain of music stores and then went on to generate over $10 million in sales during his second year in the business, or Diane McKilliop, who was recruited by my partner while she was serving us lunch at a local restaurant and blew us away by selling over $8 million in her first year.

Like tornadoes, these dynamos were off and running within days of entering the industry, cutting an unstoppable swath through the market. And then there are guys like me. When I started out in real estate, I watched, nose pressed to the glass, as my own local real estate idols, agents who were a lot like Kelley and Diane, seemed to walk on water, knocking down sales like baseball players on steroids. These agents, it seemed, could hit only home runs. They were, and still are, my personal superheroes, men and women who made their bones the hard way, during one of the toughest real estate markets imaginable, when interest rates had pushed toward 17 percent.

Now you might assume that I'm about to tell you that these agents are no different from you and me; that they put their pants on one leg at a time;

and that fundamentally, at their core, they are just like the rest of us. Wrong. After a couple of false starts, I finally worked up the courage to actually sit down and talk with a few of these agents over lunch, and coffee, and donuts, and beer.

Why Some Agents Stand Out

What I learned was that these agents are successful for a reason. And, yes, there is definitely something about how they work that's different from the way the vast majority of agents operate their businesses. It's what makes them both uniquely successful and competitively dangerous. They have an edge. In my discussions with these superstars, I found that there are, in fact, at least five key ways in which these agents SHINE. Let's take a look:

S: Sell to everyone.

H: Help others.

I: Invest in change.

N: Never fear the next step.

E: Exude confidence.

Sell to Everyone

One of the first things you notice about successful real estate agents, master presenters, business leaders, and any good beautician is their ability to sell to anyone at any time. One of my good friends, Susan Murphy, now a superstar real estate agent who closed over $8 million in sales in 2005, launched her real estate career after retiring from a hair salon where she had worked for over 20 years as a hair stylist. "With a pair of sharp scissors in my hand, I always had a captive audience!" Susan says of telling her clients about her career move. Susan is a natural-born salesperson, an engaging, high-energy person who, after only a few years in the real estate business, now works almost entirely from her referral base.

Like Susan, superstars tell everyone they know, everywhere they go about real estate. They are constantly on stage presenting their services. It's their passion. They don't think of it in terms of selling; for them it's a natural extension of their personality.

Okay, so what if you're not an extrovert? I can relate to that. To be honest, I'm not much for schmoozing, pressing the flesh, or the whole air kiss thing either. But in recognizing this about myself early on, I came to accept that allowing a fear of people to determine the success of my business and the number of times I could get in front of a buyer or seller to conduct a presentation was something that I could not allow to happen. Instead, I had to become an extroverted introvert. I had to push past my fear of rejection and, at least while on the clock in my real estate business, turn up the volume on my people skills.

According to James J. Messina, Ph.D., and Constance M. Messina, Ph.D., "Fears are irrational beliefs about how an object, event, happening, or feeling will result in negative, disastrous, life threatening, disturbing, or unsettling consequences for you." Here are a few of their suggestions for moving past your own fears:

- *Make an honest assessment of your fear and create a consistent, systematic plan of action to overcome it.* In real estate, this may include building a consistent plan for prospecting and setting a goal of conducting at least one presentation to either a buyer or a seller each day.

- *Learn to relax physically; reduce anxiety and tension by focusing on how to calm yourself in high-stress situations.* In a presentation setting, this means that you should be able to relax to the point that your voice is calm and confident, and you are able to make consistent eye contact and smile throughout your presentation.

- *Establish a sense of confidence in your ability to overcome and deal with the feared objects or events.* In sales, this can often be achieved through intensive preparation, practice, and rehearsal. Many agents role-play their presentations and prospecting techniques with a partner to gain confidence.

Help Others

It's an old truism: "*Help enough other people to achieve their goals, and you will achieve yours.*" Give and you shall receive. Do you believe that? I do. Some call it the law of reciprocity, meaning that when you give to others, what comes back is often far more valuable. Superstars apply this to real estate by digging into their clients' long-term goals and finding ways to help them achieve those dreams.

For Dennis, a veteran agent from Alaska, this means that he includes in his client notes a section dedicated to discovering his clients' long-term real estate goals, in addition to any business, investment, or personal goals. "I like to ask my clients during my first meeting where they see themselves housewise 10 years from now," he says. By asking this simple question, Dennis finds that clients often open up about all kinds of unrelated topics that are meaningful to them.

For a twist on this idea, check out the sample newsletter in Figure 10-1, which includes a shout-out to clients who have just completed a major life mission: jumping out of an airplane at 10,000 feet.

Agents who can help their clients achieve long-term goals often find that those clients instantly become referral generators. Another way to have fun with life goals is to add a link to your website like www.43things.com, a website where hundreds of thousands of people enter their aspirations and then help one another make their dreams a reality.

Invest in Change

Have you ever seen someone who refuses to change, to get with the times, to move upward and onward? For some, this may mean that they still wear parachute pants and their sunglasses at night, while for others it may mean that they're still lugging around an old-fashioned typewriter to peck out offers and counteroffers.

Real estate agents who don't adapt their technology, business model, and presentation message to meet the needs of a constantly changing real estate customer run the risk of becoming like an old home, one that hasn't been remodeled since its original construction date in 1959: obsolescent.

Master presenters are topical; their message is perishable because it changes, adapts, and contorts to fit the needs of each client. This means that, over time, an agent's message is always changing. Let's take a look at an example of this by examining a common seller concern:

Why should I list my house now?

Have you heard this question recently? I have, and it can be a showstopper if you don't have a solid response. In today's hot real estate market, sellers can have many legitimate fears about selling their home, not the least of which is finding another one to buy.

FIGURE 10-1.

The Luxury Home Expert®

June 2006

Table of Contents

● **Calif. mansion on sale for $75 million**

For $75 million, you could buy the Mighty Ducks of Anaheim hockey team in Southern California, a Boeing 737 commercial jet or 20 million large cafe mochas at Starbucks.

Or you could snap up the country's most expensive home for sale outside of the East Coast -- a 30,000-square-foot mansion perched on a cliff in Corona del Mar, Calif., south of Newport Beach.

"This is a destination resort hotel on a small scale," said Newport Beach architect Brion Jeannette, who designed the two-story home that spreads across three lots.

Mansion...

● **Jan and John Cook Parachute at 10,000 feet**

The Remley team would like to recognize Jan and John Cook for accomplishing a life goal of becoming the first in their family to parachute. The couple successful completed their training on July 8, 2006 at the Douglas County Airfield, and took to the skies the next morning. They jumped in tandem with their instructors from Air Jump School, Inc.

The ultracompetitive environment of escalation clauses, multiple offers, and endless showings is daunting for the listing agent, let alone for a seller who is considering listing his home. In making the largest financial decision of their lives, many sellers are hesitant to jump into the deep end of the pool.

So how can you, the professional real estate agent, help a seller find the courage to jump off the diving board and into the market? You can start by giving her this list of 10 reasons to market her home now.

Ten Reasons to Market Your Home Now (Seller's Market)

1. *Pricing power.* In most markets, sellers are able to sell for top dollar, as historically low interest rates and high demand have fueled a rush of buyers into the marketplace.

2. *High demand.* The low inventory in most markets means that the number of buyers competing for each home is higher than it has ever been, and thus the time it takes to secure an acceptable offer has dropped considerably.

3. *Low interest rates.* Interest rates have remained at 30-year lows, despite the fact that the Federal Reserve has hiked rates for the past several quarters. Today's low rates mean that more buyers can afford to purchase more amenities and pay higher prices than in the past.

4. *Fewer contingencies.* Because many buyers have been able to sell their former homes quickly, many of them are able to write offers that are not contingent on the sale of their home.

5. *Flexible financing.* Many buyers today are able to enjoy hundreds of different possible loan programs, from adjustable rate mortgages to reverse amortization mortgages, and even no-documentation loans. This flexibility means that more buyers can afford to buy homes than ever before.

6. *Timing control.* Sellers who need more time to move, find a replacement property, or move into a rental can be more selective in choosing the offer that best suits their needs. They can also specify their timing needs in advance.

7. *Tax savings.* Sellers who have owned their home for two of the past five years and have lived in it for two of the past five years may be able to take up to $250,000 for a single person or up to $500,000 for a married couple out of the sale as tax-free gains. See www.irs.gov for details.

8. *Nationwide market expansion.* The national housing market is now at record levels. This may mean that there are more out-of-state buyers than ever before as potential buyers for a seller's home.

9. *Homeownership rates.* The number of American families who own a home is at an all-time high—70 percent. This is good news for sellers, as it means that more families are recognizing the value and wealth-building potential of owning real estate.

10. *Discounted rental rates.* Although home prices have climbed steadily over the last several months, rental rates in most areas of the country have not kept pace. This can be good news for sellers who would like to take their time finding their next home.

As you read my Ten Reasons to Market Your Home Now, you may already be questioning some of my statements. Why? The market is changing. In some markets, and maybe yours, there has already been a dramatic downshift, with home inventories piling up like a morning traffic jam and buyers scattering in the wind. Obviously, if this is your market reality, this approach won't work anymore. Because of this, it may be time to adapt your message.

Let's take a look at how my 10-point list might change for a slower buyer's market.

Ten Reasons to Market Your Home Now (Buyer's Market)

1. *Buying power.* Many sellers are now benefiting from the ability to purchase their next home at a bargain price because of the larger inventory of homes now available. Don't miss this tremendous opportunity.

2. *Fewer showings.* Having a smaller number of buyers in the marketplace and more homes to view means fewer showings, which many sellers prefer, as the showings they do have are for serious, committed buyers, not just tire kickers.

3. *Interest rates.* Even though interest rates are rising slowly, buyers can still benefit from record-low rates. Today's low rates mean that more buyers can afford to purchase more amenities and pay higher prices than in the past. Many buyers are motivated to buy now while interest rates are still relatively low (this may change in the future!).

4. *Relocation advantages.* Many parts of the country have experienced significant real estate market slowdowns. As a buyer moving to one of these areas, you may find significant savings.

5. *Flexible financing.* Many buyers today are able to enjoy hundreds of different possible loan programs, from ARMs to reverse amortization mortgages, and even no-documentation loans. This flexibility means that more buyers can afford to buy homes than ever before.

6. *Incentives for faster sales.* Many sellers who would like to sell quickly have found that buyers in today's market respond to incentives. Many seller incentives cost nothing or very little to implement but can make a home extremely attractive to the market.

7. *Tax savings.* Sellers who have owned their home for two of the past five years and have lived in it for two of the past five years may be able to take up to $250,000 for a single person or up to $500,000 for a married couple out of the sale as tax-free gains. See www.irs.gov for details.

8. *Strong homeownership rates.* The number of American families who own a home is still at an all-time high—70 percent. This is good news for sellers, as it means that more and more families are recognizing the value and wealth-building potential of owning real estate.

9. *More time to shop for your next home.* In our current market, you may have more time to shop for your next home and less worry about competing with other buyers for your next home. This means that you can relax and take your time.

10. *Contingency sales.* Many sellers are now willing to accept offers that are contingent on a home sale. This means that you can begin shopping for your next home while your home is still on the market.

Watch out—you're in the spin zone. As a master presenter, you've adapted your message to the market and are now encouraging your clients to move forward based on this new information. By doing so, you will be helping your clients who need to sell to take the next step toward their housing goals. Let's see how top producers do the same in their real estate business.

Never Fear the Next Step

Overwhelmed. This was surely my feeling when my clients told me that they wouldn't be able to close the transaction. Through the wife's tears and the husband's anger, the elderly couple explained that they had just now learned that they owed something called "recapture" on their low-income home loan. Recapture, I quickly learned, was the amount of money that the government had paid each month to subsidize this couple's house payment, and that the government required the couple to pay back if they sold the home. Because of this, the couple wouldn't have enough cash to buy their next home.

This was a disaster. Not only did I represent both sides of this transaction, the buyer and the seller, but I also represented the sellers in their next home purchase as buyers. Three sides, three commissions, and three reasons to drink three bottles of tequila if this deal took a nosedive. Driving back to the office, I called my broker to ask for his advice. He wasn't in. So I dialed my real estate buddy Scot. His advice: Don't panic; instead, focus on the next step.

Scot was right on the money. In a tough situation during a presentation, a closing, or a negotiation, it's easy to become overwhelmed and mentally throw in the towel during a crisis. Superstars don't fall into this trap; instead, they focus on the next step. How? First they consider the outcome, the end result that everyone would like to see happen, and then they work backward by determining what steps are necessary to climb that mountain. In my case, this meant getting on the phone and talking with the couple's lien holder.

After taking a deep breath, crossing my fingers and toes, and hoping for a miracle, I dialed the lender. The lender picked up on the fifth ring, sounding exasperated. Carefully I explained my clients' predicament, trying not to sound too desperate or demanding. Near the end of the conversation, just before it seemed about ready to stall, I employed a technique I had learned from one of my veteran colleagues, a tactic that over the years I have come to call the problem-solver technique.

Check out how this simple dialogue may help you with your next real estate challenge:

The Problem-Solver Technique

Listen, knowing what I'm up against, if you were me in this situation, what would you suggest? What are my best options?

I've used this exact phraseology hundreds and hundreds of times throughout my career, and I am continually amazed at how perfect strangers will rise to my challenge, dig in, and attempt to help me find a solution to my problems. Yes, I still get the occasional idiot who cracks his gum, sneers, and then tells me to take a hike, but that is extremely rare.

Now in this case, I would love to tell you that the lender gave me good news. She didn't. But she did give me a suggestion: Why not share the pain by having everyone split up the cost and still close the transaction? It's true that this would have never worked in a hot market, but at the time the market wasn't hot; in fact, it was quite chilly—frosty really. So, hat in hand, I approached each party in the transaction (there were more players than I would have guessed) and asked for participation.

In the end, aside from the seller, who came up with a larger contribution, each of the players, myself included, pitched in less than $500 each to create a successful closing of a deal that should, by all rights, have failed. How? By never losing sight of the next step.

Exude Confidence

Consumer confidence, or the measurement of the public's likelihood of buying durable goods like automobiles or real estate, is measured in detail as an indicator of future economic prosperity or the harbinger of a possible slowdown or, worse yet, recession. Interestingly, these trend lines may do little more than reinforce false perceptions. Let me give you an example of how this might happen. A consumer, we'll call him Joe Seller, has just finished his turkey casserole and is sitting down and watching the nightly news. With glassy eyes, Joe listens as the anchor says in his deep baritone voice:

> *And now for some housing numbers. The National Association of Home Designers reports today that the number of homeowners expecting to sell their home and purchase a new home has declined by 21 percent from last year. . . .*

One of my speaker friends always likes to use this one-liner on stage: "Sixty-seven percent of statistics are made up by speakers on the spot." Normally it takes an audience a second or two to get the joke. But he makes a good point. We should always look for trends and be open to new information, but we shouldn't be fooled by false positives or statistics that aren't supported by other facts.

So what do you think—has Joe been fooled? My guess is that Joe has bought into this information hook, line, and sinker, without bothering to compare these data with other studies or his own local market statistics. He just knows one thing: "The real estate market is on the skids!" Our real estate clients are a lot like Joe; they take their cues from us when it comes to forming an opinion about the real estate market. After all, how many times have you been asked, "How's the real estate market?"

Superstars exude confidence. They have the power to make others around them become believers as well. And the one thing a real estate superstar believes in more than anything else is the power of owning real estate. So instead of saying something like, "Well, I think the market will bottom out for a few years," a top producer might say, "I think this is a terrific time to buy real estate, just like it was a great time to buy real estate 5 years ago, 10 years ago, and 15 years ago. Real estate is always a great investment!"

Our clients want us to be believers; they want us to be absolutely convinced that our product is the best investment that money can buy. They need us to give them positive reasons to move forward. Top producers exude this confidence. So the question is, Do you believe? Do you believe in your product and the value of your services? Do you buy into what you're selling?

LEARNING OPPORTUNITY

Mastering the game. Superstars have an edge that enables them to be both uniquely successful and competitively dangerous: They have mastered their presentation skills by learning how to SHINE.

S: Sell to everyone.
H: Help others.
I: Invest in change.
N: Never fear the next step.
E: Exude confidence.

Conviction: Buying Into What You're Selling

There is a new science that specializes in the study of attitude and its effect on a person's well-being and overall health. The name of this new field is psychoneuroimmunology. This fascinating new area of study, dealing with the power of belief, is beginning to catch on with mainstream scientists and institutions, as a person's attitude has been shown to dramatically affect her ability to fight off fatigue, sickness, and even disease. This may seem like common sense to the layperson: "If I'm in a good mood, I generally feel better. If I'm in a bad mood, I often feel depressed, tired, or even sickly." But health-care professionals have been reluctant to embrace this line of study unless there could be verifiable proof. Today there is, as numerous studies have shown that a person's attitude and health are strongly linked. For instance, in one study of 400 reports of spontaneous remission of cancer, the patients had one factor in common: a positive attitude and the conviction that they would survive the disease.

So do you believe? Do you have an absolute conviction that your clients can benefit from your services? The hard truth is that unless you believe in the power and value of your services, your clients never will. In the sales business, then, the first person we need to sell isn't the client but ourselves. We have to buy in, become believers, and affirm our own convictions.

Amazingly, there is a quick test to determine whether we truly think that our services have value. Why not take a minute to measure your level of faith by taking this quick conviction quiz:

1. Do I charge all of my clients the same fee for my services, or do I cut my fees in some cases and not in others?
2. Do I adjust my services by giving some clients more and some clients less?
3. Do I agree to different listing terms with some clients, like the length of the contract?

So did you answer yes to any of the questions? Congratulations; you are a mortal, like the rest of us. You bleed red, and you cry at sad movies. You bend at times when you shouldn't, and you give up things that you don't have to. You are, my friend, a sinner. But not to worry, we all are, which simply means that we can always find ways to improve and strengthen our own resolve. This is important, because when we give in to a seller who demands, for instance, a commission concession, aren't we really saying, "You know, Mr. and Mrs. Seller, you caught me. My services were never really worth X percent to begin with. I charge that only to people who don't know any better!"

I know it's not like that, right? Each situation is unique; every seller is different. But is it and is she? Or is this what we tell ourselves to justify our not holding fast to our own standards? Obviously there are times when we all have to bend or even break our own rules, but if this is a daily event, something normal rather than abnormal, what does this say about our own belief in the value of our services?

Superstars meet this challenge by preparing for confrontations with their business standards in advance, and by understanding that competition often drives the attitudes and expectations of a skeptical and often cynical marketplace. An agent's self-confidence cannot be blind faith; it must be tempered with proof, facts, and undeniable evidence that her services are the best in the marketplace. To explore how to get this done in the real world, let's look at three ways strong agents prove to their clients that they are the cream of the crop:

1. *Provide a service comparison chart.* This easy-to-build chart compares your services with those of your competitors to demonstrate why you alone can help the seller achieve his real estate goals faster and more easily, as well as how you offer the most value per dollar spent. Take a look at the sample service comparison chart in Figure 10-2.

FIGURE 10-2.

Service Comparison Chart — Sample

Service	ABC Real Estate	XYZ Realty	SOLD Realty	Franchise
Custom Sign/Riders	X	X		X
Directional Signs	X		X	X
Virtual Tours	X			X
Webpage	X			X
Office Tour	X	X		
E-mail Blast	X		X	
Open House	X	X		X
Talking House	X		X	
Home Warranty	X			X
Color Flyers	X		X	
Flyer Box	X	X	X	
Just Listed Mailing	X		X	X
Neighborhood Canvas	X	X		
Business Card Flyers	X		X	
CMA/Overall Market	X	X	X	X
30 Days Listing Review	X			

At ABC Realty we provide a full range of services that is unparalleled in the real estate industry!

2. *Provide personal statistics vs. the market.* Strong agents can almost always beat the market. For instance, if the market average is that homes sell within 45 days of being listed, but you are averaging a home sales rate of 30 days or less, this is something that you should be shouting from the rooftops. Here are three key numbers to measure:

   • Average days on market

   • Average percentage difference between list and sales price

   • Average sales price

3. *Give them evidence.* According to the 2005 National Association of Realtors Profile of Home Buyers and Sellers, the top two reasons for a client's hiring us are (1) our reputation and (2) our knowledge of the neighborhood or area. So what proves beyond a shadow of doubt that, first, you have the best track record in the industry, and second, that you really know the market inside and out? Both of these questions in clients' minds can be answered by giving them a copy of your sales track record (assuming that you have a strong track record) that demonstrates that you are, in fact, selling homes in the neighborhood.

Top Producer Tip: Are you a new agent? Don't worry; superstars weren't born with a real estate license tattooed on their forehead. If you're greener than grass, try using your office statistics compared to the overall market, which will almost always show your firm in a favorable light.

Once your clients have bought into your story and have become believers, the true test of your abilities will arrive because it's one thing to take a listing, but it's a whole different thing to keep one.

LEARNING OPPORTUNITY

"Buying in." Superstars have learned that a real estate agent's self-confidence cannot be blind faith; it must be tempered with proof, facts, and undeniable evidence that her services are the best in the marketplace.

Avoiding Crisis Addiction

There is an ailment that afflicts an astonishingly large number of real estate agents, crippling their business, paralyzing their ability to earn a living, and causing huge amounts of stress and anxiety in both their business and personal lives. I call it crisis addiction. An agent with a crisis addiction is constantly riddled with feelings of guilt, depression, apprehension, and, most of all, fear—a fear of failure.

How do you catch this debilitating disease, and, more important, how can you avoid it? For the answers, let's first see if you are already infected. Quickly, answer these five questions:

1. Do you always seem to be in a crisis or just leaving one?
2. Do your clients regularly get upset with you for not following through?
3. Do you seem to be always rushed, never able to keep up with your workload?
4. Do you feel like you're drowning in commitments that you can't possibly fulfill?
5. Do you feel guilty when you're not working?

If you answered yes to any of these questions, it's very likely that, at least in part, you have fallen victim to a crisis addiction. Like Sandy, an agent from Utah, you feel trapped in a vicious cycle of never living up to your clients' or family's expectations. As she put it, "When I started out in real estate, I always seemed to be at a dead run, never able to finish any one thing. It was pretty depressing."

In large part, the solution to curing a crisis addiction is to understand how insidious this disease can be by recognizing its symptoms, one of which is the sense of relief you feel when you solve a crisis that you have actually been responsible for creating. Sounds crazy, right? But let's look at a real-world scenario that almost every agent can identify with:

Jim is a busy guy; he is taking listings left and right, but he is failing to follow through on his promises, and now one of his sellers has finally tracked him down by phone at the office and is hotter than a firecracker on the Fourth of July. Like any good agent, Jim immediately hops in his car and rushes to the seller's home to put out the fire. Not surpris-

ingly, Jim is able to make the seller feel better by promising him even more services. Leaving the seller's home, Jim feels terrific; he has saved the listing. Another job well done! The seller is happy, and Jim is happy.

Can you see the danger in this example? Jim feels good about solving a crisis that he actually created in the first place by failing to follow through. By patting himself on the back, he may even reinforce this negative behavior. Sadly, even the best agents can fall into the trap of becoming a serial real estate arsonist by starting client fires, then returning to put out the blaze only after it threatens to destroy their relationships with their clients. It's a dangerous game, and every agent who plays with fire in this way eventually gets burned.

The good news is that you can get back control of your career by following the path of agents who have learned how to avoid a client crisis. They start by being short on commitments and long on fulfillments; in other words, they underpromise and overdeliver. For agents who are at the top of their game, this often means that it is critically important that they keep their clients in the loop when designing and implementing a marketing plan, managing client data, and ensuring the accuracy of the listing information.

For example, to accommodate the needs of sellers who are becoming increasingly more sophisticated, and technologically savvy, many superstars provide these value-added services when working with their clients:

Four Ways to Provide Exceptional Follow-Through

1. *Provide advance copies.* When designing advertising, many top producers provide their clients with an advance proof of ad copy before it is run. This ensures that the client will be satisfied with the advertising, and that there are no questions after the fact.
2. *Review MLS data.* Once the listing has been entered into the Multiple Listing Service, it is wise to either e-mail or fax a copy of the listing to the client for her review. The client can then add to the listing or correct any errors that may have occurred.
3. *Review and select property photos.* Using the highest-quality home photos is an essential aspect of the marketing plan, and choosing the right photo is critical. Allowing the client to have input into the photo selection is a terrific way to keep the seller in the marketing loop.

4. *Review and get approval for Internet marketing.* Many superstars today e-mail their clients a link to any Internet-based marketing pages that the agent produces. This allows the client to see the work being done to market his home and also gives him an opportunity to critique any errors or omissions.

To continue on the road to recovery, many agents find it wise to stay ahead of the game rather than behind the eight ball by establishing a communication plan.

LEARNING OPPORTUNITY

Crisis addiction. An agent with a crisis addiction is constantly riddled with feelings of guilt, depression, and apprehension because he is often either going into or coming out of a crisis.

Following through. To overcome this addiction, many agents start by being short on commitments and long on fulfillments; in other words, they underpromise and overdeliver.

Establishing a Communication Plan

An essential element of the success of any agent who is at the top of her earning curve is her ability to communicate with her clients on a regular basis. Obviously, different clients will have different needs when it comes to this ongoing communication (some are needier than others).

To focus on the client's need when dealing with sellers, wise agents often establish their clients' preferences at the initial seller consultation. Often they do this by asking some simple assessment questions, as shown in Figure 10-3.

Using this form, an agent can now update her contact management system and make a point of touching base with the client in accordance with the client's unique preferences and schedule.

As a part of this update process, many superstars mail (or e-mail) their clients a monthly report that shows when and how the property has been marketed. In addition, many agents establish a drip e-mail system with their clients. A drip e-mail system is a series of preplanned, prescheduled e-mails that are sent out periodically (like a dripping faucet) to keep the client updated on any planned marketing activities. For instance:

FIGURE 10-3. SELLER COMMUNICATION PLAN

Seller Communication Plan:

Seller's Name _____

Address _____

City, State, Zip _____

Primary Phone _____

E-mail _____

Business _____

Preferences:

Communication by:	Phone	E-mail
How often contacted:	Weekly	Monthly
Advertising copies:	Mailed	E-mailed
Marketing reports:	Mailed	E-mailed
Personal visits:	Weekly	Daily
Follow-up on all showings:	Yes	No

I authorize the release of my e-mail address for the strict purpose of transaction updates to third parties directly involved in the closing of any transaction:

_____ Seller

_____ Seller   Date _____

Contact Management System updated

on_____

Dear Mr. and Mrs. Homeowner,

Thank you for listing your home with my team! We're excited about your listing, and we just wanted to let you know exactly what we will be doing to market your property within the first few days:

1. Listing entered into www.rmls.com, www.Realtor.Com, www.allstate realestate.com, www.homeadvisor.com, and www.agentwebsite.com.
2. Sign placed with Ryder's.
3. Flyer box placed.

4. Directional signs placed.

5. Home warranty faxed in.

6. Written ads approved by seller (they will come shortly).

7. Lockbox placed.

8. Office tour scheduled.

9. MLS tour scheduled.

10. Open house scheduled.

11. E-mail sent to top producers.

This is just during the first seven days! Please let me know if you would like to see something that is not on the list!

Sincerely,

<Agent Name>

P.S. The highest compliment I can receive is your personal referral. Who do you know who is considering selling or buying a home?

By refining your communication plan, you can follow the lead of companies that provide first-class service, like Ritz-Carlton. Ritz-Carlton doesn't advertise. Why? Ritz-Carlton's reputation represents "brand equity that has built up over the years," says Bruce Himelstein, the company's vice president of marketing. "We mandate to our employees that they provide the finest personal service," he continues. "Each person is responsible for finding and recording the preferences of individual guests, for example, so that they can get things before the guest even knows they need it. And each employee is empowered to break away from whatever they're doing if a guest needs something. When you've built up that kind of culture over the years, it all starts to stick."

This kind of signature selling is the hallmark of first-class service and a key to mastering the presentation game. Let's find out how superstars achieve this goal by exploring your signature selling style.

LEARNING OPPORTUNITY

Communication plans. To lead with the clients' need when dealing with sellers, wise agents often establish their client's preferences at the initial seller consultation and follow up with calls and written reports.

Signature Selling

Have you ever experienced a work of art?

Perhaps it was a painting that took your breath away or a piece of literature that stirred your emotions. Just as likely, it may have been a mesmerizing photograph, or even a piece of captivating music. Now think carefully; once you had finished soaking the experience in, what was your next step?

If you're like me, your first impulse might be to tell a friend or a loved one about your discovery. But before you run for the door or reach for the phone, you probably will take just a minute to find the artist's signature. Why? Because the person who created a work of art is an essential part of the art itself. In fact, most of us are in awe of a powerful artist; we love to study, dissect, and discuss how these inspired creators are able to tap into their inner talent. As Sir Arthur Conan Doyle once wrote, "Mediocrity knows nothing higher than itself, but talent instantly recognizes genius."

So are you an artist in the field of real estate? Are you willing to sign each of your transactions or listings with your name? It's an important question. A signature is a powerful testament to your overall performance. It says that you take ownership of and pride in your accomplishments and that you are willing to allow others to admire and even critique your work.

Five Ways to "Sign" Your Work

1. *Take pride in every listing.* By taking pride in a listing, you take on ownership of your work. Ask yourself: "If my business were to be measured only by my performance in listing, would I be proud of my work?"

2. *Stop making excuses.* Any agent who justifies his failure by making excuses can fade into mediocrity and become one of the masses. Superstars rise above the horde by accepting only excellence as their finished product.

3. *Let your work stand for itself.* Just like that of many master artists, even the best agent's work may go unappreciated. Superstars realize that what's important is not always the recognition of excellence by others, but the fulfillment of their own true talent and potential.

4. *Ask for input.* Great agents often begin their career with nothing more than a burning desire to succeed. To realize their full potential, then, top producers often rely on a mentor to help them hone their skills,

find their talents, and guide their steps. By asking for input, superstars grow into the agent they wish to become.

5. *Display your talent.* Once their masterwork has been completed and the transaction closed, even the most elite agents find great satisfaction and profit in displaying their success. How? By asking for testimonials from their satisfied clients and for referrals to others who may wish to experience their unique gifts firsthand.

A strong agent is a uniquely talented individual who brings something to his craft that others can admire and experience for themselves. Thus, he is in a sense an artist, one who inspires his customers and clients to continuously refer their friends and neighbors to his work. Thus, a signature goes beyond your pride of workmanship to include a statement about the style of the work itself.

Consider Rembrandt, Hemingway, and Mozart. Each offered tremendous value and quality to his craft, but in addition, the art of each was something unique—each had a signature style that made him stand out and rise above the countless other artists of his time. Do you have a signature style—a uniqueness that sets you apart from the rest of the real estate community in your own market area?

When you look at the top agents in your city, town, or state, you will no doubt discover that many of them specialize in a particular market niche. They often play to their innate strengths by recognizing their own natural talents and leveraging those talents by specializing in the area of real estate that they are passionate about. In much the same way that a master pianist may choose to play country, rock, or classical music, a top producer who is an Internet specialist may leverage that talent by focusing on the commercial, residential, or income area of the real estate business. This powerful signature style is what supercharges many agents' success and differentiates them from the hordes of agents occupying the hypercompetitive real estate industry.

My good friends Denny and Linda Austin, a husband-and-wife team, have made all the right moves in real estate by leveraging their own natural talents. The couple had a background in retail store ownership and was used to working 80-hour weeks, so putting in long hours in their new real estate business was a breeze. Their specialization was their ability to merchandise their listings in much the same way a retail store merchandises its products. By using virtual tours, print marketing, targeted mailings, and a powerful website strategy, they were able to create over $12 million in sales during 2005.

So how can you find your own signature style? Check out these suggestions to help you develop your own signature style:

Five Ways to Develop Your Own Signature Style

1. *Identify your natural talents.* We are all born with innate abilities and strengths; some would call these our natural talents. We should embrace these natural talents as a key part of our signature style.

2. *Sharpen your skills.* What skills could help your business grow and take your natural talent to the next level—communication skills, computer skills, crisis management skills? Find out what skills could lead your business to a higher level of fulfillment.

3. *Find a path of progress.* Identify your endgame, where it is you want to be in the next 12 months, and determine what needs to happen in order to make this dream a reality. Finding this path of progress is essential to goal setting and building a signature style that actually creates results.

4. *Choose a niche.* Your market niche should be something that absolutely gets you fired up about selling real estate. It should excite you, animate you, and leave you ready to jump out of bed every morning to tackle the day.

5. *Become the best.* Measured only against your own true potential, ask yourself what it will take to become your absolute best, then commit to a plan of action to raise your standard to this level.

Your signature style is what your clients, the real estate community, and even your fiercest competitors should think about when they hear your name. It is your brand, your defining difference, the thing that separates you from the pack and makes you a shining example of an agent who is one of those chosen few who can lead instead of just follow.

LEARNING OPPORTUNITY

Signature selling. A strong agent is in a sense an artist, one who inspires her customers and clients to continuously refer their friends and neighbors to her. To accomplish this, top producers often have a signature selling style that supercharges their success.

So will you become the next Picasso, Rembrandt, or Bach of the real estate industry? As a real estate artist, you have the ability to make it happen if you make the right choices. For superstars, one of the most important choices is to design and use a powerful presentation, a presentation that inspires, captivates, and motivates a client to move forward with his real estate goals—*a real estate presentation that makes millions.*

Index

Look for These Exciting Real Estate Titles at www.amacombooks.org/realestate